Managing innovation
within networks

Consumer Research and Policy Series
Edited by Gordon Foxall

Consumer Psychology in Behavioural Perspective
Gordon Foxall

Morality and the Market
Consumer pressure for corporate accountability
N. Craig Smith

Managing innovation within networks

Wim G. Biemans

London and New York

First published 1992
by Routledge
11 New Fetter Lane, London EC4P 4EE

Simultaneously published in the USA and Canada
by Routledge
a division of Routledge, Chapman and Hall, Inc.
29 West 35th Street, New York, NY 10001

Typeset by Leaper & Gard Ltd, Bristol
Printed in Great Britain by Biddles Ltd, Guildford and King's Lynn

British Library Cataloguing in Publication Data
Biemans, Wim G. *1960–*
    Managing innovation within networks
    1. New products. Development
    I. Title
    658.575

0-415-06274-8

Library of Congress Cataloging in Publication Data
        Managing innovation within networks / Wim G. Biemans.
        p.   cm. – (Consumer research and policy series)
        Includes bibliographical references and index.
        ISBN 0-415-06274-8 (HB)
        1. New products. 2. Product management. 3. Marketing.
    I. Title. II. Series.
    HF5415.153.B54 1992
    658.5′75–dc20   91–11751
                                                                                    CIP

To Maryse

New and stirring ideas are belittled, because if they are not belittled the humiliating question arises 'Why then are you not taking part in them?'
H.G. Wells (1866–1946)

Contents

Tables and figures

TABLES

Acknowledgements

As it is with innovations, this book would never have been written if other people had not contributed substantially.

First I would like to thank the many anonymous managers who participated in the study. Their enthusiasm constantly fuelled the fire of motivation. The members of the study groups 'Commercialization of Industrial Innovations' and 'Relationships in Industrial Markets' deserve special thanks, since most of them not only took part in the investigation, but also contributed their views at meetings and criticized first drafts of papers and presentations.

I am indebted to my ex-colleagues at Eindhoven University of Technology who provided me with a stimulating environment for conducting the investigation. I want to express special gratitude to Rolf de Vries, with whom the exploratory study was conducted. His practical approach to theoretical issues provided the perfect complement to my own theoretical ideas and suggestions. I am also indebted to all colleagues at other universities and institutes, both in the Netherlands and abroad, who (often unwittingly) stimulated me to write this book.

My present colleagues at the University of Groningen earn my thanks as well, for showing interest in my work, stimulating my professional curiosity, and giving me space when I needed it.

Finally, I would like to thank Maryse Brand, who tried to teach me time and again that also in writing a book, a market-oriented strategy is clearly to be preferred over a product-oriented one.

Wim G. Biemans
Groningen

Acknowledgements are due to the publishers of the following for permission to reprint material:

Tables
(2.2) 'Marketing Research and the New Product Failure Rate', by C.M. Crawford, *Journal of Marketing*, vol. 31, no. 4. pp. 51–61, copyright 1977, American Marketing Association. (4.1) 'The Dominant Role of Users in the Scientific Instrument Innovation Process', by E. von Hippel, *Research Policy*, vol. 5, pp. 212–39, copyright 1976, Elsevier Science Publishers B.V. (4.2) 'From CAP1 to CAP2: User-initiated Innovation from the User's Point of View', by G.R. Foxall and J.D. Tierney, *Management Decision*, vol. 22, no. 5, pp. 3–15, copyright 1984, MCB University Press Ltd. (4.3) 'Strategies of User-Initiated Product Innovation', by G.R. Foxall and B. Johnston, *Technovation*, vol. 6, pp. 87–102, copyright 1987, Elsevier Science Publishers B.V. (5.3) 'The Role of Champion in Product Innovation', by A.K. Chakrabarti, copyright 1974 by the Regents of the University of California; reprinted from the *California Management Review*, vol. 17, no. 2, pp. 58–62, by permission of the Regents. (6.1) 'User and Third-Party Involvement in Developing Medical Equipment Innovations', by W.G. Biemans, *Technovation*, vol. 11, no. 3, pp. 163–82, copyright 1991, Elsevier Advanced Technology. (6.5) 'User and Third-Party Involvement in Developing Medical Equipment Innovations', by W.G. Biemans, *Technovation*, vol. 11, no. 3, pp. 163–82, copyright 1991, Elsevier Advanced Technology. (6.8) 'User and Third-Party Involvement in Developing Medical Equipment Innovations', by W.G. Biemans, *Technovation*, vol. 11, no. 3, pp. 163–82, copyright 1991, Elsevier Advanced Technology.

Figures
(2.1) 'A Dynamic Model of Process and Product Innovation', by J.M. Utterback and W.J. Abernathy, *Omega*, vol. 3, no. 6, pp. 639–56, copyright 1975, Pergamon Press PLC. (2.2) 'Analyzing Product Innovations', by D.H. Gobeli and D.J. Brown, *Research Management*, pp. 25–31, copyright 1987, Research Technology Management. (3.1) 'A Classification and Review of Models of the Intra-Firm Innovation Process', by M.A. Saren, *R&D Management*, vol. 14, no. 1, pp. 11–24, copyright 1984, Basil Blackwell Ltd. (3.2) 'Innovation Management', by A. Robertson, *Management Decision*, vol. 12, no. 6, copyright 1974, MCB University Press Ltd. (3.3) *Management of New Products*, by Booz Allen & Hamilton, copyright 1968, Booz Allen & Hamilton, Inc. (3.4) *Managing Technological Innovation*, third edn., by B.C. Twiss, copyright 1986, Pitman Publishing. (3.5) 'A Process Model for Industrial New Product Development', by R.G. Cooper, *IEEE Transactions on Engineering Management*, vol. EM-30, no. 1, pp. 2–11, copyright 1983, IEEE. (3.6) 'Criteria Changes Across Product Development Stages', by I.A. Ronkainen, *Industrial Marketing Management*, vol. 14, pp. 171–8, copyright 1985, Elsevier Science Publishing Co., Inc. (3.7) 'New Product Success in Industrial Firms', by R.G. Cooper, *Industrial Marketing Management*, vol. 11, pp. 215–23,

Preface

The last two decades have demonstrated that continuous innovation is increasingly becoming a critical success factor for corporate survival. It is no longer an activity that can be pursued at leisure; instead it requires the mobilization of resources throughout the firm guided by strategic vision. The successful firms of the 1990s excel at developing and commercializing their innovations with emphasis on speed, improved quality, and low costs. However, significant changes in the business environment place numerous obstacles on the road to success. Technological developments are both accelerating and proliferating; the development of new products requires the creative combination of various areas of expertise; markets are becoming increasingly global; and customers demand consistently better quality. These developments in worldwide markets cause many firms to establish strategic partnerships of all kinds.

A number of additional considerations led to the publication of the book you are holding now. While the continuous development and introduction of new products appear to be critical to the survival of a firm, the business of innovation still remains a hazardous one. The competitive battlefield is strewn with the remains of promising firms that ultimately failed to realize their dreams. Over the past five years I conducted an in-depth study of new product development practices of industrial firms. Quite soon I discovered that integration of marketing and product development is a prerequisite for success. Many firms try to solve the problems by cooperating with customers and various other parties within networks, but while cooperation is essential it certainly is not easy. At the same time, existing literature failed to provide management with implementable guidelines to improve their product development efforts. My empirical investigation was specifically designed to fill this gap and resulted in numerous conclusions, concepts, guidelines, procedures, and suggestions that together constitute an action guide for industrial marketing management. Therefore the first reason for writing this book is to share these findings, which are based on real-life experiences in actual cases, with managers in practice.

In addition, the book is particularly suited for students of innovation. The first three chapters provide a detailed and integrative overview of the latest theoretical developments as regards innovation, product development, adoption, diffusion, interaction, and networks. Obviously, the practical nature of my findings provides additional theoretical insights. As the French poet Paul Valéry stated 'Science is a collection of successful recipes'. By combining my own findings with what is already known, students interested in what it takes to be successful in continuously developing new products obtain an up-to-date picture of the world of innovation.

In order to satisfy both managers and students, the last chapter presents The Five Cs of innovation management, a managerial concept that captures all the essential elements into one comprehensive framework.

1 Introduction

Business has only two basic functions – marketing and innovation.
(Peter Drucker, 1959)

Thomas Alva Edison is generally considered one of the most famous innovators of all time. He patented more than a thousand inventions, including major innovations like the phonograph, the incandescent electric lamp, and the microphone. Although a technical genius, he failed time and again in his real ambition: the successful commercialization of his inventions. He had to be removed from all the businesses he had started in order to save them.

More than 150 years later, innovating has undergone change. Although innovations are still being developed by archetypical individuals like Edison (for example Jobs and Wozniak, the founders of Apple, who built their first personal computer in a garage), a large number of innovations are now being developed by teamwork within the context of organizations. This does not mean that individuals cannot perform a crucial role in these situations (see for example Thomas, 1980). For instance, despite actual discouragement from Philips headquarters, a scientist with the very appropriate name of José Solo managed to develop an innovative technology for producing chips for low-voltage equipment (*NRC Handelsblad*, 1990a). Nevertheless, the same problem still holds: the commercialization of innovations leaves much to be desired. The high-tech industry, in particular, abounds with examples of promising young firms that captured the imagination of the public with an innovative product, but failed to capture a significant part of the market and thus turn their promise into profit.

This book is the result of an empirical study addressing the problems related to developing innovations for industrial markets within networks. This first chapter explains the rationale for writing this book and introduces the empirical investigation. The research project will be positioned with respect to studies conducted by other researchers and the chapter concludes with a survey of the contents of the book.

WHY THIS BOOK ON DEVELOPING INNOVATIONS?

The last decade has seen a veritable upsurge in the number of both scientific and popular publications about innovations. Although practical interest dates back a long way, explicit attention from theorists only started with scientists like Schumpeter (1939), who was one of the first economists to focus on the innovation process. In recent years, the popular press started a real flood of publications about innovations as well. One obvious reason for all this attention is that innovations readily capture the imagination and have a certain romantic flavour. A more rational reason is the growing realization that innovations are of major importance to society. Innovations are expected to stimulate economic growth and promote employment, and thus change the quality of life, which has led to the recommend-ation to national governments to set up stimulation programmes (Industrial Research Institute, 1980). At a micro level, individual firms regard innovations as the key to productivity (Avard, Catto, and Davidson, 1982).

But why write yet another book on the subject of innovations? This question can be approached from two directions.

First, although the importance of innovations to the continuity of the firm is generally agreed upon, firms still encounter problems when it comes to developing and commercializing them. Abernathy (1982, p. 38) commented that 'the problem of deficient competitive performance really originates as a "management of innovation" problem'. Extensive research conducted among 103 Canadian firms showed that, on the average, 19 per cent of new industrial products failed after being introduced into the market, while another 22 per cent of the projects were killed before launch (Cooper, 1982, p. 218). Thus, large amounts of money are spent on unsuccessful projects. According to Booz, Allen and Hamilton (1982, p. 14), in general almost 50 per cent of new-product expenditure goes on projects that do not succeed. In the meantime, things have hardly improved since American businesses, in particular, are still characterized as being more skilled at making discoveries than at capitalizing on them (*Fortune*, 1990, p. 64).

Second, although academics stress the importance of a market-oriented product development process, they typically only provide very sketchy guidelines to indicate how to accomplish it. The most notable example is the extensive research conducted by Cooper (the results of which are summarized in Cooper (1980)). To provide such managerial guidelines, product development processes need to be studied in great detail with emphasis on manufacturer–user relationships. That is, product development, adoption, and diffusion need to be studied as interrelated processes.

The combination of both perspectives indicates the existence of a gap between what practitioners need and what is provided by the scientific literature. This book aims at bridging this gap by providing a succinct integrated survey of the relevant existing literature as regards the development of industrial innovations, and discussing in detail the results of an in-depth empirical investigation.

WHAT IS SO SPECIAL ABOUT OUR EMPIRICAL INVESTIGATION?

To understand fully both the nature of our empirical investigation and the value of its results, we will presently position it with respect to other dominant research paradigms. A first indication as to why one should be interested in yet another empirical investigation into the development of industrial innovations can be gained from the research objective. It stresses the managerial relevance of the results and can be stated as follows:

> Describing how, in practice, potential users and third parties are involved in developing innovations for industrial markets, and thus generating implementable guidelines to assist industrial firms in achieving successful product innovations through cooperation in networks during product development, as well as contributing to existing theory about the development of innovations within networks.

The matter can be further elucidated by comparing our study with two dominant alternative directions of research. Over the years the development of industrial innovations has been studied by a large number of researchers, but to explain the nature of our investigation two research paradigms are particularly relevant: the studies conducted by Cooper *cum suis* and the ones by an international group of European researchers.

During the second half of the 1970s, Robert Cooper conducted an influential study known as *Project NewProd*, which inspired many studies undertaken by other researchers (for instance, de Brentani's

(1989) recent study of success and failure in developing industrial services was largely patterned after Cooper's research). However, many differences between his research and ours can be identified. Cooper identified the general factors explaining the eventual success of new industrial products by conducting a comprehensive mail survey among more than 100 industrial firms in Canada known to be active in product development. While he concludes that 'a strong market orientation makes all the difference when it comes to separating successful vs unsuccessful industrial new products' (Cooper, 1979b, p. 135), he formulates only very sketchy guidelines to assist management in achieving market-oriented product development. Our investigation aims to remedy this situation by studying in-depth how firms cooperate with all kinds of external parties (such as industrial customers, governmental agencies, research institutes, consultants, distributors, and suppliers) to arrive at innovations that more successfully meet market requirements. The detailed study of real management situations yields a mass of qualitative data which can be used to construct guidelines with direct relevance to management practice.

The importance of relationships and networks is also recognized by the International Marketing and Purchasing (IMP) Project Group, consisting of industrial marketing researchers from various (mostly European) countries (see for example Håkansson, 1987a, 1989), and this brings us to the second direction of research in positioning our project. While the starting point of our own research is also based on the recognized importance of relationships in developing innovations for industrial markets, there is nevertheless an important difference between our research and the studies conducted thus far by the IMP Group. The IMP studies focus mainly on the network as a whole. They address matters like the structure and durability of the network, the existence and importance of individual relations, the members of the network, the activities performed within the network, and the transactions that occur. Although these studies are of importance and eventually yield a compact body of theory, our research does not consider the network as an end in itself, but as an instrument that can be used to the individual firm's advantage. This implies that, from our perspective, networks are studied to obtain implementable guidelines that can be used by firms operating within these networks. With the adjective *implementable*, we stress the fact that the guidelines should not be of a theoretical and purely descriptive nature, but instead address matters that are of direct relevance to industrial marketers.

Naturally, by structuring the observed findings and derived practical guidelines according to predetermined patterns, our investigation is also expected to contribute to existing theory about the development of innovations within networks.

CONTENTS OF THE BOOK

The concept of innovation will be described in Chapter 2. After presenting innovations from a number of different perspectives a general definition will be derived. Next, innovations will be presented according to a number of classification schemes. The chapter further focuses on innovation strategies and identifies medium-sized firms as a neglected sector. The chapter concludes with an analysis of the percentage of innovations that fail and the underlying causes of failure. Marketing-related factors are identified as the most important single cause for failure.

Chapter 3 describes the three central processes of product development, adoption, and diffusion. A large number of existing models of the product development process is classified and a specific model chosen for our research. With respect to adoption and diffusion the chapter will only present the aspects relevant to our empirical study. The three processes are shown to be closely inter-related.

Relationships are assumed to be of primary importance in developing innovations. The general concept of interaction is explored in Chapter 4. As a number of different organizations can be involved in developing innovations, product development is presented from a network perspective. A network can be described as a structure of connected relationships.

Chapter 5 presents the main results of a preliminary study of five cases taken from different areas of industry in the Netherlands. Having a prototype tested by potential users is recognized as being one of the most crucial stages of the process, something which, however, is often performed inadequately. A tentative general framework for having a prototype tested by users is proposed. Furthermore, the results demonstrate the relevance of networks.

The generalizations presented in Chapter 5 have been elaborated upon by looking at seventeen new cases involving medical equipment. Chapter 6 describes the Dutch medical equipment industry and presents the results of the empirical investigation.

Finally, Chapter 7 discusses the major managerial implications.

2 Innovation

A company must 'innovate or die'. The process of innovation is fundamental to a healthy and viable organization. Those who do not innovate ultimately fail.

(J.A. Telfer, Maple Leaf Mills Ltd)

Innovations are essential to the long-term well-being of the firm. Although most people readily agree with this assertion, the subject of innovation is the centre of controversy. For a large part this controversy can be traced back to the fact that every individual researcher uses his own specific definition of 'innovation'. Therefore, in order to clarify the subject, we feel compelled to start this chapter on innovation with a discussion of the different meanings of the term, and then present our own definition. After this, innovations will be grouped according to a number of classification schemes, followed by a presentation of innovation strategies. Next, the relationship between size and innovativeness of the firm is briefly discussed and medium-sized firms are identified as a relatively neglected sector in innovation research. Finally, the possible causes for the failure of innovations are analysed and marketing-related factors shown to be the most important single cause of failure.

DEFINING 'INNOVATION'

The beginning of wisdom is the definition of terms.

(Socrates, 470?–399 BC)

Although, or maybe we should rather say *because*, much has been written about innovations, a veritable babel of tongues has arisen and definitions of the term 'innovation' have proliferated. Each writer presents a new definition, emphasizing the elements he or she deems relevant. Van der Kooy (1988) studied seventy-six definitions of 'innovation' and concluded that (1) many investigators fail to provide an explicit definition of the term, (2) the definitions used can be divided into a number of categories, and (3) the aspects emphasized by the definitions change over time. Considering the perspective used in this book, another classification, that is the one discussed by Zaltman, Duncan, and Holbeck (1973, pp. 7–9), is especially relevant. According to them, the term 'innovation' usually refers to one of three different concepts.

1 The process of developing the new item
  The first concept of innovation refers to the creative or develop-ment process, that is the process that starts with the recognition of a potential demand for, and the technological feasibility of, an item and ends with its widespread utilization. Innovation is depicted as the creative process that results in something new. Holt (1983, p. 13) uses this perspective when he defines innovation as 'a process which covers the use of knowledge or relevant information for creation and introduction of something that is new and useful'. The same view is adopted by Haeffner (1973, p. 20) in describing innovation as 'an irrational process in which the invention idea appears first, and a completed product results after an often long and circuitous development route'. Most definitions of innovation belong to this category.
2 The process of adopting the new item
  A second perspective views innovation as the process whereby a new item is adopted, and thus implemented, by an adopter. An example is given by Knight (1967, p. 478), when he defines innovation as 'the adoption of a change which is new to an organiz-ation and to the relevant environment'.
3 The new item itself
  The third use of the term innovation refers to the item itself that has been invented and is regarded as new. The main difference from the first two views, describing innovation as a process, is that the third view defines innovation as the outcome of a process. Zaltman *et al.* (1973, p. 10) define an innovation as 'any idea, practice or material artifact perceived to be new by the relevant unit of adoption'. According to Rogers (1983, p. 11) an innovation is 'an idea, practice, or object that is perceived as new by an individual or other unit of adoption'. It should be noted that in both cases an innovation is viewed from the perspective of the adopter.

It should be clear that the three views presented above are closely related to each other. The first view defines innovation from the perspective of the developing unit. It concerns the stages of the development process and the characteristics of the developing unit. The developing unit can be an organization (for example a business firm), a social group, or an individual. The second view defines innovation from 'the other direction', that is the adopting unit, and relates to the stages of the adoption process and the characteristics of the adopting unit. The adopting unit can represent an individual, a business firm, or any other organization. It should be noted, however, that in specific instances the developing unit and the adopting unit can be one and the same (for example when a firm develops a new production machine for internal use). Finally, the third view concentrates on the new item itself, although it usually defines the innovation as being new to the unit of adoption.

In this book, we regard 'innovation' as the outcome of a development process, as something new that is being adopted by units of adoption. Nevertheless, we would like to deviate from a point of view widely adhered to by present-day researchers, that is that

> It matters little, as far as human behavior is concerned, whether or not an idea is 'objectively' new as measured by the lapse of time since its first use or discovery ... If the idea seems new and different to the [unit of adoption], it is an innovation.
>
> (Rogers and Shoemaker, 1971, p. 19)

This kind of reasoning has been attacked by Becker and Whisler (1967, p. 463) who, although defining innovation as a process, state that organizational innovation only occurs when the organization is among the first to adopt and incurs significant costs of search and risk. Later adopters undergo organizational change but not innovation. In other words, innovation processes do not occur during the later phases of the diffusion process. The same viewpoint is echoed by Knight's definition (given above) that ends with 'new to the organization *and to the relevant environment*' (emphasis added). We endorse this view because it stresses important implications for the parties involved. Let us consider the example of a firm that has developed a new product for industrial markets. The first firms adopting the new product are confronted with an innovation. They are unfamiliar with the product, do not know exactly how it functions and what it does, and cannot turn to other firms for advice because there are no references in the market yet. The manufacturer, on the other hand, is confronted with similar difficulties. The product has just been developed and is being introduced into the market. The manufacturer has no clear idea as to what firms can be considered as potential customers and cannot refer to firms already using the innovation. Furthermore, he has to solve initial implementation problems that occur at the early user sites. However, as time goes by

1 the innovation is being adopted by more and more firms,
2 the manufacturer is getting more and more experienced in marketing it,
3 the innovation is modified and various versions are introduced, and
4 similar products are introduced by competitors.

In other words, the innovation loses its uniqueness and becomes just one of the many products offered by the manufacturer, and just one of the many options available to potential adopters.

Because of these considerations, we will define an innovation as *any newly developed idea, practice, or material artefact that is perceived to be new by the early units of adoption within the relevant environment* (thus belonging to the third view discussed above).

An innovation is not synonymous with an invention. In general, an invention refers to the direct result of research activities, while an innovation concerns a commercial product. Accordingly, an invention is assumed to precede an innovation. Martin (1984, p. 2) describes it as follows: 'a scientific invention may be viewed as a new idea or concept generated by R&D, but this invention only becomes an innovation when it is transformed into a socially usable product'. Or, as one other writer succinctly put it, 'Innovation = invention + exploitation' (Roberts, 1988, p. 13). This distinction between invention and innovation is implicit in many definitions of innovation: for example, an innovation is an invention applied for the first time (Mansfield, 1968, p. 99), and 'innovation is the process by which an invention is first transformed into a new commercial product, process or service' (Saren, 1984, pp. 11–12).

CLASSIFICATION OF INNOVATIONS

Many classification schemes have been proposed by different authors to define categories of innovations. According to Zaltman *et al.* (1973, pp. 17–32) three types of classification scheme can be discerned (the following discussion is based largely on their analysis of classification schemes).

State of the system

Knight (1967, p. 484) proposed to classify innovations as programmed and non-programmed innovations. Programmed innovations are scheduled in advance and their development follows defined routines and procedures. Non-programmed innovations, on the other hand, may be of two different types: (1) slack innovations, that are developed because the firm happens to have funds available (that is slack) and (2) distress innovations, that are developed as a reaction to the lack of success of the firm (Cyert and March, 1963, pp. 278–9).

Initial focus

An obvious way to classify innovations is to define categories according to the initial focus of the innovation. Dalton (1968) mentioned three categories: (1) technological innovations, (2) value-centred innovations, and (3) structural innovations. A more important classification is proposed by Knight (1967, p. 482), who distinguishes (1) product or service innovations, (2) production process innovations, (3) organizational-structure innovations, and (4) people innovations. The importance of this scheme lies in the fact that it demonstrates clearly that an innovation is not by definition a new product. Instead, it can refer to a new production process, a new organizational structure, or new relations between people, as is also made clear by the general formulation of our own definition of innovation.

The distinction between product innovations and process innovations has also been stressed by Utterback and Abernathy (1975). Product innovations are concerned with products introduced commercially to meet a user or a market need, while process innovations involve the equipment, methods, and systems employed to produce the products. Both concepts are integrated by Utterback and Abernathy into a dynamic model of process and product innovation. As the industry in which a firm is operating matures, the emphasis changes from product innovation to process innovation (Figure 2.1). However, this seemingly clear-cut distinction between product and process innovations is in practice difficult to maintain. A computer-aided design system that is thought of as a process innovation by the user, may be considered a product innovation by the manufacturer. It all depends on the perspective from which the innovation is viewed.

Product and process innovations together can be termed technical

Figure 2.1 Innovations and stage of development

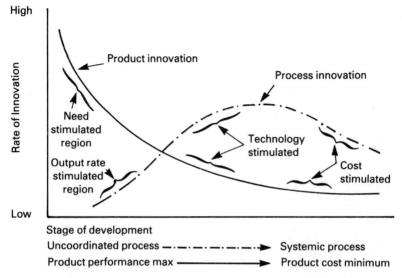

Source: Utterback and Abernathy (1975), *Omega*, vol. 3, no. 6, © Pergamon Press PLC. Reprinted with permission.

innovations, to distinguish them from the other two groups which make up the social innovations (Braun, 1980). Finally, Grossman (1970, p. 543) distinguished between instrumental innovations and ultimate innovations. The latter are ends in themselves, while the former are aimed at specific changes intended to make possible or facilitate the introduction of ultimate innovations at a later time.

Outcome or effect

A third way to classify innovations is to view them in terms of their outcome or effect. Many authors have proposed classifications of this type, all of them describing two extremes: radical and routine innovations. The central variable is the radicalness of an innovation. The more it differs from existing alternatives, the higher is its degree of radicalness. The degree of radicalness can be viewed either from the perspective of the adopter of the innovation or that of its developer, or both perspectives can be integrated.

1 The perspective of the adopter. Harvey and Mills (1970, p. 189) distinguished between routine and innovative changes. In a study of the diffusion of innovations in the flour milling industry,

Hayward, Allen, and Masterson (1977, p. 306) discovered that they fell into two distinct categories: traditional and non-traditional innovations.

2 The perspective of the developer. Inspired by Kuhn's theory of paradigms, Martin (1984, pp. 29–31) differentiated between normal and revolutionary innovations. Normann (1971, p. 205) separated product variations (minor changes) from reorientations (major changes), dividing the latter into three different types.

3 The perspectives of adopter and developer integrated. An example of an integration of both perspectives is provided by Gobeli and Brown (1987, pp. 25–7). Using the two dimensions, they arrive at four types of innovation, incremental innovations and radical innovations again being the two extremes (Figure 2.2).

Figure 2.2 A product innovation matrix

Manufacturer's view
(technological change)

Customer's view (increased benefits)	1 Incremental innovation	2 Technical innovation
	3 Application innovation	4 Radical innovation

Source: Gobeli and Brown (1987), *Research Management,* © Research Technology Management. Reprinted with permission.

When we characterize the complex innovations for industrial markets, the subject of this book, by the dimensions described above, they can be said to be (1) either programmed or non-programmed innovations, (2) technological innovations, (3) product or process innovations (that is technical innovations), or (4) ultimate innovations, and (5) positioned near the 'radical' end of the continuum.

Figure 2.3 summarizes the various classification schemes discussed above.

INNOVATION STRATEGIES

In earlier days product development projects were typically initiated in the absence of a formal strategic plan. The resulting informal planning styles, however, were not always able to cope with the multi-functional intricacies of the product development process. Thus, it is not surprising that in more recent years the importance of an explicit product development strategy has gained wider recognition (this is illustrated by Ramanujam and Mensch (1985) who present a model to improve the strategy–innovation link). Business strategies in general serve the purposes of providing synergy and coordination, aiding organization, allocating resources, motivating personnel, and permitting evaluation (Crawford, 1983, pp. 70–2). Although these general purposes of strategy also apply to new product strategies, the last-named offer two specialized values. They limit the many new product opportunities that face a firm (restricted diversion) and direct the different stages of the product development process (see also Chapter 3).

Crawford's study of the new product strategies of 125 American firms uncovered that these strategies are nowadays much more comprehensive than in earlier years. Deliberately avoiding terms like 'policy' or 'programme', Crawford (1980, p. 4) introduces the term *product innovation charter* to 'emphasize that [it] carries a directional and activity mandate'. The study demonstrated that the product innovation charter consists of

1 the target business arenas that product innovations are to take the firm into or keep it in,
2 the goals or objectives of product innovation activities, and
3 the programme of activities chosen to achieve the defined goals.

In a recent study of new product strategy practices of industrial marketers, Moore (1987, p. 12) found that 'the existence of a formal new product strategy or innovation charter was mentioned by only one-third of the participants'. The resulting informal approach, however, did not appear to be a handicap. Although not formally put down in writing, the elements of a product innovation charter were in place.

While, during the 1970s, product development was mainly regarded as a marketing problem, the 1980s have witnessed an upsurge of interest in the technology dimension (Kantrow, 1980; Pappas, 1984; Martin, 1984; Nyström, 1985; Capon and Glazer, 1987; Willyard and McClees, 1987; Spencer and Triant, 1989; Steele, 1989; Arguëlles, Miravitlles, and Nueno, 1990; Erickson *et al.*, 1990). Recently, this growing emphasis on the strategic implications of technology led Brownlie (1987, p. 56) to warn that it 'must be tempered by a healthy consideration of the market and user

Figure 2.3 Various schemes for classifying innovations

I. Types of innovations in terms of the state of the system

1 Programmed innovations ⎤ Knight (1967)
2 Non-programmed innovations ⎦
  a. Slack innovations ⎤ Cyert and March (1963)
  b. Distress innovations ⎦

II. Types of innovations in terms of their initial focus

1 Technological innovations ⎤
2 Value-centred innovations ⎬ Dalton (1968)
3 Structural innovations ⎦

1 Product or service innovations ⎤
2 Production process innovations ⎬ Utterback and Abernathy (1975)
3 Organizational-structure innovations ⎪
4 People innovations ⎦

1. Technical innovations ⎤ Knight (1967) / Braun (1980)
2. Social innovations ⎦

1. Ultimate innovations ⎤ Grossman (1970)
2. Instrumental innovations ⎦

III. Types of innovations in terms of their outcome or effect

A. Perspective of the adopter:
1 Routine changes ⎤
2 Innovative changes ⎦ Harvey and Mills (1970)

1 Traditional innovations ⎤
2 Non-traditional innovations ⎦ Hayward *et al.* (1977)

B. Perspective of the developer:
1 Normal innovations ⎤
2 Revolutionary innovations ⎦ Martin (1984)

1 Variations ⎤
2 Reorientations ⎥ Normann
   a. systematic ⎥ (1971)
   b. idiosyncratic ⎥
   c. marginal ⎦

C. Both perspectives integrated:
1 Incremental innovations ⎤
2 Technical innovations ⎥ Gobeli and
3 Application innovations ⎥ Brown (1987)
4 Radical innovations ⎦

Source: based on Zaltman, Duncan, and Holbeck (1973)

needs', thus arguing for a balance between marketing and technology. In the words of Hodock (1990, p. 5) 'an R&D focus without customer focus is a recipe for disaster'. According to Petroni (1985), the direction of emphasis depends on the type of industry.

Every organization is confronted with a range of strategic opportunities and has to select a strategy based on the specific circumstances and established goals. According to Urban, Hauser, and Dholakia (1987, p. 15) one of the first basic strategic decisions a firm has to make is whether to be *reactive* or *proactive*. A reactive product strategy deals with the initiating pressures as they occur (for example waiting until the competition introduces a product and copying if it is successful). A proactive strategy explicitly allocates resources to identify and seize opportunities and to pre-empt possible adverse events (for instance, outsmart the competition by being first on the market with a product that competitors find difficult to match). Urban *et al.* (1987) distinguish four reactive and four proactive product strategies (Table 2.1). Teece (1988) warns that the benefits of innovations do not always accrue to the innovator. When the firm that is first to commercialize a new product concept fails to control

Table 2.1 Product strategies

Reactive product strategies	*Proactive product strategies*
Defensive: Modifying existing products as a reaction to successful new products from the competition	*Research and development*: Conducting future-oriented research and development activities in order to develop technically superior products
Imitative: Copying the competition's new product before it is known whether or not the product is a success	*Marketing*: Finding a customer need and developing a product to fill it
Second-but-better: Introducing a copy of the competition's new product that offers distinct advantages over the original	*Entrepreneurial*: A special person (the entrepreneur) has an idea and realizes it by generating enthusiasm and mobilizing resources
Responsive: Develop a new product as a reaction to customer's requirements	*Acquisition*: Purchasing other firms that have products new to the acquiring firm and perhaps the market

Source: Based on Urban, Hauser, and Dholakia (1987)

complementary assets, it runs the risk of losing to followers or imitators.

Cooper (1984) studied the reported new product strategies of 122 industrial product firms in Canada and characterized every strategy on each of sixty-six strategy elements, which were subsequently reduced to nineteen strategy dimensions. Clustering of the data resulted in a classification of five new product strategies:

1 technologically driven,
2 balanced,
3 technologically deficient,
4 low budget, conservative, and
5 high budget, diverse.

The main conclusion was that 'The elite group of firms that adopted ... the balanced strategy ... achieved by far the best performance on virtually every performance criterion' (Cooper, 1984, p. 36). (The balanced strategy featured a balance between technological sophistication, orientation and innovativeness, and a strong market orientation. The programme was highly focused and new products were targeted at very attractive markets.) In fact, each of the five strategies was associated with a different performance level and type, thus establishing a strong link between the new product strategy a firm selects and the results it achieves.

INNOVATIVENESS AND FIRM SIZE

A much debated and researched issue in the literature about innovations is the link between firm size and innovativeness. Apart from a discussion of the relative importance of firm size, the question of causality has also been raised. Is firm size a determinant of innovativeness or is the size of the firm a result of the innovativeness of the firm? Although most studies assume the former position, the matter is not clear-cut. As regards the relative importance of firm size, we are confronted with a similar ambiguous situation. While many researchers discovered that small firms are more innovative than large ones and that firm size is directly related to innovativeness, others have found that large organizations are more likely to be innovative. Rothwell and Zegveld (1982) remark that any discussion of the issue is bound to be sterile when it is not conducted on an industry-by-industry basis. Ettlie and Rubenstein (1987) have tried to resolve some of the apparent contradictions by focusing on the radicalness of the innovation as an important variable. Roberts arrives at the same conclusion when he draws attention to 'the stage of development and use of the technology' as a significant factor.

> Much of the loose talk about small companies being more innovative than large ones should really be more precise statements that say small companies are likely to be the ones who are innovative at very early stages of new fields. Large companies as a group are more likely to be the primary innovation sources at later large-market stages of fields of technology.
>
> (Roberts, 1989, p. 38)

In discussing the relationship between innovativeness and firm size the discussion usually focuses on the two extremes: small and large firms. Also, when reviewing the existing literature on innovations, it becomes clear that by far the largest number of publications are written from the perspective of either the newly founded, small, emerging company that has started to make an impact on the market with an innovative product, or the established large company that has introduced another new product in order to obtain a larger share of the market. The group in between is usually lost sight of or neglected. This group consists of medium-sized companies that have been in existence for a number of years and persist in their striving to turn out innovative products.

The economic importance of the group of mid-sized companies is stressed by several authors. In his treatise 'Innovation and Entrepreneurship', Peter Drucker (1985, p. 2) points out that in the United States the *Fortune* 500 companies have been losing jobs steadily since around 1970, slowly at first, but at a much faster rate since 1977/8. All in all, by 1984, the jobs permanently lost by these companies were estimated to be at least 4 to 6 million. During this period, employment by government, universities, and hospitals declined as well. Nevertheless, during this period more than 40 million new jobs were created. As Drucker (1985, p. 3) concludes,

> And all these new jobs must have been created by small and medium-sized institutions, most of them small and medium-sized businesses, and a great many of them, if not the majority, new businesses that did not even exist twenty years ago.

Clifford and Cavanagh (1985, pp. 2–3) estimated that less than 1 per cent of all businesses in America are independent, medium-sized companies (defined as having sales between $25 million and $1 billion), and concluded that, despite their small number they 'are responsible for about a quarter of all sales and account for a fifth of all private-sector employment'. Furthermore, this segment is a mirror-image of the US economy in general in terms of industry composition, geography, and overall business and financial performance. These were the major reasons for their study of the winning performers in this 'neglected sector'.

Myers and Sweezy (1978) analysed the reasons for failure of 200 innovations and related them to firm size. With respect to medium-sized companies they found that they encounter a disproportionate share of management problems. 'Apparently, these companies are too big for innovations to command the individual attention of top management, but too small to hire the kind of specialized management that innovation needs'. Marketing and technology were also considered to be obstacles.

In Europe, some researchers have started to shift their attention away from large- to small- and medium-sized firms (for example OECD, 1982; Meyer and Roberts, 1986; Steinhöfler, 1986; Corsten and Lang, 1988; Oakey, Rothwell, and Cooper, 1988; Bahrami and Evans, 1989; Boag and Rinholm, 1989; Johne and Rowntree, 1990). In the Netherlands small- and medium-sized firms are usually grouped together (see for example Buise, 1990). Poutsma *et al.* (1987) mention a considerable decline in the number of large firms in the Netherlands during the years 1970–82, while at the same time the number of small- and medium-sized firms grew dramatically (in 1986 almost 80 per cent of all firms in the Netherlands belonged to this category). In spite of this, research into innovation processes in small- and medium-sized firms is strongly biased in favour of small firms (for example Nijverheidsorganisatie TNO, 1974; Buijs, 1984; During, 1984; Kok, Offerman and Pellenbarg, 1985).

For the reasons outlined above, ((1) mid-sized companies have been largely neglected by researchers both abroad and in the Netherlands, (2) mid-sized companies are of significant economic importance, and (3) in mid-sized companies failure of innovations is predominantly caused by management-related factors) the research reported in the second half of this book aims at taking this segment of mid-sized companies in the Netherlands out of its relative anonymity.

INNOVATION: FAILURE VERSUS SUCCESS

We all agree that innovation
Will benefit both world and nation
The question we must answer later
Is, will it help the innovator?
(Kenneth Boulding)

For industrial marketers it is of prime importance to know which factors determine the success of an innovation. This knowledge can be of assistance in setting up a product development programme and taking the right decisions during the different stages of the process. In this section we will therefore discuss the different factors influencing the eventual success of an innovation and stress the importance of marketing-related factors. First, however, we will try to answer the question of how large a percentage of innovations actually fail.

New product failure rates

Practitioners and academics alike, usually agree that many newly developed products do not become a success and that the failure rate is too high. Notwithstanding this agreement, the exact percentage of new products that fail has been the subject of discussion for many years. A variety of studies have been conducted, but the results vary widely. The fact that percentages mentioned by authors as private opinions have been cited by others as facts, only added to the confusion. According to Crawford (1979a, pp. 10–11), the differences between the percentages mentioned are mainly due to different research methods and definitions of key concepts.

1 The research method used
    The results of any kind of research are obviously very dependent on the research method used. With respect to research into the failure rate of innovations, Crawford (1979b, p. 10) mentions four different research methods.
    (a) One of the most common is to investigate *success/failure pairs.* Similar new products, one a success and the other a failure, are paired and compared. The factors influencing success can be determined by making statistical analyses of large samples. This method has been used in the widely published SAPPHO-studies (Robertson, Achilladelis, and Jervis, 1972; Szakasits, 1974), but was also used by Cooper (1979a) and Maidique and Zirger (1984).
    (b) A second method is to analyse *executive opinion.* The persons involved in the development of specific new products are asked what, in their opinion, were the most important reasons for success or failure. A disadvantage is that, except for large samples, the information obtained is often anecdotal and subjective. The most famous example of a study using this method, is the one by Peters and Waterman (1982). Other

examples are a study into innovation processes in Dutch industry (Nijverheidsorganisatie TNO, 1974) and the study
conducted by Link (1987).

(c) When the persons interviewed are experts on industry, instead
of the people directly involved, the research method is called
third-party assessment. This method is obviously very subjective and only useful when the experts are very familiar with the
industry in question.

(d) When a *generalized survey* is used, experienced marketers are
asked for their experience with failed products (as a group
instead of individual cases). An example is given by Hopkins
and Bailey (1971).

2 Key definitional decisions

The results of individual studies are also strongly influenced by the
way certain key terms have been defined. Especially important are
the following questions. What is a new product? When does the
new product come into existence? What is success? How long
should a product have to achieve success? What types of firm or
product should be studied? To illustrate the complexity of all these
definitional decisions we will take a closer look at the central
question 'what is success?'. Should just financial criteria be used in
determining the eventual success of an innovation, or should they
be combined with non-financial goals? As Maidique and Zirger
(1985) pointed out: 'while financial return is one of the most easily
quantifiable industrial parameters, it is far from the only important
one'. This observation and the results of an empirical investigation
led Cooper and Kleinschmidt (1987a, p. 216) to define three
dimensions that characterize new product performance: (a) the
overall financial performance, (b) the degree to which the product
opens new opportunities, and (c) the impact of the product in the
market.

In an attempt to determine the new product failure rate in America
by evaluating the most reliable and most recent studies, Crawford
(1979a) compared thirty-two sources which actually were reporting
on a study or which were cited as doing so. Initially he discovered that
the cited failure rates varied between 15 per cent and 99 per cent, but
closer investigation led him to drop twenty-five of these sources for
varying reasons. Based on analysis of the remaining seven studies he
came to the conclusion that 'the best estimate from available studies is
that around 35 per cent of new products fail' (Crawford, 1979a, p. 12).
Eight years later he updated the study by reviewing another seven

studies published after 1979, which resulted in a confirmation of the results obtained earlier (although the failure rate for industrial products seemed to be somewhat lower than the rate for consumer products) (Crawford, 1987).

Before we discuss the factors causing failure, we need to point out that while most researchers have studied success and failure at the product or project level, some academics have criticized this approach. They argue that the future of a firm depends on successfully pursuing a balanced programme of product developments, and incorporate this long-term view by focusing on the factors contributing to *programme* success (Cooper, 1984; Johne and Snelson, 1988).

Factors causing failure

After having determined the percentage of innovations that fails, it is time to discuss the underlying causes of failure. Or, to put it differently, what factors determine the eventual success of an innovation?

As early as 1964, the National Industrial Conference Board published the results of a study of the factors causing the failure of new products. The most important causes of failure were (in order of importance):

1 inadequate market analysis;
2 product defects;
3 higher costs than anticipated;
4 poor timing;
5 competitive reaction;
6 insufficient marketing effort;
7 inadequate sales effort, and
8 inadequate distribution.

Eight years later, Foster (1972) presented a long list of causes of product failure. However, the reasons are very similar to those cited in the NICB study and can be reduced to two main factors: (1) inadequate knowledge of market conditions and (2) managerial incompetence.

Both studies mention inadequate analysis of the market as a very important factor, which fact has also been stressed by Marquis (1969), Webster (1969), Gisser (1973), and Briscoe (1973). Crawford (1977) compared eight studies of new product success rates and listed the most important reasons cited for new product failure (Table 2.2). All studies point to lack of meaningfully superior product uniqueness as the predominant reason for failure. This could have

Table 2.2 The most important reasons for new product failure

		1	2	3	4	5	6	7	8	*Total*
1	Lacked meaningful product uniqueness (a)	X	X	X	X	X	X	X	X	8
2	Poor planning (b)	X	X		X	X	X	X		6
3	Wrong timing	X	X	X	X		X			5
4	Enthusiasm crowded on facts				X	X	X	X	X	5
5	Product failed	X	X				X			3
6	Product lacked a champion					X				1
7	Company politics					X				1
8	Unexpected high product costs						X			1

Crawford's sources:

(1) G.J. Abrams, 'Why New Products Fail', *Advertising Age*, 22 April 1974, pp.51–2.
(2) T.L. Angelus, 'Why Do Most New Products Fail?', *Advertising Age*, 24 March 1969, pp.85–6.
(3) Booz, Allen and Hamilton, *Management of New Products*, Chicago, Ill., 1968, especially p.11–12.
(4) W.J. Constandse, 'Why New Product Management Fails', *Business Management*, June 1971, pp.163–5.
(5) R.W. Diehl, 'Achieving Successful Innovation', *Michigan Business Review*, March 1972, pp.6–10.
(6) D.S. Hopkins and E.L. Bailey, 'New Product Pressures', *The Conference Board Research*, 8, June 1971, pp.16–24.
(7) M.B. MacDonald, Jr, *Appraising the Market for Industrial Products*, National Industrial Conference Board, New York.
(8) V. Miles, 'Avoid these Errors in New Product Design', *Advertising Age*, 15 July 1974, pp.26–ff.

Source: Crawford (1977), *Journal of Marketing*, vol. 31, no. 4, © American Marketing Association. Reprinted with permission.
Notes: (a) In some cases there was, in fact, no difference, but in most cases there was some difference, whose value was over-estimated by the marketers to potential buyers.
(b) Includes poor positioning, poor segmentation, under-budgeting, poor overall themes, over pricing, and all other facets of a plan.

been avoided by conducting better marketing research. Crawford offers nine hypotheses to explain the failure of marketing research to stem or stop the flow of new product failures.

Although every researcher uses a different list of criteria, the factors influencing the success of innovations can be grouped in five broad categories, that is factors related to

1 *marketing:* uniqueness of the product, benefits offered to the user, the structure/size/growth of the market, efficiency of the marketing communications, launch effort, distribution channel choice, targeting and pricing strategies, synergy with existing marketing skills, involvement of users, quality of market research, education of users, training of the sales force, etc.;

2 *management:* top management support, contacts with research institutions, planning, timing, efficiency of the development activities, internal communications, quality of management, management style, inadequate project evaluation or control, integration of the innovation project with corporate strategy, existence of a protocol, etc.;

3 *technology:* in-house expertise, contact between R&D and the production and marketing functions, practicality of the design, product defects, production problems, technical and production synergy, availability of outside technology, etc.;

4 *financial resources:* financial resources devoted to the project, etc.;

5 *external events:* reaction of key competitors, changes in user needs, changes in exchange rates, expiration of patents, government regulations, etc.

Failure cannot be attributed to one single factor, but is generally brought about by a complex set of interacting factors. Sarin and Kapur (1990) describe five new product introductions by small industrial firms in India that clearly illustrate how various factors interact in producing failure. Nevertheless, it may be clear by now that the first group of factors is the most important in determining the eventual success of product innovations. This conclusion has been underscored by Banting (1978), Cooper (1979a), Rothwell (1979), Hopkins (1981), Peters and Waterman (1982), Maidique and Zirger (1984), Voss (1985b), Twiss (1986), and Link (1987). Cooper (1976) and New and Schlacter (1979) stress the need for involvement of marketing in the development process at an early stage (indeed at every stage!), while Wilson and Ghingold (1987) offer a framework to link the R&D activities to market needs.

The above discussion implies another observation of importance to industrial marketers: that the most important causes of failure can be controlled. In their recent study, Cooper and Kleinschmidt (1987b, p. 182) concluded that 'Controllable variables, rather than situational or environment variables, are the dominant factors in success ... [This] means that the way the new product process is managed and executed ... largely decide project outcomes'. Despite all these observations, empirical studies that offer industrial marketers practical guidelines to incorporate marketing during all the stages of the product development process are scarce and usually fail to reach industrial marketers. (A recent study by Barclay and Benson (1987) showed that while only a very small minority of managers has even heard of well-publicized studies of the success and failure of new products, just 10 per cent of them had actually taken steps to apply the results!) Marketing-related factors, with emphasis on the role of market research, are mentioned as being of crucial importance. But at the same time, many critics maintain that traditional approaches to market research are inappropriate for innovative products (Tauber, 1974; Cowell and Blois, 1977; Crawford, 1977; Littler and Sweeting, 1985). Before discussing how market research can be conducted for innovations for industrial markets, and thus describing how marketing can be integrated with the development project, in the next chapter we will present the processes of product development, adoption, and diffusion.

3 Product development, adoption, and diffusion

> Only through continually bringing forth new products can most manufacturing companies sustain their long-run growth and profitability.
>
> (Samuel Johnson and Conrad Jones, 1957)

Before an innovation becomes a product widely accepted by the market it has passed through a number of stages. Even before the development process is started, a product innovation strategy must be set out. According to a study conducted by Booz, Allen and Hamilton (1982), companies that have successfully launched new products are more likely to have had a formal new product process, as well as a strategic plan, in place for a longer period of time. The new product strategy (1) links new products to company objectives, (2) aids in the search for new products (that is suggests what markets and/or technologies should be investigated), (3) identifies the strategic roles to be played by new products (for example defending a market-share position or maintaining the firm's position as a product innovator), and (4) provides general screening criteria (Booz *et al.*, 1982, p. 11; see also Chapter 2).

Typically, after the new product has been developed, it is adopted by innovative customers and a gradual diffusion into the market follows. This chapter describes the central processes of product development, adoption, and diffusion. Several types of model of the product development process are discussed and eventually one specific model is selected. The sections on the adoption and diffusion processes only discuss the aspects essential to this book, like the buying centre, the role of the purchasing agent, the speed of diffusion, adopter categories, and opinion leadership. For a more extensive review of the literature on the adoption and diffusion of new industrial products, the interested reader is referred to Kennedy

(1983). At the end of this chapter the three processes are shown to be closely interrelated.

THE PRODUCT DEVELOPMENT PROCESS

The literature on the subject of new product development abounds with models that try to capture the essence of a complex process in a relatively simple structure. When studying innovation, a general model is needed as a conceptualization of the product development process.

However, Cooper (1983a) studied the product development processes of fifty-eight new products in thirty firms and concluded that there is no 'typical process model'. Instead he found seven models, each with its own distinct set of activities and emphases. Nevertheless, it should be borne in mind that these models were based on descriptions of real situations and included processes that led to poor or just average performance. The fact that in actual situations several distinct models can be distinguished should not preclude the construction of a generalized *normative* model, which can be used to guide management in developing new products. Many studies of innovation assume such a general model.

Models of the product development process

In this section, a number of existing models are discussed and classified according to the taxonomy proposed by Saren (1984, p. 11):

1 departmental-stage models;
2 activity-stage models;
3 decision-stage models;
4 conversion process models; and
5 response models.

Within each category the models are mostly arranged in order of growing complexity. However, not all existing models fall neatly into one of the categories mentioned above. In the following survey these models are grouped according to their most salient characteristic. The advantages and disadvantages of each type of model are summarized.

However, before we continue the discussion of various product development models, we would like to comment on the function of models in general. In the literature on scientific methodology, models are frequently described as

1 being a simplification of reality, which implies that they must reflect reality, and/or

2 possessing instrumental value, which means that models do not necessarily reflect reality but can be used, for example, to predict real-life phenomena. (An example is provided by models of atoms employed in natural science.)

This goes to show that the structure and content of a model strongly depends on the objective of the model's designer. For our purposes, that is in order to have both scientific and practical value, a model of industrial product development should possess both characteristics at the same time. The model should be sufficiently realistic to reflect the intricacies involved in developing industrial innovations. At the same time, it must be simple enough to enable management to make real-life decisions. This dual objective is borne in mind in discussing the advantages and disadvantages of the models presented below. Based on both this discussion and our objectives, as stated in Chapter 1, a model is selected as a framework for presenting the results of the empirical investigation (as reported in Chapters 5 and 6).

Departmental-stage models

The simplest model represents the product development process by a series of stages referring to the departments within the firm that are involved in the process. An example is given in Figure 3.1 (Saren, 1984). According to this model an innovation enters the R&D department as an idea, moves sequentially through several other departments, and eventually reaches the market-place as a new product.

A more advanced model presented by Robertson (1974) shows an innovation as progressing from the R&D department through design, production, and marketing to emerge in the market as a new product (see Figure 3.2). Apart from progress through these departments, it also shows the influence of technological knowledge and market needs. The origin of an innovation is shown to be the result of a synthesis of knowledge–push and market–pull elements.

Figure 3.1 An example of a departmental-stage model

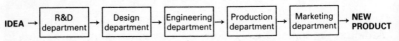

Source: Saren (1984), *R&D Management*, vol. 14, no. 1, © Basil Blackwell Ltd. Reprinted with permission.

Figure 3.2 A departmental-stage model

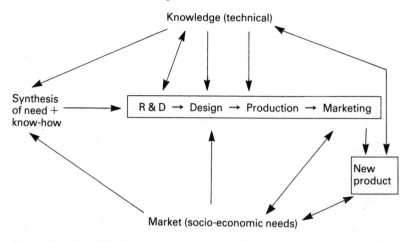

Source: Robertson (1974), *Management Decision*, vol. 12, no. 6, © MCB University Press Ltd. Reprinted with permission.

Although many more examples of departmental-stage models can be given, they all exhibit the same basic structure by showing the various departments through which an innovation moves on its way to the market-place. Differences between individual models are due to the degree of specification. As regards these models, criticism is not levelled against the number and kind of departments involved, but rather addresses the fact that they do not offer much insight into the process of product development.

1 The models only list the various departments involved and do not show the activities carried out in the course of the process.
2 This type of model shows that the innovation starts as an idea and emerges as a new product, but does not show the intermediate forms.
3 Departmental-stage models assume a sequential movement through the various departments involved. Possible overlaps between departments like R&D and production as well as feedback are ignored.
4 The models lack a general character in the way that individual models are hard to compare with each other. Different organizations use different terminology in naming their departments.

Although in some cases a departmental-stage model is all that is needed, another type of model is required to provide a more realistic representation of the product development process.

Activity-stage models

A common approach to a more realistic description is to represent the product development process by a sequence of activities. An example is given by Utterback (1974) who divides the process into three distinct stages, that is:

1 idea generation;
2 problem-solving or idea development; and
3 implementation (bringing the product to the market-place).

During (1986) presents a model, based on a model of the psychologist Kolb for individual learning, that breaks the process down into four phases that are very similar to the three stages from Utterback's model: (1) creative phase, (2) selection phase, (3) design phase, and (4) application phase. The main difference is that, whereas Utterback presented the process as a linear series of steps, During depicts a cyclical process.

The best known activity-stage model, however, is the one developed by Booz, Allen and Hamilton (1968, p. 8). It depicts the innovation as moving through six sequential stages, that are presented in a logical order and are interdependent. The explicit activity stages allow us to follow the intermediate forms of an innovation as it moves through the process. In the first stage, a number of ideas are generated that are screened in the second stage according to a number of criteria (technical feasibility, organizational fit, product mix, financial requirements, etc.). Stage three entails a commercial evaluation, that is, the innovation's future sales and costs are estimated. A prototype of the new product is developed in stage four and subsequently tested in stage five. The process concludes with the commercialization of the new product. As a result of subsequent research, the original model (illustrated in Figure 3.3) was modified to include the stage 'new product strategy development' at the start of the process. In this way, the original model became linked to the strategic objectives of the firm (Booz, Allen and Hamilton, 1982, p. 12). The Booz, Allen and Hamilton model has formed the basis for a large number of similar models (see, for example, Haeffner (1973, p. 21) and Samli, Palda, and Barker (1987, p. 49)).

These traditional sequential models have been criticized by Moore (1984, p. 11) for two reasons:

1 their inability to illustrate the interactions between the various stages of the new product development process, and

Figure 3.3 The process of product development depicted as a series of activities

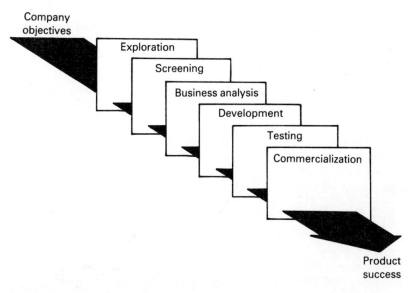

2 the assumption that each stage is completed before the next one starts.

To overcome these shortcomings, he developed a tentative model in which some of the stages occur in parallel with each other. The stages themselves, however, are essentially the same as the ones from the original Booz, Allen and Hamilton model. A more elaborate criticism of the traditional models is expressed by Takeuchi and Nonaka (1986). Based on a study of six product development processes in four Japanese multinational companies, they conclude that today's changed circumstances require a new new product development approach.

> The traditional sequential ... approach to product development ... may conflict with the goals of maximum speed and flexibility. Instead, a holistic or 'rugby' approach – where a team tries to go the distance as a unit, passing the ball back and forth – may better serve today's competitive requirements. ... Under the rugby approach, the product development process emerges from the

constant interaction of a hand-picked, multidisciplinary team whose members work together from start to finish.

(Takeuchi and Nonaka, 1986, pp. 137–8)

Recently, numerous practitioners have acknowledged the benefits of the rugby approach (Spencer and Triant, 1989, p. 38; Bronikowski, 1990, p. 35; Mitsch, 1990, p. 20), while others employ terms such as 'simultaneous engineering' (Duffy and Kelly, 1989) and 'concurrent engineering' (King *et al.*, 1990) to propagate the same concept.

Miaoulis and LaPlaca (1982) depicted the process as consisting of three broad activity stages: assessment, development, and execution. Each of these stages is made up of a large number of activities that must be undertaken. The various activities are no longer depicted as being on one level but are related to three different dimensions: market, product, and technology. The product dimension shows the progress of the innovation during the product development process. By linking the last activities of the execution phase to the first activities of the assessment phase the cyclical character of the process is acknowledged. Finally, the model allows for feedback loops as well, a phenomenon largely overlooked by the models previously discussed.

Kline (1985, p. 38) drew attention to three different types of feedback link. Sometimes work is passed from one group to another as the innovation moves to another stage. The first type of feedback is important at these interfaces. The second type of feedback relates to the fact that sometimes it is necessary to go back to previous stages of the process to correct certain aspects of the product. A third type of feedback link is distinguished because, after market introduction, the competitive position of the product should be investigated and the results used as input for the development and design of later products. So, again the cyclical character of the process is recognized.

The seven models distinguished by Cooper (1983a) are also activity-stage models. Although the models differ in the types of activity and the time spent on them, they all depict the development process as a series of activities. Like Moore, Cooper recognizes that activities can be undertaken in parallel.

More sophisticated models can be obtained through combining the two different types of model by linking the various activities with the departments involved (although the problem that different organizations use different terminology in naming their departments still remains). An example is given by Twiss (1986); apart from showing how an innovation moves from idea to product, the model also mentions the intermediate forms of the innovation (Figure 3.4).

Figure 3.4 A model of the product development process that combines activities with departments and clearly shows the innovation's intermediate forms

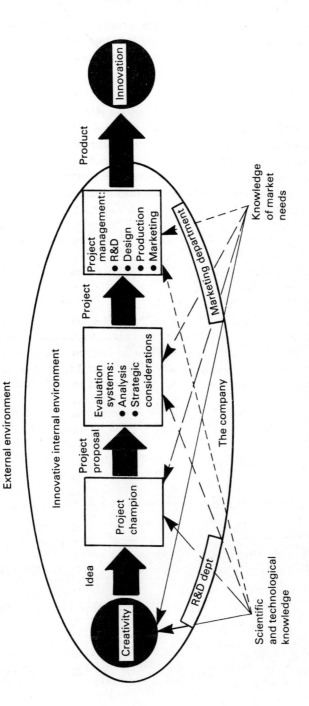

Source: Twiss (1986), *Managing Technological Innovation*, third edn, © Pitman Publishing. Reprinted with permission.

Scientific knowledge and market needs are identified as external influences on the process, with the R&D and marketing departments functioning as intermediaries.

Activity-stage models obviously improve on the departmental-stage models because:

1 they clearly show the tasks carried out during each stage;
2 they show the intermediate forms of development as the innovation progresses through the process;
3 the various stages are more clearly separated (although several of the models show that some overlap still exists); and
4 by breaking the process down into general activities, instead of departments, the resulting model is more generally applicable.

The weak point of this approach, however, is that it implies an ordered sequence by which the innovation moves through the process. Generally, there is no other alternative than to move from one stage to the next. However, some activity-stage models have incorporated feedback loops and thus implicitly acknowledge the need for evaluative decisions. The existence of different alternatives and the decisions necessary to choose among them are explicitly recognized by the decision-stage models.

Decision-stage models

Decision-stage models rest on the premise that the product development process can be broken down into a number of decisions, which are based on the information available. The process is divided into several stages, separated by evaluation points. At every evaluation point, two types of decision must be made. The first one is referred to as the GO/NO GO decision. (Should the process be continued or stopped?) Balachandra (1984, p. 96) identified some of the more important criteria to be used in GO/NO GO decisions. He divided these criteria into two categories: the absolutely critical ones (RED LIGHT variables) and the cautionary ones (YELLOW LIGHT variables). Regular and careful monitoring of these variables leads to a better insight into the likelihood of successfully completing the project. If it is decided to continue the process, a second decision concerns the next stage to be undertaken. This can be the next stage in the process, but one may also skip one or more stages or go back to an earlier stage (feedback loops). This results in a much more flexible approach as compared with activity-stage models, which generally imply that all stages are carried out in a prescribed sequence. Another advantage of decision-stage models is that they are easily constructed by taking the stages of an activity-stage model and linking them by evaluation points. Cooper (1983b) presents an elaborate example, based on an extensive review of both existing theoretical models and actual case histories (Figure 3.5). The model distinguishes between technical/production activities and market-oriented activities.

Ronkainen (1985) presented a model consisting of five broad phases (concept, feasibility, product and process development, scale-up, and standardization), with each phase broken down into several activities (Figure 3.6). The model not only incorporates many evaluation points, but also shows the consequences of every GO/NO GO decision. Thus many potential feedback loops, as well as the input necessary for each evaluation, are identified. Ronkainen emphasized that decision-makers use three basic groups of criteria, that is product, market(ing), and financial criteria. The importance of the criteria varies from one phase to another. At the outset of the process, decisions are mostly based on market criteria. During the next few phases product-related criteria start to dominate while, during the last phases, financial criteria are the most important.

Van der Kooy (1983, p. 53) suggested a model consisting of three stages, that is definition, design, and preparation, which are separated by evaluation points. Each stage is subsequently split up into three sub-stages: becoming aware of the situation, searching for alternatives, and selecting an alternative. These sub-stages are separated by interim evaluation points. The decision points are thus not only situated between the stages, but within the stages (that is between the sub-stages) as well. A similar breakdown is given by Cooper and More (1979), who split up each stage into four activities:

1 information gathering to reduce uncertainties,
2 evaluation of information,
3 decision-making, and
4 identification of remaining key uncertainties.

Decision-stage models are basically an extension of the activity-stage models, and thus enjoy all the advantages of these models (already mentioned above). An additional advantage is that, since they incorporate evaluation points, it becomes possible to apply decision theory, probability analysis, and computer simulation. Each decision point is viewed as a small process with information as input and the decision(s) as output. In the same way, the next type of model views the total development process in terms of inputs and outputs.

Figure 3.5 An example of an elaborate decision-stage model

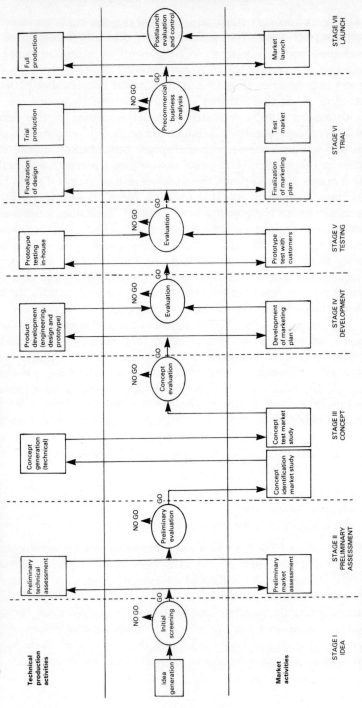

Source: Cooper (1983b), *IEEE Transactions on Engineering Management*, vol. EM-30, no. 1, © IEEE. Reprinted with permission.

Figure 3.6 A model of the product development process that shows both evaluation points and the consequences of every GO/NO GO decision

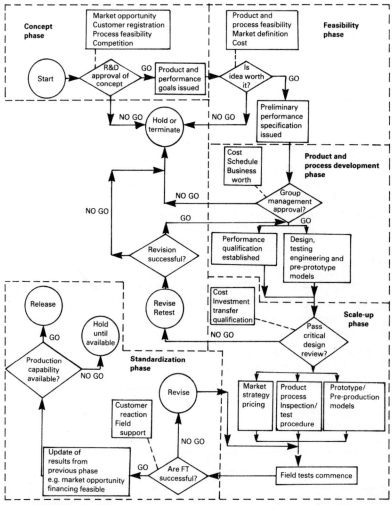

Source: Ronkainen (1985), © Elsevier Science Publishing Co. Inc. Reprinted with permission.

Conversion process models

The main criticism directed against all three types of 'stage' model is that they depict the process of product development as an orderly and logical sequence. This enables one to analyse innovations as progressing through a series of stages in a rational manner. In practice, however, there is substantial evidence that this view is a simplification of reality. The innovation process is usually not quite so rational and ordered. In an article with the revealing title 'Managing innovation: controlled chaos', Quinn (1985, p. 83) concluded that 'Innovation tends to be individually motivated, opportunistic, customer responsive, tumultuous, nonlinear, and interactive in its development. Managers can plan overall directions and goals, but surprises are likely to abound.' This consideration leads to viewing the innovation process as a system with specified inputs and outputs.

An example of this approach, given by Cooper (1982), views the product development process as using R&D spending and the firm's resources and skills as inputs to achieve new products in the market-place as outputs, while being influenced by firm characteristics (Figure 3.7). Another example is provided by Twiss (1986, p. 4).

In both cases product development is represented as a conversion process, with the process itself largely remaining a black box. The inputs may take the form of activities (for example design), information (for example scientific knowledge and customer needs), and departments (for example R&D) and are used by the firm. The order in which they are used, however, remains unspecified.

Schon also attacked what he calls 'the rational view of innovation':

> According to this view, innovation is essentially similar to other major functions of a firm. It can be managed. It must be analyzed into its component parts and made subject to rational control. It is a series of orderly steps ... intelligently directed toward an objective spelled out in advance. ... The rational view of innovation ignores or violates actual corporate experience.
>
> (Schon, 1967, p. 19–20)

Figure 3.7 Product development viewed as a conversion process

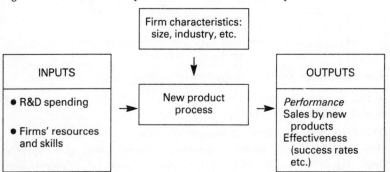

Source: Cooper (1982), *Industrial Marketing Management*, vol. 11, © Elsevier Science Publishing Co. Inc. Reprinted with permission.

Schon distinguished between uncertainty, which he considers incalculable, and risk, which he characterizes as quantifiable. Firms are unable to operate in uncertainty, but are beautifully equipped to handle risk. This led him to conclude that 'the innovative work of a corporation consists in converting uncertainty to risk' (Schon, 1967, p. 25) by both using the existing body of knowledge and adding to it when necessary.

All conversion process models are based on the same conception of the product development process: a conversion of inputs into outputs. Because the conversion process is presented as a black box, it fails to offer any insights into the activities undertaken or the stages that must be gone through. These models can be used, however, for 'externally oriented' studies of innovations, for instance studies concerning the effects or diffusion of innovations.

Response models

Innovations involve changes to which people react. This reaction can be described by a series of stages. At the outset the individual must perceive the change, he or she then searches for information about its effects and evaluates the results. Finally, he or she reacts to the change. This type of description has been termed a stimulus-response view. The individual reacts (the response) in a certain way to a change (the stimulus).

Not only individuals, but organizations as well, react to a change. Becker and Whisler (1967) compared a number of studies and concluded that most investigators agree that the process of innovation consists of the following four stages:

1 *stimulus*, that leads an individual within the organization to conceive a new idea,
2 *conception* of the idea for an innovation,
3 *proposal* of the innovation project by the individual (or others), and
4 *adoption/rejection* of the innovation.

Response models present an innovation as a reaction of the firm to a stimulus. They are radically different from the other models presented in this chapter. The product development process that is broken down into activities or stages by other models is located implicitly between the third and fourth step in response models. These models strongly concentrate on just one aspect of the innovation process, namely the early stage of inception.

Selection of a model of the product development process

From the survey given above, we can conclude that there is a wide variety of models that try to describe the product development process. All these models were developed by the authors with a specific purpose in mind, for example to examine the factors influencing success or the role of product champions and top management, and *were not meant as an accurate general description of the process.* The aspects studied by the authors determined the format of the model. In the same way, the purpose of this book and the underlying research largely determine the choice of the model to be used as a framework.

When evaluating the five broad categories, we can conclude that conversion process models do not describe the actual development process, while response models concentrate on just one stage of the process. Departmental-stage models focus on the departments involved rather than the activities, which precludes the formulation of generalizations concerning the actions to be taken during the process. Since this book primarily aims at offering managers practical guidelines regarding the actions to be undertaken during the process of product development, both the activity-stage models and decision-stage models appear to be suitable. Because (1) decision-stage models are in fact extensions of activity-stage models (making them more flexible and realistic) and (2) the decisions underlying the actions undertaken during the product development process are of primary importance, a decision-stage model is clearly to be preferred. Furthermore, decision-stage models can easily be adapted to account for involvement of users and third parties in product development.

The choice of a specific decision-stage model further depends on the degree of specification of the models available. The model presented by Cooper (1983b) (Figure 3.5), based on extensive research findings, an analysis of previous normative models, and a review of sixty flow charts of case histories of new product projects, seems to offer a sufficiently detailed and realistic description of the product development process with respect to industrial products to act as an action guide to managers (a description of the individual stages can be found in appendix A).

Nevertheless, some criticism can be raised against this model. Stage V of the model (testing) includes both in-house testing of the prototype and testing the prototype with customers, these being undertaken in parallel. In our opinion this seems highly improbable: a firm will perform the internal test (in-house test or alpha test) before performing the external test (product test by customers or beta test) because of the different objectives of both activities. The purpose of the in-house test is to test the technical functionality of the product, while testing with customers is done as a last check to see whether product characteristics meet customer requirements. As a result of the in-house test the prototype may be modified before being tested by customers. It should be stressed here that, in practice, the various stages will not be as sequential and as neatly separated from each other as the model suggests. Overlapping stages and feedback loops will be the rule rather than the exception. As mentioned before, each GO decision may result in going back to a previously completed stage. However, for the sake of clarity, all these potential feedback loops have not been included in Figure 3.5.

THE ADOPTION PROCESS

If anyone advances anything new, people resist with all their might; they act as if they neither heard nor could comprehend; they speak of the new view with contempt, as if it were not worth the trouble of even so much as an investigation or a regard; and thus a new truth may wait a long time before it can make its way.

(Johann W. von Goethe, 1749–1832)

In the third edition of his classic work 'Diffusion of Innovations', Rogers (1983, p. 21) defined adoption as 'the decision to make full use of an innovation as the best course of action available'. The adoption process is the process that a potential customer goes through to reach the decision to adopt a new product. More (1984) proposed a comprehensive model of the industrial buying process which revolves around adoption-stage activities and outcomes. The process starts with recognition of a need and the eventual result is the adoption of an innovation. In addition to these adoption stages and outcomes the model incorporates buying-centre behaviour, the choice process, risk and information handling, and finally, seller interfacing.

After having described the stages of the adoption process, the discussion will focus on the concept of the buying centre and the role of the purchasing agent in buying processes.

Stages of the adoption process

Rogers (1983) has presented the adoption process as a series of stages similar to the ones distinguished by More. Rogers, however, stresses the fact that rejection (that is the decision not to adopt an innovation) is also a conceivable outcome of the decision process. For this reason he prefers the more neutral term *innovation-decision process.* (The complementary process of product development he calls 'innovation-development process'.) Whatever the outcome of the decision process, it may be reversed afterwards. For example, 'discontinuance' is the decision to reject an innovation after it has previously been adopted. The innovation-decision process is described as '*a series of actions and choices over time through which an individual or organization evaluates a new idea and decides whether or not to incorporate the new idea into ongoing practice*' (Rogers, 1983, p. 163).

The adoption process consists of the following five stages (Rogers, 1983, p. 164; Figure 3.8).

1 Knowledge
   This stage starts when the decision-making unit is confronted with the innovation and gains some understanding of how it functions. The knowledge relates to the existence of the innovation, how it should be used, and how it works.

2 Persuasion
   At the second stage the decision-making unit forms a favourable or unfavourable attitude towards the innovation, which is based on the information acquired. Matters such as the kind of information needed and where it can be found are important here, but the way information is interpreted (selective perception) plays a major role as well. The information sought at this stage of the process has a typical evaluative character and aims to reduce the uncertainty regarding the innovation's expected consequences.

3 Decision
   At the decision stage the decision-making unit engages in activities that lead to the choice of adopting or rejecting an innovation. A small-scale trial of the innovation is quite often a major determinant of this decision. The trial can be performed by the decision-making unit itself or a third party (particularly if the third party is considered to be an opinion leader).

4 Implementation
   Implementation is the actual use of the innovation by the decision-making unit. This stage follows the preceding one naturally, but has been rather neglected by researchers. As Wood and Elgie (1976, pp. 32–54) demonstrated, many start-up problems may occur at this important stage. Therefore, information necessary at

Figure 3.8 A model of stages in the adoption process

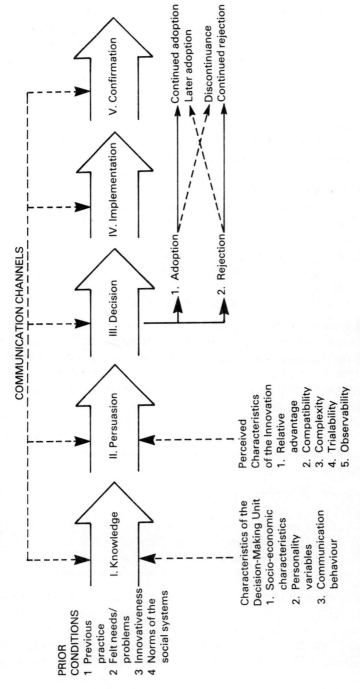

COMMUNICATION CHANNELS

PRIOR
CONDITIONS
1 Previous practice
2 Felt needs/ problems
3 Innovativeness
4 Norms of the social systems

I. Knowledge → II. Persuasion → III. Decision → IV. Implementation → V. Confirmation

1. Adoption
2. Rejection

Continued adoption
Later adoption
Discontinuance
Continued rejection

Characteristics of the
Decision-Making Unit
1. Socio-economic characteristics
2. Personality variables
3. Communication behaviour

Perceived
Characteristics
of the Innovation
1. Relative advantage
2. Compatibility
3. Complexity
4. Trialability
5. Observability

Source: Rogers (1983) © The Free Press, division of Macmillan Inc. Reprinted with permission.

this stage relates to the operation of the innovation, the problems that may occur, and the ways to prevent or solve them. Training and assistance by the seller may be necessary where complex industrial innovations are concerned (see also Biemans and de Vries, 1988, p. 45). During the implementation, the innovation may be changed or modified by the user (re-invention). This phenomenon has been neglected by researchers for many years (Agarwala-Rogers, 1978, pp. 138–41).

5   Confirmation

Although most investigators consider implementation to be the last stage of the process, Rogers distinguishes another one: confirmation. At this final stage the decision-making unit seeks information to reinforce the decision made. However, the information may also lead to reversal of the decision. Discontinuance, the decision to reject an innovation after having previously adopted it, can be very difficult when considerable investments were involved in the decision to adopt it in the first place. This may lead the decision-making unit to seek only information that will support the original decision (selective exposure).

Following the description of the adoption process a few observations are in order. First, the decision to reject an innovation is not limited to the decision-stage. In fact, rejection may occur at any stage of the process. For example, if the knowledge gained at the first stage does not rouse any interest, the innovation can be effectively rejected by just forgetting about it. As pointed out earlier, rejection may also occur after the decision to adopt the innovation has been made. Thus we would like to make a distinction between three different kinds of rejection (unlike Rogers (1983, p. 173), who lumps the second and third category together):

1 *passive rejection* (or non-adoption), which occurs when use of the innovation is never really considered,
2 *a priori active rejection*, which occurs when adoption of the innovation is considered but later decided against, and
3 *a posteriori active rejection* (or discontinuance), which occurs when reconsideration of adoption of the innovation results in rejection.

Second, the adoption process, as described above, assumes a linear sequence of stages. In practice this is not always the case, as decision may precede persuasion. Think of the company that is 'forced' to follow the competition in adopting innovative production machinery. Finally, the description shows that the gathering of information is not limited to the knowledge stage but is at the centre of all stages of the process (as the model presented by More (1984) also acknowledges). Ozanne and Churchill (1968, p. 359) reported that personal sources (in particular personal selling) were more important at the early stages, while impersonal sources were paramount at the evaluation. Their research also showed that as the final decision approaches, the need for informational inputs increases. Empirical evidence furnished by Moriarty and Spekman (1984, p. 145) suggests that, under certain conditions (for example in selling to smaller organizations), impersonal information sources may be a substitute for a personal sales call. A study conducted by Chakrabarti, Feinman, and Fuente-villa (1982, p. 203) demonstrated that the desired information depends on the function; managerial personnel demand evaluative information whereas technical personnel prefer problem-specific information. Differences regarding the way information is diffused inside the organization were also found: managers were mostly involved in downward communication, while design engineers showed more utilization of lateral communication channels. Because the technical personnel were found to be under time constraints, easy access is of prime importance regarding information targeted at this group.

The buying centre

In his writings about diffusion, Rogers uses the description 'an individual or other unit of adoption'. Since we are discussing the adoption of products for industrial markets, the unit of adoption is the so-called *buying centre.* Some authors use the term 'Decision-Making Unit' (DMU) to refer to the same concept. However, we will consistently use the term 'buying centre' to differentiate it from 'Decision-Making Unit' which has more general connotations (Rogers, for example, refers to the decision-making unit when discussing the innovation-decision process to include the adoption of abstract ideas as well as the purchase of concrete products). The buying centre was originally defined as *all the organizational members involved in the purchase decision for a particular product or service* (Wind, 1967; Webster and Wind, 1972). Webster and Wind (1972) distinguished the following roles in a buying centre:

1 *users,* who will be using the innovation,
2 *gatekeepers,* who control the information to be received by other members of the DMU,

3 *influencers,* who affect the purchasing decision by supplying information for the evaluation of alternatives or by setting down buying specifications,
4 *deciders,* who actually make the buying decision, whether or not they have the formal authority to do so, and
5 *buyers,* who have the formal authority for selecting a supplier and implementing all procedures connected with securing the product.

The *initiator,* who identifies a problem and starts the buying process, is a sixth role added to the list by Bonoma (1982, p. 113). Webster and Wind did not overlook this role, but incorporated it in the user as 'in many cases the potential users are those who initiate the buying process'. (Webster and Wind, 1972, p. 78).

Although different roles can be discerned within a buying centre, this does not imply that a buying centre always consists of more than one person. In specific instances the roles mentioned above may be incorporated in one person; at the other extreme lies the extensive buying committee consisting of several persons from several functional areas. Based on interviews with respondents in fifty-five industrial customers for reprographic equipment, Newall reported that

> In the case of large companies, there is an element of constancy about the size of the buying group, where a number of roles are common ... In the case of smaller companies, the fact that a single member may fulfil more than one buying role ... means that a smaller decision group emerges.
>
> Newall (1977, pp. 185–6)

A review of existing literature led Mattson (1988) to formulate a model to analyse and predict the composition of a buying centre.

The existence of a multi-person buying centre has important consequences for research into organizational buying behaviour. After having studied the industrial adoption process, Ozanne and Churchill (1971, p. 327) remarked that 'the use of a group as the typical unit of adoption complicated the analysis'. Taking an individual as the unit of adoption, however, appears to be an unjustified simplification. Based on extensive literature research, Smith and Taylor arrived at the conclusion that

> the most that can be said about the composition of a buying centre is that it is typically made up of members drawn from between three and ten functional areas with almost 40 per cent of purchase decisions being influenced by at least three persons.
>
> Smith and Taylor (1985, p. 59)

Moriarty and Bateson (1982) discuss the need to use exhaustive snowballing in the study of complex buying centres and present a telephone and mail-based method that is both effective and cost efficient. When there is more than one person involved in the buying process, the interaction between the members becomes important. An early study that shows flow charts and interaction patterns is presented by Harding (1966). Johnston and Bonoma (1981) formulated five structural and interactive dimensions of the buying centre and demonstrated how they can be quantified.

The original definition of a buying centre leaves some room for discussion. For example, the definition of 'involvement' should not be formulated in such a way as to include only casual involvement as well. This would lead to the inclusion of a large number of people and thus to an impractical utilization of the concept. Only those individuals with direct major involvement in the given purchase decision should be included. A second matter of interest concerns the possible inclusion of outsiders. Most authors limit the membership of the centre to members of the buying organization, as implied by the original definition. Although Webster and Wind (1972) define the buying centre in their classic *Organizational Buying Behavior* initially as 'all those individuals and groups who participate in the purchasing decision-making process' (p. 6), further on they describe it as '*members of the organization* who interact during the buying decision process' (p. 77) (emphasis added). In a later publication, however, Wind (1978a, p. 69) argues that 'as long as the outsiders have a stake in the decision, there is no reason why they should be excluded'. We endorse this reasoning because outsiders can indeed be significantly involved in the ultimate buying decision. Weigand (1968, p. 45) mentions as examples of outside influencers 'engineering consultants, insurance firms, testing laboratories, construction firms, governmental units, or simply respected firms in an industry who unwittingly perform part of the buying function for those who follow their lead'. Zaltman and Bonoma (1977, p. 57) gave evidence of other firms in the role of influencers when they stated that 'the importance of purchase-related word-of-mouth communication among buying firms is greatly underestimated'.

A major determinant of the structure of the buying centre is the specific buying situation. Robinson, Faris, and Wind (1967) in their BUYGRID model defined three principal buying situations, that is the new task, modified rebuy, and straight rebuy. As the buying situation becomes more complex and novel, there is a greater likelihood that a special buying centre will be established to carry out the purchasing decision (Wind, 1978a, p. 71), the average number of persons within the buying centre increases (Doyle, *et al.*, 1979, p. 8; Crow and Lindquist, 1985, p. 54), buyers are more actively searching for information (Grönhaug, 1975, p. 20), and other purchasing criteria are used (Krieger and Meredith, 1985, p. 279). Spekman and Stern (1979, p. 58) reported a strong correlation between environmental uncertainty and the participation of buying-group members in purchasing-related decisions. Finally, Johne (1984, pp. 191–3) drew attention to a possible link between the innovative behaviour of firms and the departments involved in buying decisions.

The role of the purchasing agent

Several studies have been conducted to determine the relative influence of members of the buying centre during the buying process. The buying decision is usually depicted as a process consisting of several stages. Ozanne and Churchill (1971) proposed five stages, while Wind (1978b) increased this number to twelve. Most researchers, however, postulate a model of the buying process based on BUYPHASE, the eight-step approach proposed by Robinson, Faris, and Wind (1967):

1 anticipation or recognition of a problem and a general solution,
2 determination of characteristics and quality of a needed item,
3 description of characteristics and quantity of needed item,
4 search for and qualification of potential sources,
5 requisition and analysis of proposals,
6 evaluation of proposals and selection of supplier(s),
7 selection of an order routine, and
8 performance feedback and evaluation.

Some studies have focused explicitly on the relative influence of the purchasing agent on the buying decision. Bellizzi (1979) found that the purchase of expensive capital equipment appears to be dominated by top managers at most stages of the buying process. Purchasing agents were found not to exert great influence on most stages, but did rank quite high on some of the later stages of the process. For operating supplies and major materials, on the other hand, the influence of the purchasing agent was reported to be much more significant. Thus it seems that the product type is one of the major factors determining the purchasing agent's influence during the buying process. This conclusion is supported by Giunipero (1984, p. 247) when, in a study of computer buying, he points out significant differences in the perceived role activity between public and private purchasers and shows that these differences vary across product categories. Similar conclusions were arrived at by other researchers (for example Erickson and Gross, 1980). However, the results of a study by Jackson *et al.* (1984, p. 79) demonstrate that purchasing agents perceived themselves to have a greater influence on decisions to select a *supplier* than decisions aimed at selecting a product. Bellizzi provided empirical support for the hypothesis that industrial buying behaviour is partly determined by the size of an organization. His study of buying in the commercial construction industry showed that the influence of a purchasing agent increases with organizational size (Bellizzi, 1981, p. 19). The purchasing agent's influence also seems to depend on the buying situation. Doyle *et al.* (1979, p. 9) reported that the purchasing agent tended to be strongly involved in nearly all buying phases for straight rebuys, whereas his role in new-task buying situations had a more coordinating character. Mogee and Bean (1978, p. 136) remarked that if an innovative purchase becomes a routine one, primary responsibility is shifted to the purchasing department.

Considering the above, it seems that concerning complex, industrial innovations in particular, the purchasing agent only plays a minor role during the buying process. Bonoma and Zaltman maintained that

> As the rate of technical change increases, the importance of the purchasing manager in the organizational acquisition process decreases. At the same time, the importance of technical and engineering individuals making up the buying center increases rapidly, and they may well become the sole, or at least major, authorizers of purchases.
>
> (Bonoma and Zaltman, 1978, p. 22)

Abratt (1986, p. 295) lends further support to this finding when, as the result of a study of buying behaviour of purchasers of high technology laboratory instrumentation, he concludes that 'the involvement of the buying department is mostly administrative and involves some information gathering'.

Traditionally, the purchasing agent has been regarded as an 'order writer', one who only becomes significantly involved during the later stages of the buying process. This negative view has caused resentment among the members of the purchasing profession. More than twenty-five years ago, Strauss (1964) already reported on the friction between purchasing agents and engineers. The conflict was primarily over the purchasing agent's attempts to gain more control over decisions on what to buy; he wanted more control over specifications. Purchasing agents also felt that top management pays too little attention to the purchasing function. A survey of 750 US industrial managers conducted by Ammer (1974) disclosed negative perceptions of the purchasing function on the part of top management.

Almost twenty-five years ago it was foreseen that 'the trend of purchasing practice is likely to be towards greater centralization, with larger and more responsible purchasing departments, increasingly embodying technical and specialist staffs and skills', thus enhancing the status and calibre of the purchasing department (Lister, 1967, p. 198) and resulting in greater professionalism (Strauss, 1964). During the last decade, this view has been confirmed when authors pointed out that purchasing managers are upgrading their skills (Upah and Bird, 1980, p. 119) and a new class of professional buyer is coming into existence (Giunipero and Zenz, 1982, p. 21) that can add immensely to the level of profitability of the firm (Williams and Smith, 1990, p. 316). The implications of these purchasing trends for industrial marketers were spelled out. However, no clear picture emerges. Barath and Hugstad (1977, p. 304), for example, warned that an increased professional status can restrict rather than expand the role of purchasing agents in the industrial buying process.

The theme of professionalizing purchasing agents has also been discussed extensively in the Dutch and Belgian media (de Rijcke and van Weele, 1980; de Rijcke and Faes, 1982), even as recently as 1987. As a result of a study of purchasing management in Dutch industry it was concluded that most industrial purchasers

> function as order-takers for engineers in the production department. They are the ones that need materials, that formulate the technical requirements and very often even say where it should be bought. The role of the purchasers involved is reduced to negotiating about price.
>
> (*FEM*, 1987, p. 33)

Upgrading of the purchasing function is mentioned as a general remedy. Another study (van Weele and van Hespen, 1987) arrives at similar, although somewhat less negative, conclusions: although the purchasing function was not found to be largely neglected, (1) the role during the buying decision is mostly restricted to administrative actions, (2) the involvement in buying innovative products is quite low, and (3) increasing professionalism of the purchasing department is thought to be necessary.

Considering the above, the conclusion that purchasing agents only play a minor administrative role in the adoption of industrial innovations seems to be warranted. There is, however, another role traditionally attributed to the purchasing agent: the *gatekeeper*.

According to Mogee and Bean (1978, p. 135) 'the purchasing agent plays an important gatekeeper role in industrial innovation but is not the principal decision maker'. When the purchasing agent performs a gatekeeping function, the firm is better equipped to stay involved in technological innovations (Zaltman and Bonoma, 1977, p. 55). Situations of great environmental uncertainty in particular, offer the purchasing agent the opportunity to fulfil this central gate-keeping role (Spekman and Stern, 1979, p. 60), which makes the purchasing agent less of an order-taker than previously suggested (Spekman and Ford, 1977, p. 402). This unique gatekeeper position implies that the seller's representatives are generally required to go to the purchasing agent before contacting and influencing other parties in the buying organization (Mogee and Bean, 1978, p. 136; Berkowitz, 1986, p. 42; Bellizzi and Walter, 1980, p. 140; Biemans and de Vries, 1987b, p. 36). Nicosia and Wind (1977, p. 368) argue that, as the buying process grows more comprehensive and complex, the purchasing agent is the ideal person to plan and coordinate such a process. Basically, his task is to understand the different points of view and needs within the organization and to resolve conflicts. Williams and Smith (1990) take the involvement of purchasing employees in the adoption process for granted, and stress the gate-keeper role in their argument for involving purchasing agents in the product development process as well.

THE DIFFUSION PROCESS

Diffusion is defined by Rogers (1983, p. 5), who conducted a comprehensive review of the literature on diffusion and summarized the findings into an integrated framework, as 'the process by which an innovation is communicated through certain channels over time among the members of a social system'. Robertson (1971, p. 32) has expanded this definition to make it more applicable to the marketing of new products: '*diffusion is the adoption of new products or services over time by consumers within social systems as encouraged by marketing activities*'. This definition illustrates the close link (and difference!) between adoption and diffusion: adoption is an individual decision-making process, while diffusion reflects a series of adoption decisions by individual units within the social system (see also the last section in this chapter). Although we will concentrate on the diffusion of new products in industrial markets, it must be kept in mind that, according to Rogers' more general definition, diffusion research may also relate to subjects like the dissemination of ideas within the firm (see for example Vandermerwe, 1987).

According to Rogers, research on diffusion of innovations originated independently within several distinct disciplines, such as sociology and anthropology. Although each discipline used its own approach, remarkably similar results were found. For example, that the diffusion of an innovation followed an S-shaped curve over time and that innovators had higher socio-economic status than later adopters (Rogers, 1983, p. 38). Indeed, the lack of diffusion of diffusion research was mentioned by Rogers as one of the main reasons for writing the first edition of *Diffusion of Innovations* (Rogers, 1962).

For a considerable time, the field of diffusion has been dominated by rural sociology. An early study that has had a major influence on (1) the methodology, theoretical constructs, and interpretations of later students of diffusion in the rural sociology tradition, and (2) diffusion research in general, is the hybrid-seed-corn study conducted by Ryan and Gross (1943). One of the main findings was the important role of interpersonal networks in the diffusion process.

During the 1960s, diffusion research caught the attention of the marketing discipline as well. The large percentage of new consumer products that fail prompted marketing managers to conduct diffusion studies. Despite its late start, diffusion research in the marketing field has really spread. According to Rogers 'by 1981, there were 304 marketing (diffusion) publications, 10 percent of the total, and marketing ranked fourth in its contribution to diffusion research!' (Rogers, 1983, p. 74). A survey of innovation diffusion models in marketing is given by Mahajan and Muller (1979) and, more recently, Böcker and Gierl (1988). Mahajan, Muller, and Bass (1990) evaluate the developments in innovation diffusion models for the past two decades and conclude with a research agenda to make diffusion models theoretically more sound and practically more effective and realistic. Sultan, Farley, and Lehmann (1990) analysed 213 applications of diffusion models from fifteen articles in an attempt to formulate quantitative generalizations. Although diffusion research seems to be well established in marketing, little research has been conducted into the diffusion of industrial innovations. In 1966 the lack of research relating to adoption and diffusion of new industrial products was pointed out (King, 1966, p. 684). This conclusion was repeated by Ozanne and Churchill (1968, p. 352), Cook (1970), who mentioned that out of 708 publications on diffusion studies only five (!) were concerned with the industrial field, and later similar views were expressed by Abu-Ismail (1976, p. 2). Even as recently as 1990, marketing scholars still have to conclude that, with respect to the diffusion of innovations 'research studies in the major marketing journals have focused almost exclusively on consumer goods and services... [Furthermore] diffusion models developed in consumer product marketing may have little or no relevance in industrial marketing' (Day and Herbig, 1990, pp. 261–2).

Elements of the diffusion process

After analysing the definitions of diffusion given by Robertson (1971, p. 32) and Rogers (1983, p. 5) we can distinguish the following six elements of the process of diffusion of industrial innovations.

1 Adoption
  The adoption process has been discussed in the preceding section.
2 The innovation
  The subject of innovations has been covered extensively in chapter 2 and needs no further elaboration.
3 Time
  Time is an important element of the diffusion process. It is used to separate early from late adopters of an innovation and to identify an innovation's speed of diffusion.
4 The units of adoption
  As regards industrial innovations, the buyer is an organization instead of an individual. That means that one has to consider a group of people involved in the purchasing decision: the buying centre (see also the preceding section).
5 A social system
  Diffusion of an innovation occurs within a social system, that is a set of interrelated units that are engaged in joint problem-solving to accomplish a common goal (Rogers, 1983, p. 24). The social system constitutes the boundary within which the innovation diffuses, provides norms and values, defines roles, and evaluates the consequences of the diffusion.
6 The communication channels
  Communication is the process by which participants create and share information with one another in order to reach a mutual understanding. Diffusion can be considered a special type of

communication in which the information concerns new ideas. Communication channels are the means by which messages proceed from the sender to the receiver. When studying the diffusion of industrial innovations, two kinds of communication channels are important. First, channels whereby the industrial marketer sends information to potential buyers (marketing activities). Second, channels used for communication between potential buyers (word-of-mouth communication, opinion leadership). Another distinction is the one between mass media channels and interpersonal channels. The former are those that involve a mass medium, while the latter involve a face-to-face exchange. According to Rogers (1983, pp. 198–9) interpersonal channels play an important role at the persuasion stage. Ozanne and Churchill (1968, p. 359) found that personal sources (personal selling) were important at the earlier stages, while impersonal sources (tooling proposals and price quotations) dominated at the evaluation. Mass media were found to be of minor importance.

The speed of diffusion

Many studies have been conducted to discover why some innovations gain acceptance faster than others, that is to determine the factors that influence the speed of diffusion. Rogers (1983, p. 23) terms it, somewhat confusingly, the rate of adoption and defines it as 'the relative speed with which an innovation is adopted by members of the system'. According to Rogers (1983, p. 233), there are five categories of variables that influence the speed of diffusion:

1 perceived attributes of the innovation,
2 type of innovation decision,
3 communication channels,
4 nature of the social system, and
5 extent of the change agents' promotion efforts.

Here we will only describe briefly the first category, because it is by far the most important. Rogers (1983, p. 232) maintains that 49 to 87 per cent of the variance in the speed of diffusion can be explained by the variables belonging to this category. The following five attributes of innovations are of importance.

1 Relative advantage
   The relative advantage of an innovation is the degree to which an innovation is perceived as being better than the idea it supersedes.

This relative advantage can be expressed in many ways, such as cost savings or increased prestige. Hayward (1978, p. 195) drew attention to differences in perception of an innovation's characteristics between adopters and non-adopters. The substitution that is the result of the relative advantage of a new technology compared with the existing one, is explicitly incorporated in a diffusion model by Norton and Bass (1987).

2 Compatibility

Compatibility is the extent to which an innovation is perceived as consistent with the socio-cultural values and beliefs, past experiences (for example with previously introduced products), and needs of potential adopters. An innovation with a high degree of compatibility means less uncertainty to the potential adopter. Hayward *et al.* (1977, pp. 303–4) discovered that 'the innovations which were adopted most rapidly were ... [those] innovations which are very similar to existing methods and practices' and called these 'traditional innovations'.

3 Complexity

The complexity of an innovation refers to the degree to which it is perceived as relatively difficult to understand and use.

4 Trialability

The speed of diffusion is influenced by the degree to which an innovation may be experimented with on a limited basis. More (1984, p. 195) studied the diffusion of a computer-assisted-learning system and concluded that a trial situation could involve the seller providing the buying centre with an available 'canned' teaching program at a modest price, which could allow the buying centre to simplify their comparison of alternatives and reduce many barriers.

5 Observability

The last characteristic of an innovation to be mentioned is the degree to which the results of the innovation are visible and can be communicated.

The attributes of innovations mentioned above are to some extent interrelated. For example, new application software is an innovation with a low degree of observability. This is one reason for the conclusion of Voss (1985b, p. 127), that 'the purchaser places a strong reliance on the information gained from seeing a demonstration of a working system' (that is a trial of the innovation on a small scale).

Apart from the five categories of variables enumerated by Rogers, numerous other variables that influence the speed of diffusion are mentioned by other researchers. Mansfield (1968, p. 120) drew attention to the adopter-industry competitive environment, while Robertson and Gatignon (1986) expanded this to include the supply-side competitive environment as well. Later they worked out these variables in more detail and empirically tested the competitive effects (Gatignon and Robertson, 1989). Brown (1981) also emphasized the supply aspect of diffusion by presenting it from a market and infra-structure perspective, which focuses on the ways in which innovations and the conditions for adoption are made available to the potential adopters. Johne (1984) focused on one specific characteristic of the adopter industry, namely the innovative behaviour of firms, while Nooteboom (1989) stressed the importance of firm size. Both Cohn (1981) and Boorsma and van Kooten (1989) named the attitudes of the decision makers towards change and risks as a relevant variable. Nooteboom and Boorsma (1990) modelled the diffusion process by explicitly taking into account rapid technical progress and the risks of implementation. Wood and Elgie (1976) also emphasized the import-ance of the ease of start-up. Finally, the policies of labour unions and the size of the investment (Mansfield, 1968, pp. 120–3) as well as the role of third parties (Mantel and Rosegger, 1987) have been mentioned as factors that influence the speed of diffusion. In an international context, Nabseth and Ray (1974, pp. 311–15) enumer-ated a large number of factors that may explain differences between the speed of diffusion in different countries.

More (1984) has stated that a quick diffusion may not be realized because of several potential barriers to adoption. He mentioned thirteen different kinds of barriers (based on his model of the organiz-ational adoption process), and suggested how they can be overcome by improved interfacing with the potential buyer's adoption process (see also Rabino, 1983).

Adopter categories

The time variable, which occupies such a central place in diffusion theory and research, can be used to make a distinction between adopters who adopt an innovation when it has just been introduced and adopters who only adopt after the innovation has been around for a considerable time. In other words, adopters can be categorized according to their innovativeness (that is the degree to which an adopter is relatively earlier in adopting new ideas than other members of a system). Rogers (1983, p. 246) distinguished five adopter categories (Figure 3.9):

Figure 3.9 Adopter categorization on the basis of innovativeness

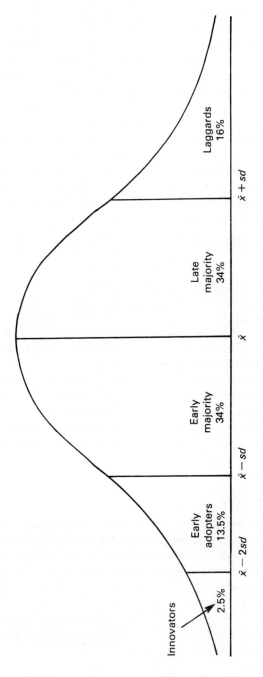

$\bar{x}$ = mean value of x (variable measuring time)
sd = standard deviation

Source: Rogers (1983), © The Free Press, division of Macmillan Inc. Reprinted with permission.

1 innovators,
2 early adopters,
3 early majority,
4 late majority, and
5 laggards.

A great deal of research has been conducted to determine the characteristics of adopter categories. Some generalizations are presented by Rogers and Shoemaker (1971, pp. 352–76), who analysed approximately 900 empirical publications, dealing with the diffusion of innovations, available in July 1968. Although many studies have been conducted since then, the general conclusions still seem to hold (Rogers, 1983, pp. 260–1).

Webster argued that those firms which are first to adopt an innovation are those

a for whom the innovation offers the largest relative advantage ...,
b that can best tolerate the risk involved in adoption ...,
c that have the highest level of aspiration ..., [and]
d for whom information relating to the innovation ... has the greatest value.

(Webster, 1969, p. 39)

In a study of the diffusion of product and process innovations among 352 small- and medium-sized manufacturing companies in the Netherlands, Docter and Stokman (1987) found that early adopters differed from late adopters with respect to the sector of industry, size of the firm, age of the firm, average level of educational qualification within the firm, long-term orientation, market position, degree of exportation, characteristics of the market, cooperation with other firms, and search for and use of information.

The innovators and early adopters are extremely important in the diffusion process. They provide the supplier of the innovation with an initial level of penetration, can be used as references, and, hence, influence other potential adopters (Robertson, 1971, p. 112; Foxall, 1984, p. 93; Webster, 1968). This influence can be exerted in three ways (Turnbull and Meenaghan, 1980, p. 10).

1 Social display
   Potential adopters will be encouraged by conspicuous new products to interpersonal communication with the owner, thereby creating awareness and knowledge.

2 Legitimation

The fact that the innovator group has already purchased the innovation reduces the perceived risk with risk-averse potential adopters.

3 Encouragement

The first buyers of the innovation can in conversation urge other members of the social system to adopt it. Their motive may be the desire to reduce their cognitive dissonance following the purchase.

The role of opinion leaders

It is not best that we should all think alike; it is difference of opinion which makes horse races.

(Mark Twain, 1835–1910)

Closely related to the concept of adopter categories is the notion of opinion leadership, which we will define as *the degree to which an actor (be it an individual, group or organization) is able informally to influence other actors' attitudes or overt behaviour in a desired way with relative frequency* (based on Rogers, 1983, p. 271). Robertson (1971, p. 35) writes about the same phenomenon when he states that 'the interaction effect refers to a process of influence and imitation among consumers by which adopters of a new product lead others to purchase'.

In a study of the US presidential election in 1940, Lazarsfeld *et al.* (1948) discovered to their surprise that almost no voting choices were directly influenced by the mass media. Instead, people appeared to be much more influenced by face-to-face contact with other people. Thus, they formulated the *two-step flow model* of communication: the first step being from sources to opinion leaders (a transfer of information) and the second step from opinion leaders to their followers (information plus influence).

Many studies have been conducted to determine the characteristics of opinion leaders. In general, they are thought to have greater social participation and higher socio-economic status, and to be more cosmopolite and innovative than their followers. Rogers (1983, p. 284), however, warns that opinion leaders are not necessarily innovators: 'when a social system's norms favor change, opinion leaders are more innovative, but when the norms do not favor change, opinion leaders are not especially innovative' (see also Summers (1971) for an investigation into the relationship between innovativeness and opinion leadership).

Little work has been done on the question of opinion leadership in industrial markets compared to consumer markets (Lancaster and White, 1976, p. 288). Webster (1968, p. 458) commented that industrial marketers can use the concept of opinion leadership by giving widespread publicity to the first successful installations of their product. He also hypothesized that the opinion leaders would be expected to be the early adopters instead of the innovators (the very first adopters), which is supported by Rogers (1983, p. 259). He concluded, however, that in industrial markets word-of-mouth communication may be of less importance than in consumer markets. In a later publication he confirmed this conclusion when he stated that 'informal patterns of communication relating to new products appear to be weak in the industrial market' (Webster, 1970, p. 189). Twenty years later this view is echoed by Day and Herbig (1990, p. 265) who state that 'the use of opinion leaders is primarily a consumer phenomena [*sic*]. In industrial markets, there exist counterparts but not of the power and numbers that exist in consumer markets'. Back in 1971, Webster already warned that

> such concepts as opinion leadership and word-of-mouth which implicitly assume interpersonal interaction simply do not fit the industrial context very well without considerable reworking ... It is simple-minded to assume that interpersonal interaction is the only basis for influence among firms in an industry.
>
> (Webster, 1971, p. 187)

Other forms of influence among firms are, for example, managers' professional associations, industry trade associations, technical seminars, trade journals, etc. In our opinion, however, Webster unnecessarily diminishes the significance of opinion leadership in industrial markets by equating it with interpersonal interaction and excluding from the concept other forms of interorganizational influence.

Opinion leadership may be less common in industrial markets than in consumer markets for a number of reasons (Lancaster and White, 1976, p. 293; Webster, 1968; Webster, 1970).

1 The supplier provides more complete information.
2 The supplier is more likely to provide information about the product's limitations and negative consequences so as to avoid possible misuse of the product.
3 Consumer purchasing decisions often contain psycho-social problems which can be answered by peers; these problems are rare in industrial purchasing.

4 The motives and rewards for opinion leadership found in consumer markets would appear to be less relevant in industrial markets. Individuals in firms who may wish to volunteer information may be prevented from doing so as a result of company policy.
5 Consumers are closer in the spatial sense, which simplifies personal communication. For competitive reasons firms in the same industry are less likely to communicate directly.

However, there is also evidence in support of opinion leadership in industrial markets. Martilla (1971) investigated paper buying practices of 106 converting firms and emphasized opinion leadership within firms, an area which Webster ignored. His study led him to conclude that 'contrary to Webster's findings, buying influentials in the converting markets also reported seeking information and opinions about paper from persons in competing firms, in much the same way as within the firm' (Martilla, 1971, p. 175). Similar results were found by Hayward who, after having studied diffusion of innovations in the flour milling industry, stated that

> purchasers and potential purchasers repeatedly stated that they gained information from colleagues after having obtained initial details of new products from sales engineers, advertising leaflets and trade journals. Further study demonstrated that these people were visited time and time again ... These opinion leaders play a major role in the successful introduction of new products and highlight the importance of good communication.
>
> (Hayward, 1978, p. 198)

In studies of farmers' purchasing decisions, opinion leadership was found to be a relevant factor (Foxall, 1979, p. 305) and to be associated with innovativeness (Foxall, 1980, p. 80).

An investigation of the diffusion of a continuous-casting process in the steel industry led Czepiel (1974, p. 177) to conclude that early adopters exhibited greater opinion leadership. The study focused on the social system and showed the existence of a functioning informal community linking the firms together. Consideration of his remarks about situational influences might offer an explanation for the seemingly inconsistent results found by other researchers with respect to opinion leadership in industrial markets (Foxall, 1984, p. 122).

Interrelated processes

In the first section of this chapter it was accentuated that there is (or at least should be) a close relationship between the product innovation strategy and the product development process. This link is also evident in the model of the product development process presented by Booz, Allen and Hamilton (1982, p. 13). The processes of product development, adoption, and diffusion are closely inter-related as well. This is clearly demonstrated by Figure 3.10. The process of adoption can be regarded as complementary to the process of product development. The development and introduction of the innovation by the manufacturer are the logical counterparts of the purchasing and implementation of the innovation by the adopting firm. A detailed knowledge and understanding of the adoption process can assist the industrial marketer in introducing the innovation and overcoming barriers to adoption (Barnes and Ayars, 1977; Rabino, 1983; More, 1984). When we defined diffusion, we

Figure 3.10 The relationship between product development, adoption, and diffusion

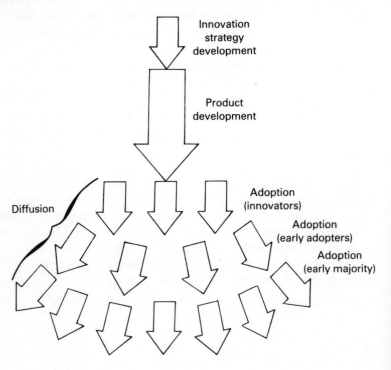

drew attention to the link between adoption and diffusion by mentioning that adoption is an individual decision-making process, while diffusion reflects a series of adoption decisions by individual units within the social system. The close link between adoption and diffusion is also reflected in the terminology employed by different authors. Descriptions like 'speed of diffusion' and 'rate of adoption' are used interchangeably, while 'adopter categories' are generally employed to describe diffusion processes.

The close interrelationship between the product development process and the adoption process is reflected in the statement by Bonoma and Johnston (1978, p. 215) that industrial buying behaviour can not be studied in isolation from industrial marketing behaviour. Selling and buying are two closely related subjects and thus the industrial marketing researcher must use a dyadic approach, based upon relational variables (see also Wood and Elgie, 1976, p. 72). They conclude that industrial marketing must be viewed as the interaction between buyer and seller.

4 Interaction and networks

Marketing can be seen as relationship management: creating, developing, and maintaining a network in which the firm thrives.
(Evert Gummesson, 1987)

After having discussed several aspects of innovations in general terms, in chapter 3 we discussed the process of product development. A large number of models were categorized and reviewed. Looking back on the models proposed by different authors, we note that most of them seem to presume that innovation is the sole province of the manufacturing firm. The models are conceptualized from the manufacturer's perspective.

1 Department-stage models: the development of an innovation is traced by enumerating the departments through which it passes within the manufacturing firm.
2 Conversion models: the development process is depicted as a black box with several resources as inputs and the innovation as output of a conversion process within the firm.
3 Response models: the process of developing an innovation is regarded as a process of change, whereby a firm responds to stimuli from its environment.

In practice, however, activities relating to the development of innovations are not always performed by the manufacturing firm alone. In specific industries, users of the innovation may play an important role. This was already noted more than seventy years ago by Alfred Marshall when he observed that

[in industries that have] been long established on a large scale ... improvements in machinery are devised almost exclusively by machine makers ... But this is not the case in industries that are as yet in an early stage of development or are rapidly changing their form ... In all such trades, new machinery and new processes are for the greater part devised by manufacturers for their own use.

(Marshall, 1920, p. 280)

This observation was subsequently ignored for many years. During the latter part of the 1970s seminal research in this area was conducted by von Hippel. As a result of a number of empirical studies, he discovered that in some industries users play a dominant role in the innovation development process. This time, the notion was picked up by other researchers and elaborated upon.

When we argued that most models seem to be drawn up from the perspective of the manufacturing firm and neglect possible inputs from users, we left out the activity-stage and decision-stage models. Although these models are also formulated from a manufacturer's perspective, by describing the process as a series of subsequent general activities they can be easily modified to account for user involvement. Take, for example, the model we selected for the research reported in this book. Even though specific reference to the user is only made in the step 'testing prototype with customers', the general formulation of the various activities allows the consideration of more fundamental involvement of users in the process. If, for example, a manufacturer and a user jointly develop a prototype which is subsequently made into an industrial product by the manufacturer, who also produces and markets it, the model can still be used to describe the development process.

In this chapter we argue that product development in industrial markets needs to be looked at from a network perspective. In order to understand the essential elements of the network concept fully, we present a survey of various theories that clearly shows how the original concept of buyer–seller interaction evolved into a network approach. This survey starts with the studies of von Hippel that pointed out the dominant role of users with respect to idea generation in some industries (in von Hippel (1988) the results of the studies are summarized and integrated). We go on to discuss some of the conceptual extensions and refinements of von Hippel's theory proposed by other investigators. The main conclusion is that the process of developing innovations for industrial markets should generally be regarded as an interactive process in which both manufacturers and users may play a significant role. After having presented the central concept of interaction, we stress that parties other than manufacturers and users may also be involved in developing industrial innovations. All these parties are connected into networks by individual relationships. Thus, the process of developing innovations for industrial markets is viewed from a network perspective.

THE STUDIES OF VON HIPPEL: MANUFACTURER-ACTIVE PARADIGM (MAP) VERSUS CUSTOMER-ACTIVE PARADIGM (CAP)

Idea generation: MAP or CAP?

As we already noted in Chapter 2, market-related factors discriminate most strongly between successful industrial innovations and the ones that fail. Indeed, the most important single factor is a lack of accurate understanding of user needs. Furthermore, three out of four successful industrial innovations are developed in response to a perceived user need, rather than as the result of some new technological advances and opportunities (Utterback, 1974). Nevertheless, it is unclear how a manufacturer acquires the necessary 'accurate understanding of user needs'. How users can provide 'need input' to the innovation process is also unclear. Questions such as these were what led von Hippel to study idea generation for innovations in several industries.

His first study concerned a sample of 111 successful innovations in scientific instruments, which were divided into three categories: basic innovations, major improvements, and minor improvements (von Hippel, 1976, p. 217). The innovations investigated all belonged to either one of four narrowly defined classes of scientific instruments. Von Hippel's most important conclusion was that the innovation process in scientific instruments is a *user-dominated* process: 77 per cent of the innovations studied were developed by users (Table 4.1).

Table 4.1 Source of scientific instrument innovations by innovation significance

Innovation significance	User developed (%)	Innovation developed by			
		User	Manufacturer	NA	Total
First-of-type	100	4	0	0	4
Major improvement	82	36	8	0	44
Minor improvement	70	32	14	17	63
Total	77	72	22	17	111

Source: von Hippel (1976), *Research Policy*, vol. 5, © Elsevier Science Publishers B.V. Reprinted with permission.

In the large majority of cases it was the user, not the instrument manufacturer, who

1 perceived that an advance in instrumentation was required (that is recognized the need),
2 invented the instrument,
3 built a prototype,
4 proved the prototype's value by applying it, and
5 diffused detailed information on the value of his invention and how his prototype device may be replicated, via journals, symposia, informal visits, etc. to both user colleagues and instrument manufacturers.

After a manufacturer got interested in the developed prototype, his contribution would be

1 to perform product-engineering work on the user's device to improve its reliability, convenience of operation, etc. (that is, transform the user's device into a commercially viable product) and
2 to manufacture, market, and sell the innovation.

A second study arrived at similar results: 67 per cent of the new process machines used by the semi-conductor industry were developed by users (von Hippel, 1977a, p. 67).

Both studies led von Hippel to hypothesize that there are in fact two different paradigms describing the idea-generation stage of the product development process. The *Manufacturer-Active Paradigm* (MAP) underlies idea generation for consumer products and is described by him as follows:

> In the MAP, the role of the customer is essentially that of respondent, 'speaking only when spoken to'. It is the role of the manufacturer to select and survey a group of customers to obtain information on needs for new products or modification of existing products; analyze the data; develop a responsive product idea; and test the idea against customer perceptions and purchase decisions.
>
> (von Hippel, 1978, p. 40)

This description is clearly relevant to product development processes in consumer goods markets, where there is a large number of potential users that can be identified relatively easily, where user requirements change but slowly, and the manufacturer typically has a relatively long time span to develop and market his new products.

In industrial markets, however, the situation is quite different. The number of potential customers is relatively small, user requirements are changing quickly, and new products need to be developed quickly in response to urgent problems. If no manufacturer can be found to meet these requirements, the user may be forced to develop the innovation in house. Thus, based on his studies of idea generation for industrial innovations, von Hippel hypothesized that a *Customer-Active Paradigm* (CAP) provides a better fit with observed reality:

> In the CAP, it is the role of the would-be customer to develop the idea for a new product; select a supplier capable of making the product; and take the initiative to send a request to the selected supplier. The role of the manufacturer in this paradigm is: to wait for a potential customer to submit a request ...; to screen ideas (not needs) for new products; and to select those for development which seem to offer the most promise from the manufacturer's point of view.
>
> (von Hippel, 1978, p. 40)

According to this paradigm, the user generally provides more than merely an idea for a new product. In specific instances, users may supply a manufacturer with

1 an identification of a problem or need,
2 a general type of solution,
3 product-functional specifications,
4 product design specifications, or
5 a complete product design.

A number of studies by other investigators support these observations (Meadows, 1969; Peplow, 1960; Utterback, 1971; Robinson, Faris, and Wind, 1967). Both paradigms are shown in Figure 4.1.

Although CAP seems to fit more closely to industrial product-idea generation practice than MAP, the issue is not so clear cut. Von Hippel (1978, p. 44) argues that the answer to the question whether MAP or CAP is more appropriate in a given situation depends on the nature of the customer need and the accessibility of the new-product opportunity to manufacturer-managed action (Figure 4.2).

In the article in which von Hippel presented the MAP and CAP paradigms, he also reported on some anecdotal evidence of a third paradigm, 'one in which "everyone knows" what the customer wants, but progress in technology is required before the desired product can be realized' (von Hippel, 1978, p. 48). Despite his concluding remark that 'further research into the matter should be of value' his subsequent studies have not elaborated this point.

Figure 4.1 Typical steps in the development and diffusion of a scientific instrument innovation

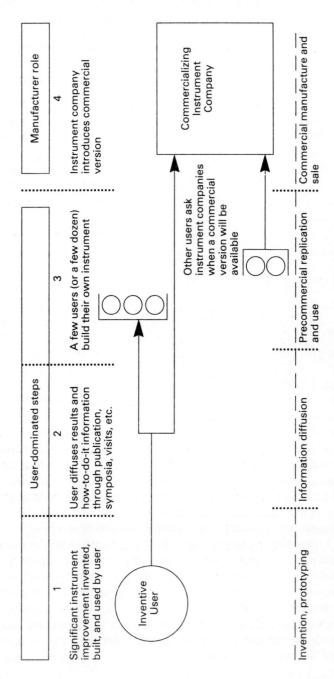

Source: von Hippel (1976), *Research Policy*, vol. 5, © Elsevier Science Publishers B.V. Reprinted with permission.

Figure 4.2 Characteristics of new industrial product opportunity appropriate to CAP and/or MAP

Nature of customer need	Accessibility of new product opportunity to manufacture-managed action	
	Low	High
Overt	Customer-active only	Customer-and/or manufacturer-active
Latent	Neither	Manufacturer-active only

Source: von Hippel (1978), *Journal of Marketing*, vol. 42, no. 1, © American Marketing Association. Reprinted with permission.

Implications of CAP for the manufacturer

The fact that CAP generally fits the circumstances in industrial markets better than MAP holds two important implications for manufacturers of industrial innovations (von Hippel, 1977b, pp. 20–1). First, manufacturers can suffice with primarily employing engineers skilled at product engineering instead of R&D. Second, market research strategies should focus on finding user *solutions* with attractive market potential rather than finding user 'needs'. However, a manufacturer following this strategy needs to keep in mind that (1) a large user population only develops a relatively small number of new products, of which but a fraction will be commercially promising, and (2) user–innovators often have no incentive to take their developed devices beyond their own company.

Von Hippel (1982, pp. 120–1) mentions two general strategies to find the innovating users. The first, the *user-stimulus strategy*, consists of (1) defining the desired product as precisely as possible, (2) specifying an appropriate award, and (3) informing likely innovators only (these potential innovators are not restricted to the manufacturer's own customer base). The second, the *user-analysis strategy*, relies on analysing the self-screening and self-identification behaviour of users to identify the innovators. New-product ideas need to be analysed like any other internally generated idea; user-developed devices need to be evaluated like any other product prototype developed in the manufacturer's own laboratory. Based on this analysis, the manufacturer may decide to adopt the user-developed solution, adopt only certain aspects of it, or characterize the whole idea as commercially non-viable.

In more recent publications (von Hippel, 1985, 1986) the innovator users have been termed *lead users* and characterized as follows.

1 Lead users face needs that will be general in a market-place, but do so months or years before the greater part of that market-place encounters them, and
2 they are positioned to benefit significantly by obtaining a solution to those needs (von Hippel, 1986, p. 796).

The concept of lead users provides a solution to the problem briefly mentioned in chapter 2. How should marketing research be conducted for innovative products when traditional methods are inappropriate? In the words of von Hippel,

> average users have a poor ability to identify novel product attributes accurately because they do not have real-world experience with them. But *lead users* are *well* positioned by the very same reasoning: They have real-world experience with the needs that future profitable products must serve and with attributes they must contain. Clearly, therefore, systematic utilization of lead user data in marketing research will allow practitioners to identify profitable new product opportunities, attributes, and concepts that are invisible today.
>
> (von Hippel, 1985, p. 317)

Quinn observed that the potential of lead users is increasingly being recognized by both small and large companies.

> Many experienced big companies are relying less on early market research and more on interactive development with lead customers. Hewlett–Packard, 3M, Sony and Raychem frequently introduce radically new products through small teams that work closely with lead customers. These teams learn from their customers' needs and innovations, and rapidly modify designs and entry strategies based on this information.
>
> (Quinn, 1985, p. 80)

According to von Hippel (1986, p. 797), lead users can be incorporated into marketing research by a four-step process:

1 identify an important market or technical trend,
2 identify lead users who lead that trend in terms of (a) experience and (b) intensity of need,

3 analyse lead-user-need data, and
4 project lead-user data onto the general market of interest.

CAP: CRITICISM, REFINEMENTS, AND CONCEPTUAL EXTENSIONS

After publication of von Hippel's studies, a number of other researchers have demonstrated user involvement in innovation processes in areas as diverse as industrial machinery (Foxall and Tierney, 1984; vanden Abeele and Christiaens, 1987), medical instruments (Shaw, 1985; vanden Abeele and Christiaens, 1987), applications software (Voss, 1985a) and machine tools (Parkinson, 1982). However, in this section we will review some of the criticism and conceptual extensions to von Hippel's customer-active paradigm made by researchers of innovation processes.

In order to test his new paradigm (that is CAP) von Hippel investigated two necessary preconditions: (1) there is a customer request and (2) the request provides the 'idea' for the new product to the manufacturer. Vanden Abeele and Christiaens (1987, pp. 33–4) argued that these conditions need to be refined and put forward four necessary preconditions:

1 the customer must develop an innovative idea either for an existing or a new product,
2 transfer of the idea must occur (on the initiative of the customer, the manufacturer, or even a third party),
3 the manufacturer must be receptive, and
4 the compensation offered by the manufacturer to the customer for the innovation must be less than the price of proper technology transfer (if the customer has to be paid in full for the innovation it would not be different from the existing concept of 'technology transfer').

Foxall and Tierney (1984, p. 6) remarked that the customer-active paradigm, as hypothesized by von Hippel, assumes that the eventual manufacturer benefits most from user-initiated innovations. First, the manufacturer gains most significantly from the almost costless reduction in uncertainty which surrounds the earlier part of the new product development process. Second, during subsequent product development and commercialization, the manufacturer/marketer benefits from reductions in the costs of market research and R&D design which derive from their being targeted specifically towards the refinement of existing ideas or prototypes. Third, the manufacturer/

marketer benefits from the acceleration of the innovation diffusion process. Finally, by the time competitors are able to enter the market, the manufacturer will have gained the benefit of experience in production and distribution, which can result in his enjoying cost and margin advantages and which may forestall competitive entry.

A case study of a user-initiated innovation at British Aerospace questions the implicit assumption that the major benefits must inevitably accrue to the manufacturer/marketer. The case study describes how a division of British Aerospace plays the role of user-initiator but goes further than this by actively seeking out markets and marketing arrangements for its internally generated innovations. Thus, a second paradigm of customer activity, called CAP2, is proposed.

> CAP2 describes a user–innovator, who also takes an active, entrepreneurial role in the successful commercialisation of the new item, while CAP1 (von Hippel's Customer-Active Paradigm) actually describes customer-led invention/innovation but tends to ignore the possibility of customer-initiated entrepreneurship involving the alertness to opportunities for product innovation.
>
> (Foxall and Tierney, 1984, p. 13)

Foxall and Tierney suggest that CAP2 probably only applies to larger industrial companies. The differences between MAP, CAP1, and CAP2 are summarized in Table 4.2. Foxall (1986, pp. 23–4) further suggests that user/manufacturer interactions in industrial new-product development should not be regarded as a simple MAP/CAP dichotomy. Instead, there is a continuum of possible interactions, in which both MAP and CAP1 would appear nearer the manufacturer-dominated extreme, while CAP2 approximates the other extreme.

Table 4.2 Loci of invention, innovation, and entrepreneurship in MAP, CAP1 and CAP2

	MAP	*CAP1*	*CAP2*
Locus of invention	Manufacturer	Customer	Customer
Locus of innovation	Manufacturer	Customer/ manufacturer	Customer
Locus of entrepreneurship*	Manufacturer	Manufacturer	Customer/ manufacturer

Source: Foxall and Tierney (1984), *Management Decision*, vol. 22, no. 5, © MCB University Press Ltd. Reprinted with permission.
Note: *with respect to product innovation

Investigation of a number of case studies led Foxall and Johnston (1987) to refine further the continuum of scenarios for development of innovations for industrial markets (Table 4.3). They distinguish the following five categories.

1 *Manufacturer-initiated innovation (MII)*: the manufacturer performs all the stages of the new-product development process. This is essentially the same as von Hippel's MAP.
2 *User-initiated innovation I (UII1)*: the user develops a new device for internal use.
3 *User-initiated innovation 2 (UII2)*: the user-initiator of an internally implemented process innovation approaches a manufacturer with an idea, design, or prototype and requests him to produce and deliver further supplies of the item.
4 *User-initiated innovation 3 (UII3)*: in addition to the steps from UII2, the user also acts entrepreneurially in the commercial exploitation of his process innovation. This situation corresponds with CAP2.
5 *User-initiated innovation 4 (UII4)*: the user is responsible for all stages in the new product development process, including consumption.

Table 4.3 Locus of responsibility for creation and marketing of innovations

| | Stage of product development process | | | | |
	MII	UII1	UII2	UII3	UII4
Development of new product strategy	M	—	M	M/U	U
Idea generation	M	U	U	U	U
Idea screening	M	—	U	U/M	U
Business analysis:	M	—	M	U/M	U
concept testing	M	—	M	U/M	U
financial appraisal	M	—	M	U/M	U
Development	M	U	M	M	U
Market testing	M	—	M	M	U
Test marketing	M	—	M	M	U
Commercialization	M	—	M	M	U
Consumption	M	U	Users	Users	U+Users
Diffusion	M	—	M	M	U

Source: Foxall and Johnston (1987), *Technovation*, vol. 6, © Elsevier Science Publishers B.V. Reprinted with permission.
Notes: M = the manufacturer; U = the user; Users = other customers who make use of the innovation as process or product

In a recent publication, Foxall (1989, p. 95) groups UII3 and UII4 together under the heading of 'reverse innovation'.

Similar notions of a range of user-initiated innovations have been reported by Voss (1985a, pp. 114–15) and Shaw (1985, p. 288), although these researchers describe the development process from the manufacturer's (instead of the user's) point of view.

Reviewing the literature discussed above, we note that the initial concept of CAP has evolved into a broad spectrum of *manufacturer– user interactions*. The focus of research has shifted from identifying the innovation process as either manufacturer-active or customer-active, to determining the role of users during the process of product development. The involvement of users is no longer restricted to the idea-generation stage, but extended to all stages of the process. For example, Mantel and Meredith (1986, p. 34) discovered that an early customer sometimes even assists the manufacturer in marketing the innovation. Here it should be noted that, while most academic research into user-involvement concerns industrial new products, many examples from practice illustrate that users may contribute to the development of consumer products as well. For instance, Oliver markets its squash rackets by stressing that the 100 best squash players in the world test their new models. Philips involved a large number of teenagers in designing their Moving Sound, a modern line of audio equipment for young people. This emphasis on innovative design was pursued in the recently launched Helmet Television.

The interaction between manufacturer and users becomes especially important in the case of major innovations. As Gemünden (1985, p. 137) concluded, 'a *delegation-to-the-seller paradigm* is efficient for a small innovative step, whereas for a big innovative step an *intensive-interaction paradigm* is needed'. In the next section we will present the theoretical background of this central concept of interaction.

SUPPLIER–CUSTOMER INTERACTION IN INDUSTRIAL MARKETS

Industrial markets can be characterized by long-lasting relationships instead of short business transactions. This observation led to the establishment of the *International Marketing and Purchasing Project Group*. Researchers from France, Italy, Sweden, West Germany, and Great Britain initiated an international joint research project in order to study supplier–customer relationships in international industrial markets. Based on a theoretical interaction model, a number of case

studies were conducted (Håkansson, 1982). The theoretical framework (illustrated in Figure 4.3) consists of four groups of variables
that describe and influence the interaction between buying and selling
companies, that is variables describing

1 the *interaction process,*
2 the *participants* in the interaction process,
3 the *environment* within which the interaction takes place, and
4 the *atmosphere* affecting and affected by the interaction.

The interaction process encompasses the longer-term aspects of a
relationship as well as the individual episodes in a relationship. The
episodes involve the exchange between two parties, consisting of (1)
product or service exchange, (2) information exchange, (3) financial
exchange, and (4) social exchange (Håkansson, 1982, p. 16).

Instead of discussing the results of the study exhaustively, we will
focus on the way supplier–customer relationships develop in industrial markets. Supplier–customer relationships do not come into existence overnight, but rather evolve over time. According to Ford
(1980), the development of such relationships can be described by
five stages. Differences between the stages can be characterized by
the variables experience, uncertainty, distance, commitment, and
adaptations. The stages are summarized in Figure 4.4.

1 The pre-relationship stage
   Obviously, the first stage is the pre-relationship stage. There are a
   number of reasons for a customer to look for a new source of
   supply, for instance dissatisfaction with an existing source or
   marketing efforts of a potential supplier. As regards the new
   supplier, there is no experience, no commitment, considerable
   uncertainty, and at least some social distance (unfamiliarity with
   each other).
2 The early stage
   At the early stage, the potential supplier is in contact with the
   customer to negotiate or develop the specifications for the
   purchase. Both parties have little experience of each other, there is
   considerable uncertainty and still the same distance, there is little
   or no evidence on which to evaluate the level of commitment, and
   adaptations relate to high investments of management time.
3 The development stage
   The development stage starts after the signing of the contract for
   the major capital purchase. It is characterized by increasing experience and therefore reduced uncertainty and distance. The firm's

Figure 4.3 The IMP interaction model

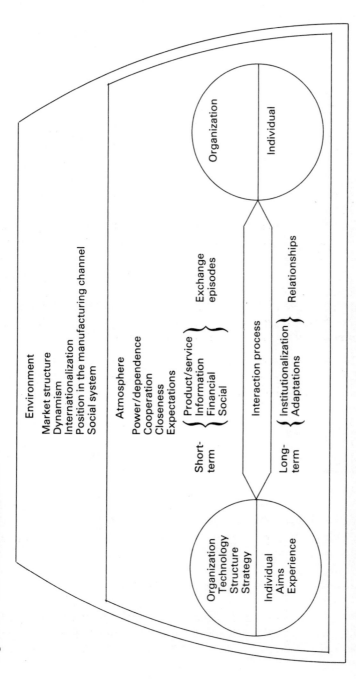

Source: Håkansson (1982) © John Wiley & Sons Ltd. Reprinted with permission.

Figure 4.4 The development of buyer–seller relationships in industrial markets

	1 The pre-relationship stage	2 The early stage	3 The development stage	4 The long-term stage	5 The final stage
	Evaluation of new potential supplier	Negotiation of sample delivery	Contract signed or delivery build-up scale deliveries	After several major purchases or large scale deliveries	In long-established stable markets
Evaluation initiated by: – particular episode in existing relationship – general evaluation of existing supplier performance – efforts of non-supplier – other information sources – overall policy decision		**Experience** – Low	– Increased	– High	
Evaluation conditioned by: – experience with previous supplier – uncertainty about potential relationship – 'Distance' from potential supplier		**Uncertainty** – High	– Reduced	– Minimum development of institutionalization	Extensive institutionalization
		Distance – High	– Reduced	– Minimum	
Commitment – zero		**Commitment** Actual: Low Perceived: Low	Actual: Increased Perceived: Demonstrated by Informal Adaptations	Actual: maximum Perceived: reduced	Business based on industry Codes of Practice
		Adaptation High investment of management time. Few cost-savings	Increasing formal and informal adaptations. Cost savings increase	Extensive adaptations, Cost savings reduced by institutionalization	

Source: Ford (1980), *European Journal of Marketing*, vol. 14, no. 5/6. © MCB University Press Ltd. Reprinted with permission

evaluation of its partner depends on the perceived commitment to the relationship. There is an increasing number of both formal and informal adaptations.

4 The long-term stage

The long-term stage is marked by the firms' importance to each other. There is considerable experience at this stage, while uncertainty and distance are reduced to a minimum. The level of commitment to the relationship is indicated by the extensive formal and informal adaptations which have occurred.

5 The final stage

The final stage can be reached in stable markets over long periods of time. It is characterized by an extension of the institutionalization process to a point where the conduct of business is based on industry codes of practice.

An alternative model for developing buyer–seller relationships that has received much attention was recently proposed by Dwyer, Schurr, and Oh (1987). However, the stages they mention (awareness, exploration, expansion, commitment, and dissolution) closely correspond to the stages of Ford's process. No matter which framework is adopted, supplier–customer relationships in industrial markets are invariably described as being long term and based on cooperation, trust, and loyalty. In other words, commitment is the key concept. A three-stage process model of the development of commitment has been presented by LaFief and O'Neal (1987).

When operating in international markets, one should keep in mind that there may be considerable differences between supplier–customer relationships in different countries (Campbell, 1985). A fairly recent IMP study demonstrated the importance of supplier–customer relationships by showing that 'the ability of a company to ... establish close social and business relationships with clients is a major factor for success in international industrial marketing' (Ford, 1984, p. 109). Nevertheless, managing a portfolio of customer relationships involves specific problems and challenges (Campbell and Cunningham, 1985; Jackson, 1985).

NETWORKS

The International Marketing and Purchasing (IMP) Project Group studied relationships between selling and purchasing firms in industrial markets in the broadest sense, that is the relationships were not studied within a more specific context. Although relationships are of importance to the marketing of industrial products, they are crucial in the context of innovations as well.

Consider, for example, the area of *stimulating innovative activity.*

> Creating a dynamic high-tech region is not a matter of combining ingredients. It is one of building institutions and relationships – both locally and nationally – that support the development of innovative enterprises ... It is these relationships between the individuals, firms and institutions in the region that matter – not their simple presence.
>
> (Saxenian, 1988, pp. 74, 75)

And, to return to the subject of our investigation, supplier–customer relationships may play a central role in *developing innovations for industrial markets.* Earlier in this chapter we presented a number of studies demonstrating the involvement of users in product development. Many industrial innovations were shown to be developed through interaction between the manufacturer and potential users. The Swedish branch of the IMP Project Group, in particular, however, has gone beyond simple manufacturer–user relationships and postulates that other parties may be involved as well. In these situations, the manufacturer operates within a network consisting of a number of organizations linked together by individual interactive relationships. We will present below some important theoretical studies with respect to networks and conclude by summarizing the relevance of the network concept to the subject of this book: the development of industrial innovations.

From sole focus on the manufacturer to functioning within networks

Thus far, we have seen that over the years product development has been viewed from a number of different perspectives.

1 Product development initiated by the manufacturer
   The overwhelming majority of studies focuses on the manufacturer as the initiator of the product development process (see chapter 3 for examples). Much attention is paid to determining ways of increasing the rate of success of new products. The process of product development is usually divided into a series of subsequent stages and specific recommendations to the manufacturer are formulated. The manufacturer is considered the main actor who controls the process and influences the environment.

2 Product development initiated by the user

Von Hippel focused on the user as the initiator of the product development process and he developed a customer-active paradigm in contrast to a manufacturer-active paradigm (von Hippel, 1978). The customer-active paradigm has been supported by many empirical studies.

3 Product development as an interaction process between user and manufacturer

According to the first two views, the initiative for product development is located in one actor only. More recent research (Håkansson, 1982) has combined both views and proposed an interaction approach.

The three types of product development study are complementary but to some extent also overlapping, as is shown in Figure 4.5 (Håkansson, 1987b, p. 86).

The main criticism of the three perspectives outlined above is that each of them focuses on only one or a few actors. While the first two

Figure 4.5 The initiator of product development

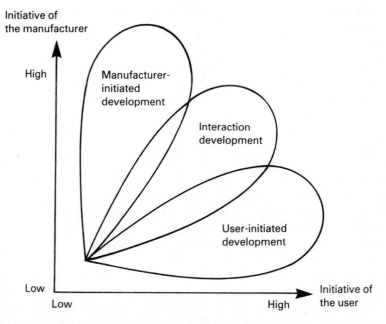

Source: Håkansson (1987), *Industrial Technological Development: A Network Approach*, © Croom Helm Ltd. Reprinted with permission.

are oriented towards one specific type of actor, the third directs itself towards the interplay between two actors. Thus, all three viewpoints restrict themselves to a limited number of actors. These views are considered to be too narrow in their approach: product development should be regarded as the interplay between a number of actors, that is, as taking place within networks. New knowledge in terms of new product or process ideas often emerges at the interface between different knowledge areas. The specialized development resources of individual development units (such as firms and research institutes) need to be coordinated through a series of exchange relationships linking all these units together (Håkansson, 1987a, pp. 4–5). Shared values and unifying ideas are the most important elements holding the decentralized segments of a network together in a dynamic pattern of interaction (Lipnack and Stamps, 1987, p. 23).

Although companies may consider technical cooperation as the only possible opportunity for developing new products, it is also stimulated by changes in the environment (see Ohmae, 1989).

> The significant change in the business environment due to economic conditions, high costs, the globalization of business and increasing political control has changed the focus of alliance strategies to the point where they are now becoming the rule rather than the exception.
>
> (James, 1985, p. 76)

For instance, the integrated European market intended for 1992 will push for more international cooperation (Riedle, 1989, p. 221). At the end of 1989 the idea of a future unified Europe led Bova and DAF, two Dutch manufacturers of buses, to join forces by founding United Bus with the explicit objective of 'establishing an international group of manufacturers of buses and touringcars which will play an important role in Europe'. Since their start they have already been joined by Optare (Great Britain), Den Oudsten (The Netherlands), and Dab-Silkeborg (Denmark) (*Carrière*, 1990, p. 11). The need for cooperation with external parties is increasingly mentioned as an essential element of a firm's business strategy. For example, in August 1990, as the basis of the much needed radical reorganization, Philips president J.D. Timmer launched *Operation Centurion*. The wording of the new Philips gospel, as published at the end of October, stresses reduced vertical integration and increasing collaboration as critical measures in eliminating the existing problems (*NRC Handelsblad*, 1990c). Michael Spindler, the new Chief Operating Officer at Apple per January 1990, announced in September a plan to take care of the problems confronting the firm by accelerating the market launch of new products through cooperation with suppliers, amongst other things (*Business Week*, 1990).

Both the motives prompting collaboration and a large number of situational factors lead a firm to choose from a broad range of alternative cooperation modes, each differing in economic relevance and effects (Hagedoorn, 1990).

Depending on the type of counterpart, interaction with the objective of cooperating in developing technological innovations can be divided into three categories (cf. Håkansson, 1987a, pp. 6–8). *Vertical interaction* concerns all cooperation between partners belonging to the same production chain, for example manufacturer–customer relationships. There are often good reasons for manufacturers and customers to cooperate in developing an innovation. Through interaction with a major customer, a manufacturer can develop a product that fits the needs of the market segment better, develop technical ability, share the substantial development costs, gain access to the necessary application know-how, reduce total development time (faster market launch!), and use the name and reputation of the customer as a reference when selling to other customers. The customer, on the other hand, acquires an advanced technology at an early stage, resulting in an improved competitive position, obtains a product better fitted to its market or production requirements, may enjoy a price discount and/or exclusive use during a specified period, and establishes or maintains an innovative reputation. Lyons, Krachenberg, and Henke (1990) provide an extensive survey of the various costs and benefits of buyer–supplier relationships in general. A recent study of 123 companies in Sweden showed that customers and suppliers made up almost 75 per cent of the cooperation partners (Håkansson, 1990, pp. 375–6).

Horizontal competitive interaction relates to cooperation between companies which are basically competitors, for example Philips and Siemens who teamed up to develop the megachip. In the autumn of 1990 this truly gigantic project gained wide publicity because of Philips' withdrawal after five years of cooperation. While the project brought Philips many technological benefits, it is generally considered to be a commercial failure (*NRC Handelsblad*, 1990b). A more recent example involves Philips Medical Systems and Hitachi, who announced in October 1989 that they would cooperate in developing and producing computer tomography systems for the American market (and thus share the high costs involved). Through this type of interaction the manufacturers may gain access to specialized technological knowledge, reduce the costs of development and production, reduce the risks, speed up the development process, improve the product's quality, increase market potential by making market agreements (for example, with respect to global standards), learn basic skills and knowledge, and acquire new and more precise benchmarks of a partner's performance (cf. Frey, 1986, p. 295). However, if the parties involved should differ considerably in size or contribution to the project, the interaction may be detrimental to the weaker party. In general, owing to cultural differences and the type of skills traded, Western companies face an inherent disadvantage in alliances with Asian competitors (Hamel, Doz, and Pralahad, 1989, pp. 136–8).

Finally, *horizontal complementary interaction* encompasses cases where manufacturers of complementary products cooperate. An example is presented by DSM and Peugeot who jointly started a project to develop new materials. Other examples can be found in systems selling or large turn-key projects. Elements of both horizontal competitive and horizontal complementary cooperation can be found in such large-scale cooperation programmes as Eureka, which was initiated to integrate European industry and has brought together scientists and engineers from over 600 industrial companies and public research institutes in more than 165 R&D projects (Dickson, 1988, p. 27). For example, more than thirty European firms cooperated in developing a European High Definition Television system and, in April 1989 announced their intention to cooperate in the development of the corresponding television sets, video-recorders, and studio equipment as well. More than 100 firms collaborating in Joint European Submicron Silicon (JESSI), the large-scale European technology programme with a total budget of approximately 8,000 m. Dutch guilders, needed four years to select fifty-four projects that are essential for the survival of an independent European chip industry. Souder and Nassar (1990a, 1990b) investigated twenty-one American R&D consortia, listed the various advantages and disadvantages of ten types of R&D consortia, developed a model for selecting compatible consortia partners, and formulated guidelines for effectively managing such R&D consortia. Although these are examples of extremely complex and comprehensive networks, in developing innovations for industrial markets manufacturers typically deal with networks in one form or another.

No matter what mode of interaction is selected, cooperation with external parties always has several potential side benefits, such as building a long-term relationship (with potential future benefits), demonstrating an overall cooperative attitude, and improving the overall working environment, while sometimes the cooperation may turn out to be an unexpected source of strategically relevant information ('serendipity').

The network approach

Interactive relationships connect individual companies into structures that can be analysed by means of network concepts. A network is described by Cook and Emerson (1978) as 'sets of two or more connected exchange relations'. However, we define a network so as to include the case of manufacturer–user interaction discussed previously, this being a network in its most simple form. According to Håkansson (1987a, pp. 14–17), a network contains three basic elements (Figure 4.6).

1 *Actors*, defined as those who perform activities and/or control resources within a certain field. Actors can be individuals, a group of persons, a division within a company, a company, or a group of companies.
2 *Activities*, which are performed by actors. There are two main categories of activities: transformation activities (carried out within the control of one actor and characterized by one resource being improved by the use of other resources) and transaction activities (linking transformation activities and creating relationships with other actors).
3 *Resources*, which consist of physical assets (machinery, material, etc.), financial, and human assets (labour, knowledge, and relationships).

The network approach implies two important theoretical extensions of the original interaction concept.

First, *the parties involved* are no longer restricted to the buying and selling firms. Although the relationship between the manufacturer and the user can still be of major importance in developing an innovation, many other parties can be involved as well. The government can stimulate innovation through subsidies, universities and other research institutes can carry out basic research that leads to new technologies, knowledge brokers and transfer centres can bring the relevant parties together, and competitors can share the risks and costs of large development projects. Third parties may even be involved in the diffusion of innovations. Mantel and Rosegger (1987, pp. 124–8) presented a typology of third-party institutions that intervene, with varying intensity of influence, in the adoption decision of

Figure 4.6 A network model

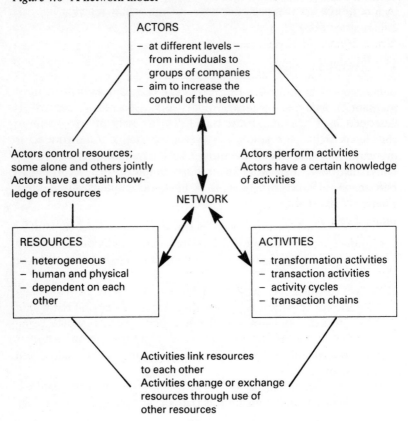

ACTORS
- at different levels –
  from individuals to
  groups of companies
- aim to increase the
  control of the network

Actors control resources;
some alone and others jointly
Actors have a certain knowledge of resources

Actors perform activities
Actors have a certain knowledge
of activities

NETWORK

RESOURCES
- heterogeneous
- human and physical
- dependent on each
  other

ACTIVITIES
- transformation activities
- transaction activities
- activity cycles
- transaction chains

Activities link resources
to each other
Activities change or exchange
resources through use of
other resources

Source: Håkansson (1987), © Croom Helm Ltd. Reprinted with permission.

others. Through the network concept, the individual buyer–seller
relationship is put into the context of other relationships. Although
technological cooperation with local partners has obvious advantages,
internationally operating firms often cooperate with foreign companies as well. Håkansson and Laage-Hellman (1984, pp. 228–32)
discussed a continuum of R&D cooperation strategies.

The second conceptual extension relates to *the kind of relationship*. Apart from direct relationships, that is the straightforward
relationship between the focal firm and its partner, one should distinguish indirect relationships. Mattsson (1987, p. 128) defines an
indirect relationship 'from a focal firm A's point of view to be a
relationship between two firms of which A is not one of the counterparts'. Thus, if the focal firm A has a direct relationship with B, while

B has a direct relationship with C, B–C is an indirect relation for A; A has an indirect relation to C. The concept of indirect relationships can best be elucidated by an example (taken from Biemans and de Vries, 1988). Suppose a manufacturer in the machine industry has developed a new process machine in close cooperation with one of its leading customers. In this case, the direct relationship is the one between the manufacturer and its leading customer. When implementation of the new process machine influences the quality of the end product produced with it, the leading customer will want to test the changed end product with its own customers. These relationships are termed indirect from the manufacturer's perspective. Similarly, considering the viewpoint of the leading customer, the relationships between the manufacturer and its suppliers are indirect relationships. Figure 4.7 depicts a hypothetical situation involving these and other indirect relationships.

Every firm has a certain position in a network that can be defined by (1) the functions performed by the firm for other firms, (2) the relative importance of the firm in the network, (3) the strength of the relationships with other firms, and (4) the identity of the firms with which the firm has direct relationships. The present network position can be regarded as the firm's 'strategic situation' (Mattsson, 1987, p. 128). Indirect relationships are of importance because,

1 given the strategic situation, they influence the direct relationship and
2 changes in the strategic situation can change the firm's position both with regard to the direct and indirect relationships (see also the discussion on second-order functions of relationships (Håkansson and Johanson, 1989, p. 220))).

The relationships connecting companies into networks are among the most valuable resources a company possesses. As we have already seen, the relationships can be analysed according to the interaction model (Håkansson, 1982) and are of a long-term character. The development of relationships takes time and resources, involves commitments for the future and creates assets that can be used by the firm. Thus the development of relationships should be treated like any other investments made by a firm (Johanson and Mattsson, 1985). These investments in relationships are made to increase productivity or technical efficiency, to serve as information channels, and to increase control (power). The relations between organizations can be regarded as bonds of different types and strength (Mattsson, 1985, p. 265):

Figure 4.7 Direct and indirect relationships in a network

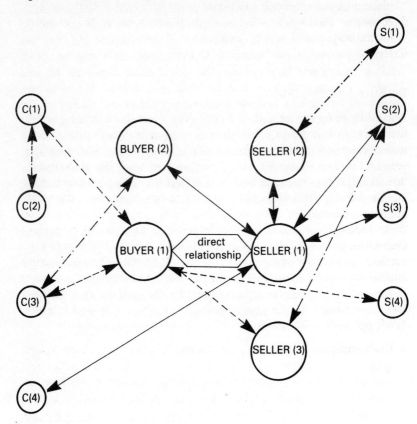

C(i) : customer i
S(i) : supplier i
←——→ direct relationship for SELLER (1) / indirect relationship for BUYER (1)
←---→ indirect relationship for SELLER (1) / direct relationship for BUYER (1)
←-·-→ indirect relationship for SELLER (1) / indirect relationship for BUYER (1)

1 *technical bonds:* two companies have technical bonds when they have adjusted to each other in some technical sense;
2 *time-based bonds:* there is a need for temporal coordination between sequential activities in a production process involving separate firms;
3 *knowledge-based bonds:* through exchange of information over a period of time two organizations build up knowledge about each other;

4 *social bonds:* to a great extent contacts between organizations take place on a person-to-person basis;
5 *economic bonds:* companies can sometimes be united in more formal ways (investment, credit);
6 *legal bonds:* common ownership and contracts of all kinds.

Research into networks

According to Fombrun (1982, p. 281) there are three approaches to the analysis of networks. The *nodal* strategy decomposes the original network into component nodes, where the focus is on the network as seen by the node occupant. The *dyadic* strategy leads to a decomposition of the network into nodal pairs, with a focus on the relationship among pairs. Finally, the *triadic* strategy results in an inventory of all possible triads in the network, with a focus on the composition of these triads in terms of the relationships linking the three nodes. Current research into product development through networks mostly employs a dyadic strategy, although, by taking indirect relationships into account as well, some elements of a triadic strategy are present.

Despite all the opportunities offered by the analysis of networks, there are some inherent methodological problems, too (Kennedy, 1987, pp. 102–3; Mattsson, 1985, pp. 284–7).

1 Each study of networks is confronted with the issue of *boundary specification*, that is, where does one set the limits for collecting data when in reality a network may have no real limits? Each study of networks should explicitly state the way the boundaries of the network were set so that individual studies can be compared to each other.
2 When the total network is too large to study in its entirety, the investigator is confronted with the problem of *sampling* elements to estimate existing relationships.
3 A third issue relates to *measurement.* Networks can be investigated by using direct observation, analysis of archival records, and survey data. Too many studies rely on survey data (in the form of personal interviews) only. Ideally, one should combine the different methods of data gathering to obtain a complete and realistic picture.

Looking back at the last three IMP Conferences, held at respectively the University of Manchester (Turnbull and Paliwoda, 1988), Penn State University (Wilson, Han, and Holler, 1989), and S.D.A. Bocconi, Milan (Fiocca and Snehota, 1990), a number of interesting conclusions and viewpoints with respect to the current state-of-the-art of interaction and network research can be submitted (see also Biemans and Brand, 1989).

Research into interaction and networks: increase followed by stabilization?

The original IMP model of interaction has served as the basis of a large number of empirical studies into buyer–seller interaction. The results of these studies are increasingly being presented at the annual IMP Conference. While at the 4th IMP Conference in 1988 about half of the total number of papers (approximately thirty, including hand-outs) discussed interaction and/or networks, this share increased to approximately two-thirds in 1989, and dropped again to about 50 per cent in 1990. However, due to the sharp increase of papers (the total number of papers presented at the last three conferences respectively was approximately thirty, forty-five, and sixty), the initial increase in absolute numbers seems to have stabilized. Papers are increasingly addressing individual relationships in the context of networks, with most of the research in this area still being conducted by Swedish investigators. For instance, during the 6th IMP Conference, the concepts of interaction and networks received about equal attention. The second large-scale empirical study recently conducted by the IMP Group investigated relationships in the context of networks and without a doubt will prove to be a stimulus for much subsequent research.

Research into interaction is no longer limited to Europe

Despite the fact that the original interaction model was developed by European investigators, research into this area has spread to other continents. In the United States, in particular, interaction has become the central theme of many congresses, seminars, and workshops, and many publications on interaction have seen print by now. For a survey of these American publications the interested reader is referred to Wilson and Möller (1988).

Broader field of application

At present, research into interaction and networks is no longer exclusively applied to the buying and selling of industrial products. This was most clearly shown at the 5th IMP Conference. In addition to the traditional subjects, investigators applied the concepts to the study of services (agency–client relationships in advertising), distribution (buyer–supplier relationships in retailing), and international issues (East–West trade). Of particular interest was the announcement of a large-scale international investigation into the interfaces between various functions within organizations (Specht, 1989).

Time to strike a balance

After a decade of research, the time for striking a balance has arrived. A first attempt was made by Möller and Wilson (1988), but the recent review presented by Easton (1989) shows that much work still remains to be done. A similar point was raised during the final discussion at the last IMP Conference. Problems arise because (1) many investigators define the same theoretical concepts in varying ways and (2) a significant part of the existing research is only available in a language that is not easily accessible (mainly Swedish).

Research into networks is only partly quantifiable

An important issue concerns the question whether research into networks can be quantified. To elucidate the matter the existing publications can be divided into two categories.

1 A considerable number of the available publications is very general in nature and strongly oriented towards generating or integrating theoretical concepts. Most of them are based on a very limited number of in-depth case studies or even lack any empirical basis at all. The purpose of these studies is to generate rather than quantify theoretical constructs (Mattsson, 1985, p. 286). Examples can be found in the proceedings of each IMP Conference (for example Easton and Lundgren, 1988; Ford, 1989; Rajagopal and Deans, 1990).
2 Other publications do not address networks in their entirety, but instead concentrate on very limited and narrowly defined aspects of networks. Thanks to this narrow focus, quantification is possible (Gadde and Mattsson, 1987; Nelson, 1988; Wigand and Frankwick, 1989).

All in all, the annual IMP Conference is gradually changing into a general platform for discussing all aspects of industrial marketing and purchasing. While the importance of relationships is increasingly being recognized, the group of researchers actively investigating interaction and networks is being supplemented by an increasing number of academics with broader interests and new focal areas of investigation emerge. For instance, while in 1988 only one of the papers concerned the subject of purchasing, this number grew dramatically to five in 1989 and ten in 1990, with more and more emphasis on the strategic implications! Other emerging areas of interest include export, logistics, and industrial services.

Relevance of the network concept to the development of industrial innovations

We will conclude this chapter on manufacturer–user interaction and networks by summarizing the relevance of the network concept to the development of innovations for industrial markets. Nowadays, a number of trends can be observed in industrial markets.

1 Technological developments have accelerated to a level where product life cycles have shortened considerably. This implies that a manufacturer can no longer count on a steady demand over many years for a newly developed product. Instead, he must continually be actively searching for innovative products to succeed the existing ones, while the time available to reap the benefits has been significantly reduced (cf. Foster, 1986). Both academics and practitioners emphasize the need to speed up the product development process, and several studies provide guidelines for cutting the amount of time required in half (*Fortune*, 1987; Duffy and Kelly, 1989; *Fortune*, 1989; Bronikowski, 1990; Gupta and Wilemon, 1990; Stalk and Hout, 1990; van den Muyzenberg, 1990).
2 New products are becoming increasingly complex and their development necessitates the combination of different areas of knowledge. For example, sometimes part of the technical knowledge is not available in house and must be obtained from external sources, such as research institutes and possibly competitors. In other situations the development of an innovation demands application know-how that exists with customers.
3 The increasing complexity of industrial products has also resulted in a demand for standardization. Customers no longer want each manufacturer to develop his own version of a product but prefer the development of industry standards.
4 Industrial markets are becoming increasingly global. The manufacturer can no longer confine himself to developing a product for a local market only. More and more, the product should be aimed at

international markets, which may not always be easily accessible to the manufacturer.

5 Because of the increasing complexity of industrial products, the growing competition, and the shortened product life cycles, developing industrial innovations has become an expensive and high-risk activity.

Because of these current tendencies in industrial markets, manufacturers are increasingly developing innovations through cooperation with other organizations. These potential partners are not limited to the firm's present customers or potential users of the innovation. In addition, many other organizations, such as competitors, research institutes, and distributors may contribute to the product development process (for example an industry standard may be developed through cooperation between a number of competitors and major customers). By means of these interactive relationships manufacturers can shorten the duration of the total product development process, share the costs and risks involved, obtain the necessary technical, market and/or application knowledge, gain access to international markets, and create industrial standards. Cooperation during product development is regarded by manufacturers as a means to attain an innovation process that is both more effective and more efficient. Therefore the most compelling reason for discussing the development of innovations from a network perspective is that it *matches reality* (cf. Bradbury, 1989, p. 7).

Despite this reality, Dutch researchers of industrial marketing have paid only limited attention to the network concept. This could partially be due to the abstract and theoretical nature of most publications about networks to date. In a broader perspective, however, an increasing number of articles and books about networks is being published by Dutch researchers, evidence of recognition of the relevance of the network concept. The sociological, economic, geographical, logistic, and management aspects of networks are considered in Boekema and Kamann (1989). Some recent empirical studies concern coordination mechanisms in horticultural networks (Kamann and Strijker, 1991) and dynamics and countervailing power in charter networks (Kamann, 1991). Commandeur and Taal (1989) investigate networks in connection with the firm's production processes. However, application of the network concept to the area of developing innovations is still quite limited. Beije (1989) attempted to integrate information-transfer within and between organizations with traditional economic theory at an abstract theoretical level.

Wissema and Euser (1988) studied a number of widely varying case studies (involving both consumer and industrial innovations) and discuss the functioning of networks from a managerial point of view at a relatively high level of abstraction. Although, as Mattsson (1985, p. 286) stated, 'at the present stage of development of the network approach we are more interested in description and understanding of complex processes than empirical generalizations', the ultimate purpose of research into networks should be to generate guidelines that can assist managers in their decision-making, for example with respect to product development within networks. Just as research into interaction processes has generated results relevant to industrial marketing practice, the network approach holds potential in that direction too. Before describing the functioning of firms within networks in the Dutch medical equipment industry, the next chapter will present the results of an exploratory investigation analysing cases of user involvement in product development from various industries.

5 User involvement in product development

Listening to customers must become everyone's business.

(Tom Peters, 1987)

During the years 1985 to 1989 we conducted an extensive study of interaction patterns in developing industrial innovations in the Netherlands. This empirical investigation consisted of two parts. First, an *exploratory study*, involving five cases of industrial new product development from various sectors of Dutch industry, was carried out by conducting in-depth semi-structured interviews with the persons most closely involved in the projects. While the study focused on the involvement of potential users in product development, the results clearly indicated the relevance of the network concept. Next, partly because of the results of the exploratory study, the Dutch medical equipment industry was selected for conducting a *follow-up investigation*. Seventeen cases of new product development within thirteen firms were studied in great detail. The results both confirmed the initial tentative conclusions concerning user involvement and provided substantial insight in the functioning of firms within networks.

The subject of user involvement in developing industrial innovations is treated in the present chapter by presenting the main findings of the exploratory study. Chapter 6 elaborates on this theme by showing how Dutch manufacturers develop medical equipment innovations through interaction with various parties within a network. The book concludes with discussing the major managerial implications in Chapter 7.

The results of the exploratory study are based on in-depth personal interviews with the people involved in both the manufacturing and buying organizations. Third parties, such as distributors and advisers, in so far as they contributed significantly to the product development process, were interviewed too. In some cases it was necessary to interview competitors and industry experts to obtain information about the current developments in the market in question (for more details on the research methodology employed the reader is referred to Appendix B).

For the exploratory study we looked for Dutch manufacturers conducting their product development activities in the Netherlands, which are of medium size (that is having between fifty and 500 employees), enjoy an innovative image in the market, and are willing to discuss a recent innovation project in great detail. Eventually, we selected a sample of five firms that satisfied all or most of these criteria: Ammeraal Conveyor Belting B.V., Packitt*, Dräger Nederland B.V., the N.V. Nederlandsche Apparatenfabriek Nedap, and Grenco Process Technology B.V. The firms and the innovations studied are described in Table 5.1 (detailed case descriptions can be found in Biemans (1989)). Although the five cases involve very different firms, products, and situations, some general conclusions can be formulated. However, when reading these conclusions it should be borne in mind that they are based on the five cases only, which were investigated to explore the subject, so that broad generalizations should be made wth the utmost care. Nevertheless, as these conclusions are based on in-depth case studies, they may be of great practical value to other industrial firms in similar situations. Additional support is lent to the conclusions because they (1) partly concur with the findings of other investigators and/or (2) are confirmed by the results of the follow-up investigation in the medical equipment industry.

The conclusions presented in this chapter relate to the following topics:

1 product development as a phased process,
2 differences between having industrial and consumer products tested by users,
3 derived demand,
4 product champions,
5 networks,
6 marketing of knowledge, and
7 having potential users test industrial prototypes.

The conclusions are clearly illustrated by examples from the cases investigated.

*The name of the firm has been disguised for reasons of confidentiality.

Table 5.1 Brief descriptions of the five firms participating in the exploratory study

---

AMMERAAL CONVEYOR BELTING B.V.: A new belt for conveying products
Ammeraal is a Dutch manufacturer of process and conveyor belting. It has subsidiaries in ten different countries, while its products are sold in more than sixty countries all over the world. Worldwide, Ammeraal is one of the major suppliers of process and conveyor belting, which are used in various industries, for example airports, postal services, industrial bakeries, and agriculture. Innovative developments concerning belting usually involve the use of new materials that result in improved product characteristics. Requirements of customers in the food industry led Ammeraal to develop a new belt made of synthetic material. Both suppliers and users were involved in the development process. In the course of the development process various problems arose concerning the production of the high-quality belt.

PACKITT: Steel drums, a new design
Packitt is an international company with a long history in manufacturing packaging for all kinds of products sold to industrial customers. The largest division manufactures and sells steel drums (mostly to industrial firms who use them for oil and chemical products). The market for steel drums can be characterized as being very traditional and not very innovative. Nevertheless, the last decade has witnessed an increasing tendency to use large containers to transport steel drums. This development led Packitt to develop a new steel drum which makes optimal use of the space available in the standardized containers. Lack of serious management support was one of the causes that ultimately resulted in scrapping the project.

DRÄGER NEDERLAND B.V.: A pulse oximeter for monitoring oxygen
From a global viewpoint, Dräger is one of the leading manufacturers of breathing equipment for hospitals. Dräger Nederland is the Dutch distributor of an innovative monitor developed in the United States with the help of local users. The pulse oximeter offers advantages to the specialist, nurse, and patient. That the new monitor was developed in the United States did not preclude users in the Netherlands from improving on the original design. Leading specialists who were dissatisfied with the quality of the sensors complained to Dräger. When action was not directly forthcoming they developed their own improved sensors.

N.V. NEDERLANDSCHE APPARATENFABRIEK NEDAP: An advanced electronic access-control system
Nedap started as a manufacturer/supplier of electrotechnical parts, but for some years now it has been developing and selling its own products. Ever since its establishment, Nedap has been actively searching for potential new products. Approximately 70 per cent of sales is generated by products developed during the last five years. The most important innovations recently developed involve systems for the identification of animals, people, and goods, which all depend on the same basic technology. The hands-free access-control system proved to be a moderate success. However, its success is largely based on the absence of competitors offering alternative solutions of comparable quality.

Table 5.1 contd.

GRENCO PROCESS TECHNOLOGY B.V.: A freeze-concentration process for the food industry

Grenco Process Technology, a relatively young subsidiary of Grasso's Koninklijke Machinefabrieken N.V., which has a long history as a manufacturer of industrial machinery, is specialized in engineering and assembling industrial process installations. The innovative freeze-concentration process is used for removing water from aqueous solutions and is based on an advanced technology, of which Grenco is the sole supplier. This monopoly rests on the exclusive possession of advanced technological know-how, co-developed by the present managing director. The new technology has been applied to diverse sectors in the food industry, with Grenco continually searching for new applications. The basic technology needs to be adapted to every new application, which necessitates a joint development project with a key customer.

PRODUCT DEVELOPMENT AS A PHASED PROCESS

The model of the product development process, selected as a basis for our empirical investigation, consists of a series of distinctly separated stages. When we selected this model in Chapter 3, we drew attention to the fact that in practice this distinction between separate stages may be very unclear and somewhat artificial. This remark is unequivocally supported by the cases investigated.

Consider the distinction between developing a prototype and testing it. When the innovation is jointly developed by the manufacturer and a major user, the two stages are no longer clearly separated. The development and testing activities may even be conducted at the user's premises with assistance from the manufacturer's engineers. When this occurs, the frequent instant feedback loops and close manufacturer–user interaction result in a continuous and iterative development–internal testing–external testing cycle.

> The case of Grenco illustrates the point. The basic technology incorporated in the process installations can be applied to various markets. Every potentially profitable market is analysed carefully to (1) gather detailed market information and (2) identify the potential user that appears most promising as a partner for jointly developing the application. The development activities take place on the user's premises. A pilot plant is built that imitates the production process on a small scale and the application is developed and tested. Grenco engineers work

full-time at the user's premises to start up the pilot plant and debug the installation. This results in an iterative process in which it is hard to distinguish between the development and testing stages.

Another distinction with overtones of artificiality is the one between having the innovation tested by users and introducing it into the market. The names and reputations of major users, who tested the new product under real-life conditions, can be used in promotional material and during sales presentations. These users can also be employed to demonstrate the product in operation to potential purchasers, thus accelerating diffusion of the innovation. The users who participated in the external testing stage are quite often the initial buyers of the innovation, too. Moreover, as a result of the external testing stage, the innovation is unlikely to remain confidential. Testing in the market is a means by which information is disseminated as well as gathered (Foxall, 1984, p. 222). This is also recognized by Rabino and Moore (1989, p. 38) who mention, in their study of the new-product announcement process, that beta tests serve the important function of alerting selected users to an imminent product launch.

In the case of Ammeraal, sales representatives got over-enthusiastic and were already selling the new belt at the time of external testing. That is, before it was actually introduced into the market (before it was even decided that the new belt would in fact be introduced!). This resulted in serious problems with some customers and points to the need for an extensive internal communication programme that includes careful briefing of all sales personnel.

DIFFERENCES BETWEEN HAVING INDUSTRIAL AND CONSUMER PRODUCTS TESTED BY POTENTIAL USERS

In this chapter we specifically address the testing of industrial proto-types by potential users (beta tests; see also the last section of this chapter). This external testing stage, however, is relevant not only to industrial products. New consumer products are generally also tested by potential users before being introduced into the market. Some differences between field tests in industrial versus consumer markets are enumerated below.

Number of potential users involved

In general, a relatively large sample of users is selected to test new consumer products. However, due to the typically limited number of potential users of new industrial products, the latter are usually tested by only a few users (such as industrial firms or research institutes).

Number of persons involved

New consumer products are usually tested by a single person. People are asked individually to taste a new variety of soup or try a new vacuum cleaner. With industrial products, however, the number of people within the organization testing the innovation can become quite large. Often, persons from various departments and levels are involved.

> The new monitor introduced by Dräger in the Netherlands was tested by both specialists and the nursing staff, while the technical department was quite often involved as well.

Personal relationship

In general, the testing of new consumer products does not involve a personal relationship between the manufacturer and the persons testing the new product. As industrial innovations (1) are often of great importance to the user's competitive position, (2) may represent a vital part of the user's production process, and (3) may necessitate detailed instructions (and sometimes even training) to understand their operation, the personal relationship between the manufacturer and the organizations testing the new product strongly determines the value and significance of the test results.

Employing users as reference

Due to the usual anonymity of the people testing new consumer products, their names will not be used as references during market introduction. Instances where famous people are used for testing the new product (for instance, a renowned sportsman testing new equipment) are obvious exceptions. However, potential users testing new industrial products are frequently selected because their names, reputations, and test results can be used in promotional material and during sales presentations. Therefore these initial customers are also referred to as *launching customers.*

In introducing the new pulse monitor in the Netherlands, Dräger placed monitors with recognized opinion leaders. Three different kinds of opinion leaders can be distinguished: (1) hospitals where teaching takes place, (2) specialized (parts of) hospitals, and (3) specialists who publish regularly. These three categories were used as references and functioned as a source of free publicity.

Distinction between product testing and market introduction

When developing new consumer products, the product testing and market introduction stages are clearly separated. With industrial innovations this distinction becomes artificial since the firms testing the new product are generally the first buyers too and are used as commercial references. In these situations the *testing customers* will be *launching customers* as well.

The external organization testing a new industrial product need not necessarily be a potential *buyer.* For instance, Packitt had its new steel drum tested extensively by both (1) an external research institute (to obtain the necessary 'seal of approval') and (2) a shipping company with whom it had been doing business for years. While the second test concerned a real external test (that is, a test of the new product under real-life circumstances), the first one is better characterized as another 'internal test', because it concerned a series of technical tests identical in character and objective to the tests conducted by Packitt.

Use of external research organizations

Manufacturers wanting to test new consumer products often hire an external market research organization to conduct the product tests. These organizations have the specialized knowledge and staff to perform such tests and often use established consumer panels for these purposes. Only the large manufacturers of consumer goods have the expertise and facilities to perform the external tests themselves (that is, to arrange having users test their prototypes). Nevertheless, they also often use external agencies to obtain objective results. On the other hand, the complexity of industrial innovations and the importance of personal relationships with users make it imperative for manufacturers to perform the tests themselves (thus running the risk of distorted information).

The reader should take care not to confuse external testing with test marketing, a concept that can often be found in the literature concerning consumer goods. Test marketing refers to testing a new or modified product *together with the marketing mix* by introducing it into a limited area of the total market. The purpose is not just to identify and correct possible weaknesses in the product, but also evaluate the marketing mix and estimate the sales potential (Cadbury, 1975).

DERIVED DEMAND

As opposed to consumer products, industrial products are faced with what is called a derived demand (Hutt and Speh, 1989, p. 6). This may have important additional implications for having the products tested by users. Industrial products are bought by industrial customers and used for the production of either consumer products or other industrial products; sometimes industrial products are incorporated in consumer products (for instance, electronic integrated circuits that are bought by a manufacturer of consumer electronics and used as components for a video-recorder). When the use of an innovation by the industrial customer results in changes in his own end product, the manufacturer cannot confine himself to having only his own customers test the innovation. In these situations, the manufacturer should take care that his customers' customers are involved as well, since they indirectly influence the acceptance of the innovation.

Packitt had its new drum primarily tested by a shipping company and some large customers. However, in so doing, it overlooked the fact that not only Packitt's customers, but also the customers' customers influence the acceptance of the new drum. Packitt's customers use the drums for shipping their products (mostly oil and chemicals) to their customers. As these final customers are located, virtually without exception, in less developed countries, they do not possess equipment suitable for handling the new drums. This proved to be one of the major obstacles for a successful market acceptance.

In other instances, the customer testing the innovation will take the initiative himself and test his changed end product with his own customers before he decides whether or not to purchase the innovation.

The best example is provided by the case of Grenco. In some cases, using the new process installation resulted in a changed quality of the customer's product or even in completely new products. In these instances, the potential buyers tested the new installation extensively and, in addition, wanted to test the changed/new product with their own customers too.

This aspect of derived demand is of importance:

1 when the innovation is used for the production of the end product and results in changes in the product's characteristics (for example a numerically controlled production machine),
2 when the innovation is used as a component of the end product and thus changes its characteristics (for example a transistor),
3 when the innovation is sold in combination with the end product (for example a form of packaging), and
4 when use of the innovation offers the opportunity of producing completely new products (for example a new process installation).

PRODUCT CHAMPIONS

An innovation is a new product that represents a change. To the user it represents a change from using one kind of product to using another. This new product may be technically complex and require adaptation from the people that have to use it. To the manufacturer, the innovation may represent a new production technology that disrupts the normal course of activity. Due to the product's innovativeness, potential customers could be reluctant to buy it or become convinced of its superiority. The change represented by an innovation is accompanied by uncertainty, which relates to:

1 its technological functioning (it is uncertain whether the innovation will be technically feasible),
2 its yield (the financial returns are difficult to estimate at the start of the development process),
3 the costs (the total development costs can only be estimated very roughly), and

4 the time span (at the outset it is not clear how long the process will take).

This uncertainty is even increased in the case of technically complex innovations.

People, as well as organizations, try to resist that change and uncertainty. For an organization a certain amount of resistance against change is not only normal, but even desirable. Without it an organization would continually be put on another track and be unable to function optimally. To overcome this inner resistance to innovations, someone within the organization has to feel strongly committed to the new product. According to Schon (1963, p. 84), the following pattern is often observed:

1 at the outset, the innovation encounters sharp resistance from within the organization,
2 to overcome this resistance, the innovation is strongly promoted,
3 for the introduction, promotion, and development of the innovation, informal communication channels are used, and
4 in most cases, one man emerges as champion of the innovation.

Such a person is not only important at the start of the innovation process, as suggested for example by Chakrabarti (1974, p. 58), but also plays a crucial role during later stages. For example, when the attention within the organization to the innovation project diminishes or problems concerning the development crop up which lead to costs higher than those originally estimated. To prevent potentially successful projects from being terminated prematurely, a person is needed who continues to believe in the project despite the initial setbacks.

This central person is often referred to as a *product champion* and defined as an individual who is intensely interested and involved in the overall objectives and goals of the innovation project and who plays a dominant role in many of the interaction events through some of the stages, overcoming technical and organizational obstacles and pulling the effort through its final achievement by the sheer force of his will and energy (adapted from a Materials Advisory Board study, 1966). He believes in the potential of the project, shows total commitment and is willing to take risks for the sake of the innovation. This identification with the innovation often goes far beyond the requirements of the job. For many of them the price of failure means professional suicide. According to Peters (1987, p. 248) product champions are characterized by energy, passion, idealism,

pragmatism, cunning, towering impatience, an unrealistic unwillingness to allow any barrier to set him back, and love–hate relationships
among his subordinates. To accentuate their strong commitment to
the innovation they are called *crusaders* by Davidow (1986, pp. 150–
2) and described as follows: 'They are easy to spot. They're the ones
with fire in their eyes and blood on their swords'.

Our investigation shows that we can distinguish between two
different kinds of product champion. The *buyer's product champion*
is someone within the potential buying organization who is convinced
of the innovation's use and potential.

> In the case of Dräger, medical specialists who are enthusiastic
> about the ease with which patients can be monitored functioned
> as buyer's product champions.

The product champion's enthusiasm and belief in the new product
can act as the driving force behind the buying organization's interest
in the innovation. He spends a lot of time trying to convince his
superiors to try the new product and, at a later stage, when there may
be some problems, to keep the project going. According to
Gemünden, buyers' product champions

> are very influential, but they show a janus-face. On the one
> hand they are partners in developing and implementing an
> innovative solution, advocates who sell a product in the buying
> organization, fund raisers who look for the money, and allies
> against opponents to innovation. On the other hand they
> demand more problem-solving support, bargain harder, and
> interact more intensively with competitors.
>
> (Gemünden, 1985, p. 146)

The *seller's product champion* is the person within the manufacturing
organization who motivates people inside the company to keep
investing (not just money, but time and energy as well) in the new
product.

> The managing director of Grenco, who co-developed the new
> technology, was frequently a key figure. He promoted the tech-
> nology and motivated his staff to develop new applications. This
> role was based upon his expertise in technological aspects,
> commercial capabilities, and hierarchical position. In many
> instances he had to take care of initial problems that occurred

> too. This combination of technological and commercial knowledge is a big advantage to Grenco, but also makes it very vulnerable.

Both kinds of product champion fulfil the same role: to establish and maintain the organization's interest in the innovation project.

Product champions can be characterized as occupying central positions in both formal and informal networks and using them extensively (for example influential engineers). Many studies have argued that top management support has a positive influence on the success of the innovation. From this it can be concluded that we can distinguish between

1 a *product champion by power*, who is influential because of his hierarchical position within the organization, and
2 a *product champion by know-how*, who is able to exert influence because of his specific expertise (Gemünden, 1985, p. 141).

> One of Nedap's customers bought the access-control system because the director was charmed by the advanced technology, while a less sophisticated solution would have functioned just as well (product champion by power). The medical specialists wanting to purchase Dräger's new monitor had a strong position since they were the only ones able to evaluate the medical aspects of the innovation (product champion by know-how).

In a recent publication, Chakrabarti and Hauschildt (1989) elaborate on these concepts by separating the champion aspect from the power and know-how positions, and focusing on the interaction between the three functional roles in innovation management.

Referring to the two types of product champion mentioned above, an organization can have the following product champion structures.

1 A *know-how-based structure:* a product champion by know-how is able to exert influence, but is rather restricted by the absence of power based on his hierarchical position (Jervis, 1975, p. 23). This makes him less interesting to sales representatives of the seller.
2 A *power-based structure:* a product champion by power has great opportunities for influencing the project, but is dependent on others for its technical aspects. Since he is in a position to authorize expensive purchases, he offers the seller more opportunities.

However, due to his lack of expertise, he is also very dependent on the problem-solving abilities of the seller.

3 A *tandem structure:* the combination of a product champion by know-how and a product champion by power offers many opportunities, especially within large organizations. This seems the ideal structure, because it combines the problem-solving capabilities of the product champion by know-how with the authority to make decisions of the product champion by power.

4 A *personal-union structure:* both types of product champion combined in one person can be highly effective and is found especially in smaller firms (for instance the director/owner of a small company).

The concepts presented above can be recognized in the individual cases, as summarized in Table 5.2. It clearly demonstrates the existence of product champions. The less complex products show either no product champion at all (Ammeraal) or only a product champion

Table 5.2 The occurrence of product champions in the individual cases

	Ammeraal	Packitt	Dräger	Nedap	Grenco
At the seller:					
Product champion by power	O	+	n.a.	+	++
Product champion by know-how	O	O	n.a.	+	++
Product champion structure	O	Power-based	n.a.	Tandem	Personal union
At the buyer:					
Product champion by power	O	O	+	+	+
Product champion by know-how	O	O	+	+	++
Product champion structure	O	O	Personal union	Power-based or know-how based	Personal union

Notes: O product champion (structure) not in evidence
 + product champion in evidence
++ product champion strongly in evidence
n.a. information not available

in the selling organization who bases his influence on his hierarchical position (Packitt). As the innovation becomes more complex (1) product champions can be discerned at the buying organization as well and (2) their influence is no longer solely based on power; specific expertise starts to be relevant too. The most complex innovation investigated offers strong evidence of the importance of having a product champion at both the selling and buying organization (Grenco). The quality of the personal relationship between both product champions strongly influences the success of the innovation project.

> While Grenco's managing director functions as a product champion at the seller, he recognizes the importance of a product champion at the buyer as well. For this reason, he considers the initial contact with the right person within the potential buying firm to be of major importance. In most cases, the ideal person is an R&D manager who is situated neither too low (lacks the power to make decisions) nor too high (has the power to take action, but the people at the lower levels will not feel committed to his decisions) within the organizational hierarchy. He has to be prepared for resistance within the organization and he should be able to keep the project going despite initial set backs. As one manager remarked: 'There were times when I felt terribly lonely'. Particularly during the early stages of the development process, the personal relationship is of prime importance. At this point, the actions of the individuals involved are not so much dictated by the terms of a formal agreement as by an open and trusting atmosphere. This feeling of mutual trust is a prerequisite for successful cooperation.

The importance of product champions has also been demonstrated by Rubenstein *et al.* (1976, p. 18) who reported that 'an overwhelming majority of the projects studied indicated that certain individuals had played (often informal) roles in their initiation, progress and outcome'. A recent study by Ettlie (1986) showed that the most important factor for a successful implementation of advanced industrial products was the supplier–user relationship, while the existence of a product champion at the user was mentioned as a separate factor in explaining its success. Chakrabarti (1974, p. 59) compared forty-five cases of new industrial products and found a strong correlation between the presence of a product champion and the eventual success of the new product (Table 5.3).

Table 5.3 Identification of a product champion in forty-five cases

	Number of relatively successful cases	Number of less successful cases	Total
Number of cases where the presence of a product champion was identified	16	1	17
Number of cases where a product champion could not be identified	1	27	28

Source: Chakrabarti (1974), *California Management Review*, vol. 17, no. 2, © the Regents of the University of California. Reprinted by permission of the Regents.

In a study of the development of applications software, Voss (1985b, p. 126) found that the development and commercialization stages often had separate champions. The results of his study also indicated a positive relationship between the existence of a product champion and the success of the new product. Finally, Kuczmarski (1988, p. 264) went so far as to conclude that 'the importance of a product champion to the success of new product development cannot be overstated'.

NETWORKS

The cases studied during the exploratory study stress the relevance of the network concept. Due to the derived demand of industrial products, several parties may be involved in the product development process and/or the purchasing decision and complicated networks may be the result. Take, for example, the network concerning the development, adoption, and diffusion of a relatively simple product like a steel drum (Figure 5.1).

Packitt developed the new drum because of problems ventilated by major customers. The prototype was tested internally as well as by an external research institute. After having been success-fully tested by a shipping company, the product was introduced into the market. Apart from these major parties, a number of other persons/organizations influenced the eventual market acceptance: (1) insurance companies, who may lower the insurance premium because the new drum results in less

Figure 5.1 The parties involved in the development, adoption, and diffusion of a new steel drum

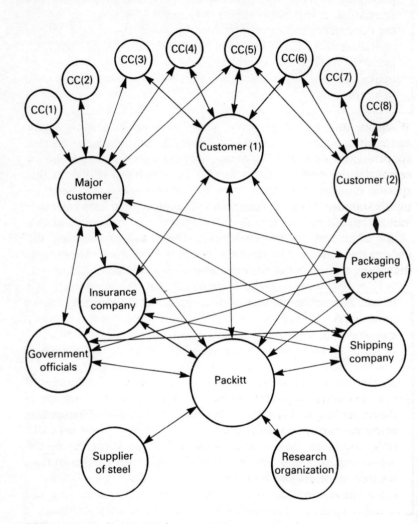

CC(i) = customer's customer i

damage, (2) government officials, who draw up regulations as regards the transportation of dangerous chemicals, (3) packaging experts, who are consulted by Packitt, insurance companies, government officials, and major customers, and (4) the customers' customers, who must be able to handle the new steel drum as well. The last-named category is very important in industrial markets and should be involved in the product development process (for example during concept testing or testing of a prototype).

When we take a look at a very complex innovation, such as the extremely complex process installation developed by Grenco in close cooperation with a major customer, we find a network consisting of essentially the same elements as the one described above. In this specific situation, both the customers' customers and the manufacturer's suppliers play a crucial role, thus stressing the importance of indirect relationships even more (Biemans and de Vries, 1988, p. 46).

All other cases exhibit elements of networks as well, while the importance of specific parties within individual networks depends on the circumstances and situation involved.

In the Ammeraal network the key customers are clearly the most important counterparts, while distributors and original equipment manufacturers also have a role to play. The network in which Dräger functions is completely different; in this case opinion leaders are of great importance. Product diffusion is accelerated by demonstrating the new monitor to leading hospitals that have a positive influence in the market (such as university hospitals and specialized regional hospitals). The case of Nedap hardly shows the operation of a network, contrary to what would be expected, considering the complexity of the access-control system. Nevertheless, the product is successful because it offers the customer unique product benefits that cannot be matched by competitors (yet).

MARKETING OF KNOWLEDGE

The marketing of technically complex industrial innovations involves much more than the marketing of a mere new product. Apart from the physical product, considerable attention should be paid to the knowledge embodied in the innovation as well. This knowledge component plays a role during all stages of the product development process.

When jointly developing an innovation with a major potential customer (for example the case of Grenco), the marketing starts *early in the product development process*, namely when the manufacturer selects a potential customer. Both the manufacturer and the customer are expected to invest in a project whose outcome is uncertain; they do not know whether the innovation will function and be commercially interesting. Thus, the manufacturer is in effect marketing a solution that has not even been developed yet. The quality of the buyer–seller relationship at the individual level and the extent to which mutual trust is successfully developed greatly influence the success of the collaboration and continue to play a central role during the *prototype development* stage. However, as the development process continues, attention shifts from a vague subjective feeling of trust to a more objective evaluation of each other's contributions to the project (Vollering, 1986, p. 8). From the customer's point of view, confidence and trust refer to the feeling of certainty that the manufacturer will do what he promises and spare no effort, that his claims with respect to his product and service can be accepted without serious question, and that he can be counted upon to go all out to give aid in emergencies (Hill *et al.*, 1975, p. 11). These assurances may more than offset significant price concessions offered by less trustworthy suppliers. The manufacturer must earn this confidence either by good performance over a long period of time or the display of extraordinary commercial skills. On the other hand, from the manufacturer's perspective, confidence refers to the feeling of certainty that the customer will do his stint of the duties, share in the total costs of the project, and demonstrate continuing commitment by devoting the time, manpower, money, and energy to the project that it requires. This dominating influence of trust, confidence, and integrity has been noted with respect to existing complex products too. Davidow (1986) argues that, as high-tech products are becoming more and more alike and at the same time incomprehensibly complex, the manufacturer is increasingly obliged to differentiate on the basis of other characteristics than the product itself. The key ingredient in selling the product is no longer the product itself, but the direct relationship between the customer and the seller.

The innovation's knowledge component is also of importance when *testing a prototype with potential users*. The manufacturer who intends to have a technically complex innovation tested by product users should make sure that they are, at the very least, familiar with the way it works. Neglecting to educate the users concerning the product's correct operation may significantly reduce the usefulness of the test results.

Naturally, close attention should be paid to the knowledge embodied in the innovation during *market introduction and subsequent selling*. When potential customers are confonted with an innovation that is based on a new advanced technology, they will have difficulty in evaluating the offered advantages and opportunities. Therefore the manufacturer must try to translate the innovation's technological characteristics into quantified benefits and present them to the real decision makers within the Decision-Making Unit (Berry (1980, p. 33) calls this 'managing evidence').

Grenco supplied potential customers with detailed calculations that showed the savings in costs which could be realized by implementing the new technology in their specific situation. The necessary numbers were obtained by detailed study of the customer's operations.

Confidence and trust, based on the buyer–seller relationship and the seller's commercial capabilities, reputation, and image become important factors influencing the purchasing decision. Considering the importance of personal buyer–seller relationships, technically complex industrial innovations place specific demands on the manufacturer's sales representatives. In addition to their commercial skills they should have some technical training, so that they can initiate the buyers into the basic technical aspects of the innovation. At the same time, the manufacturer's engineers should be able to think in commercial terms, in order to be able to communicate effectively with customers during product development. The buying organization, on the other hand, should provide its employees with enough technical background to be worthy interlocutors.

The knowledge embodied in the innovation can even be of importance *after the sale*. For example, if a potential customer is convinced of the advantages of innovative, complex machinery and decides to use it in his production process, he will be interested in guaranteed future delivery and servicing. If the manufacturer of the innovation is in sole possession of the embodied technology and (for some reason) should go out of business, the buying organization could be in trouble. Measures may be taken to prevent this from happening.

> One of Grenco's customers solved the problem by contractually arranging for transfer of knowledge in case Grenco should for some reason be unable to deliver in the future. If this should happen, Grenco could be obligated to transfer the knowledge to either the customer or a competing supplier.

Marketing of the innovation's knowledge component is quite similar to the more general field of marketing of services. With services as well, the intangibility of the 'product' is of critical importance. As Gelderman and Leeflang (1988, p. 100) point out, a customer orientation in a service organization can only be effective if its contact personnel is customer oriented. The organization should be involved in *internal marketing*, that is 'applying the philosophy and practices of marketing to the people that serve the external customer so that (1) the best possible people can be employed and retained and (2) they will do the best possible work' (Berry, 1980, p. 32).

TESTING INDUSTRIAL INNOVATIONS WITH POTENTIAL USERS: A TENTATIVE FRAMEWORK

Always push for a field trial, ... there's nothing like a customer saying, 'Hey, this stuff really works like you said it would and I want to buy some'.

(Michael A. DeSesa, NL Chemicals)

As most of the firms studied experienced various problems with the testing of industrial prototypes by potential users, we will presently address this issue in great detail. However, there are additional reasons for discussing this particular stage of the product development process.

1 Testing the prototype with users functions as a last crucial check (before production is started) to ensure that product characteristics meet customer requirements.
2 In industrial markets the personal relationship between manufacturer and customer is of major concern. Introducing a product that does not meet customer requirements may be detrimental to existing relationships. In addition, testing with potential users emphasizes the manufacturer's market orientation.
3 The many uncertainties surrounding industrial innovations stresses the importance of external testing.

4 Every firm that attaches great significance to interaction with users during product development engages in external testing. Both Cooper and Kleinschmidt (1986, p. 79) and Moore (1987, p. 14) found that approximately 70 per cent of the firms studied had new products tested by potential users.

Various authors have stressed the critical importance of the external testing stage. As Leiva and Obermayer (1989, p. 48) remarked, 'Evaluation, which must be performed under "live" conditions using real customers, is a key to minimizing surprises at market entry'. The collective experiences of the managers interviewed were used to derive a general framework regarding testing industrial innovations with potential users. The framework (based on Biemans and de Vries, 1987a) consists of nine activities (Figure 5.2), which are briefly discussed.

Activity 1: Timing

The first activity concerns determining when the tests by potential users should be conducted (that is the timing of the external tests). On the one hand, the external tests should be conducted after the prototype has been tested internally with positive results. At the same time, the external testing stage must be concluded with positive results before full-scale production is started. Conducting the external tests too early entails the risk of testing a product that is not yet fully developed: its characteristics may still change as a result of the internal tests. Starting it too late means running the risk of facing large and costly changes in the production process.

In the course of developing the innovative access-control system Nedap started negotiations with a major service company. This led to the decision to accelerate market acceptance by installing the prototype and having it tested under real-life conditions. At the time of installation, however, Nedap was unable to deliver the central processing unit (CPU), which forced the customer to buy the CPU and the necessary software from other suppliers. Nedap had to return to the development stage and concentrate on developing the missing parts. Based on the customer's experiences, the hardware needed to be modified as well.

Figure 5.2 A tentative framework for having potential users test a developed prototype

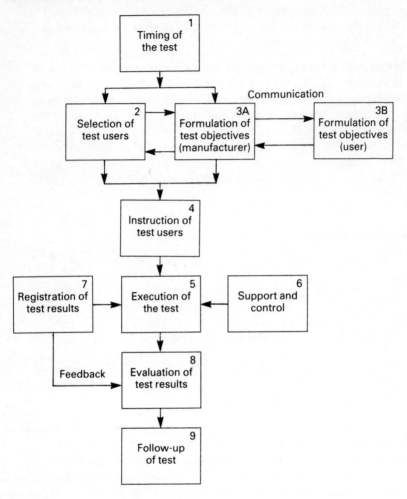

Activity 2: Selection of the test users

Picking the right potential users to test early versions of a product can be critical to the product's ultimate success (McKenna, 1985, p. 77). But what exactly is meant by *right* in this context? We asked a limited number of firms, taking part in a group discussion, to determine the most important criteria in selecting potential users to test an innovation. As it concerned just a handful of firms, the results of the discussion should be considered indicative rather than conclusive. In order of decreasing importance the following criteria were agreed upon:

1 objective of the test,
2 user's representativeness of the specific (segment of the) market,
3 willingness to cooperate and/or innovation orientation,
4 market position and/or firm size, and
5 existence of a relationship (Biemans and de Vries, 1987a, p. 28).

The first criterion refers to the distinction between technical and commercial objectives. When the purpose of the test is purely technical, the manufacturer must select a user capable of evaluating the technical performance of the product. In this situation, the representativeness of the user is of minor importance, since the external test is in effect an extension of the technical tests performed in-house by the manufacturer. Afterwards, the innovation still needs to be tested by a number of representative users to test the innovation's functioning in practice. If, on the other hand, the test stresses the commercial aspects, the manufacturer should select users with a positive image and influence in the market. In the ideal situation, these users are representative of the market (segment) as well. In practice, there is no dilemma in choosing one test objective in preference to the other; in fact, the selection of the test objective is determined by the complexity of the product and situation in question. Frequently, manufacturers try to combine both objectives and need to compromise.

Ensuring that the selected users are representative of the market segment in question, is of the utmost importance as it determines the managerial value of the test results. In industrial markets, the matter of representativeness may be quite complex. Due to the derived demand, the manufacturer must not limit himself to his own customers when identifying the persons influencing the purchasing decision (Biemans and de Vries, 1987b, p. 35).

Criterion 3 mentions a combination of the willingness to cooperate and the innovation orientation of the user. It assumes that potential users who are innovative themselves are more inclined to cooperate (Johne, 1984, p. 194). Innovative users have the added advantage that they often play a central role in the diffusion process (Midgley, 1977, p. 51). The importance of having new products tested by innovative users has also been observed in connection with expensive consumer products (Samli, Palda, and Barker, 1987, p. 49). The criterion of innovativeness seems to be in contradiction to the demanded representativeness. Sometimes, however, both criteria can be combined, for example, when a selected innovative user is representative with respect to a specific application. In other instances, the manufacturer must look for a meaningful trade-off between both criteria.

Market position and size are combined in one criterion because of the obvious relationship between both variables. Sometimes it is advisable to select a large firm that is able to quantify the innovation's advantages, such as reduced maintenance costs.

It is remarkable that the existence of a relationship is only mentioned in fifth place, while in practice this criterion is often given much higher priority.

The most important external test of the new drum developed by Packitt (the test was quite elaborate and employees of Packitt were actually present to supervise the test's progress) was conducted by a shipping company selected for this task because of an existing and good personal relationship of long standing. However, this turned out be a major error because the company was not representative of Packitt's customers in general. While the shipping company experienced no problems handling the new drum, this proved to be an exception. Not even the major customers in Packitt's home market possessed equipment suitable to handle the new drum.

Activity 3: Formulation of objectives

Although test objectives must be formulated by both the manufacturer (activity 3a) and the potential users who test the innovation (activity 3b), they do not need to be identical. The manufacturer's objective may be either technical or commercial, while the user may simply wish to keep up to date with technological developments. Whatever they may be, explicit objectives are necessary to allow for evaluation of the results. To avoid misunderstandings, both the manufacturer and the users should be informed about each other's objectives.

In formulating its test objectives Ammeraal did not always formulate them very clearly. Sometimes tests were conducted while it was unclear what aspects of the new belt were being tested. Since Ammeraal's test users did not need to pay for the new belt, they often did not formulate any test objectives at all. For them it was just a matter of receiving a new belt free of charge, which meant that they did not need to buy a new one for the next couple of years!

Activity 4: Instruction

Even though the actual testing takes place at the customer site, it does not mean that the manufacturer does not need to be involved. Due to the innovative character of the product, the manufacturer may have to give detailed operating instructions to the user in order to prevent negative test results that are in fact caused by incorrect handling of the product. The manufacturer needs to instruct the user on the nature of the various tests to be undertaken, while he should also be familiar with any additional tests performed by the user.

The external testing of Grenco's new process installation is an integral part of an iterative development–internal testing–external testing cycle that takes place at the customer's premises. Due to the extreme complexity of the technology, a great deal of time is spent on the instruction and training of the customer's engineers. They are the ones who will have to operate the installation and need at least an understanding of its basic principles and a working knowledge of the process.

Activity 5: Execution

The fifth activity of the framework, the actual execution of the external test, is carried out by the test user. However, the manufacturer may be involved indirectly (see activity 6).

Packitt paid insufficient attention to the execution of the test by the potential users. Packitt shipped a sample batch of the new drum to its major customers, who tested them on their own sites. In contrast to the extensive test by the shipping company, these tests were not attended by employees from Packitt. Therefore the firm was unable to check whether the new drums were handled correctly. Packitt was not even aware of the nature of the tests conducted by these customers!

Problems during execution may partly be prevented by careful instruction of the user by the manufacturer's sales representatives.

Ammeraal was confronted with serious problems because one of its sales representatives had not stressed that the new belt, to be tested by a major customer, was just a prototype and that its addition to the existing range of belting was by no means certain yet. The customer tested the new belt, found it to be the perfect solution for an existing problem, and placed a large order at once. In the meantime, however, Ammeraal had run into production problems which necessitated postponement of market introduction. Several meetings at top management level were necessary to restore the good relationship between the two firms.

Activity 6: Support and control

As the external test involves a prototype, there is always the possibility of things going wrong, which can be very serious if the innovation involves the heart of the user's production process. Therefore the manufacturer is expected to guarantee quick corrective measures.

The belts of Ammeraal are typically a vital part of the user's production process. Therefore, participation in the testing of a newly developed prototype entails certain risks. In order to get the user's cooperation, Ammeraal guarantees fast replacement of broken or malfunctioning belts and bears all expenses.

Under normal circumstances, a representative of the manufacturer could visit the user to check on the progress of the test. Such a regular inspection serves to (1) demonstrate the manufacturer's commitment to the test, (2) check whether the test is actually performed correctly, (3) get a first impression of the test results, and (4) encourage the user to mention minor problems.

Activity 7: Registration

When the manufacturer is not actually present during the test, it is of the utmost importance that the user (1) knows what to measure and how to measure it and (2) passes the information in the desired format on to the manufacturer. To obtain objective test results it is desirable to have the test users fill in standardized evaluation forms.

Activity 8: Evaluation

The test results can only be evaluated when the objectives of the tests have been stated unequivocally. To avoid misunderstandings, the results should be evaluated by the manufacturer together with the test user. Naturally, the test results need to be evaluated in the light of the test objectives as they were previously formulated.

> One of the customers testing Ammeraal's new belt was a large chemical firm. Initially, the test results were judged negatively because certain acids caused delamination (separation of the various layers of the belt). However, it was *known in advance* that the acids in question would cause delamination. The belt was tested by this specific customer for other reasons having nothing to do with acids and delamination!

Activity 9: Follow-up

The final, and often forgotten, activity concerns the follow-up of the test. 'Follow-up' is a general term that can imply many different things. For example, the manufacturer should inform the potential user who performed the test of

1 the general results of the tests performed with other potential users,
2 what will be done with the test results, and
3 the termination of the test (naturally, if the user is actually involved in the evaluation of the test results, he will be aware of the fact that the test has ended).

> Ammeraal neglected to supply its test users with all these kinds of information. One customer was indeed not even aware that the test at his facility was already finished; he thought it was still going on!

A totally different form of follow-up consists of using the names of the customers who performed the tests successfully, together with their experiences regarding the innovation, in promotional material and sales presentations. It is up to the industrial marketer to take the initiative in these matters (Webster, 1970, p. 189). McKenna (1985, p. 77) mentions that an impressive customer list can give the company a reputation as an innovator or a technological leader.

The above description could suggest that the individual activities should be taken one after the other. Figure 5.2, however, shows the selection of potential users and the formulation of the test objectives drawn in parallel, since the manufacturer cannot clearly separate these two activities. For instance, when the sole objective of the test is to discover whether the product realizes the specified functions, the manufacturer will select a user who is able to evaluate the product from a technical and functional viewpoint. When, on the other hand, he plans to use the user's name as an important promotional tool at the time of market introduction (the *launching customer principle*), he will choose a user who is well known in the market and enjoys a good reputation. Small firms that are technologically advanced, but rather unknown in the market, can be used to test the product's functioning but are useless as commercial references. The link between selecting the test users and formulating the test objectives is also expressed by the fact that 'objective of the test' was mentioned as the most important criterion for selecting potential users to test an innovation. Activities 5 (execution), 6 (support and control), and 7 (registration) concern parallel activities, too.

The framework presented above should not be treated as a rigid model, a description of reality that can be used under all circumstances. Clearly, the relevance and content of the activities depend on the specific product and market situation. When a firm introduces a modified product into a market segment in which it has been selling for a long time, the whole procedure will be rather routine. The firm is familiar with the market structure, has relationships with major product users, and has probably tested new products with them before. When, on the other hand, a company introduces a very complex and innovative product into a market that is totally new to the firm, it has to conduct a detailed market study both to determine the structure of that market and identify the potential users most suitable for testing the innovation. The framework must be looked upon as a general scenario that offers guidelines to management that will prevent them from overlooking important aspects and will improve their decision-making with respect to testing prototypes with potential users.

This chapter presented some results concerning user involvement in product development. The next chapter elaborates on the subject by discussing some empirical findings as regards the development of complex medical equipment innovations from a network perspective.

6 Development of innovations within networks

No company is an island.

(Håkan Håkansson, 1990)

The findings presented in Chapter 5 demonstrate the existence of networks in various situations and stress the importance of personal relationships. Having prototypes tested by potential users was found to be of major importance to the eventual success of an innovation but lacking a structured approach. Based on the individual cases, a tentative framework was proposed to provide practical guidelines to management. To elaborate on the theme of user involvement in product development, a follow-up investigation was undertaken in the field of medical technology. This chapter presents the results of this investigation which focused on the functioning of firms within networks. First, however, we will provide some illustrative background information by discussing the Dutch medical equipment industry and reviewing some theoretical studies about the development, adoption, and diffusion of innovative medical equipment, with explicit attention to the role of networks. While the adoption and diffusion processes are not the focus of our research, some basic insight is needed fully to understand the intricacies of developing medical equipment innovations within networks.

MEDICAL EQUIPMENT

The Dutch medical equipment industry was selected for several reasons. Because of its strategic importance and great potential, an Advisory Committee on Industry Policy selected it as a major area for special attention, leading to the initiation of an extensive stimulation programme (Wagner, 1981). In addition, the field of medical technology has been characterized as one with a relatively high level of innovative activity (Shaw, 1986, p. 53; vanden Abeele and Christiaens,

1987, p. 52), while the external testing stage, which was found to be essential in the preliminary investigation, is of crucial importance with respect to medical equipment innovations. Furthermore, an empirical investigation of the British medical equipment industry demonstrates the critical role of manufacturer–user interaction (Shaw, 1986, p. 53; see also Roberts, 1989, p. 37) and networks (Shaw, 1988, pp. 516–17) in developing innovative medical equipment. Finally, although increasing budgetary constraints force the Dutch public health sector to operate commercially, the intensity and quality of the relationships between users, manufacturers, and research institutes are often found wanting (Ackermans, 1987; Zijlstra, 1985, p. 63; Ministry of Economic Affairs, 1986, p. 15).

For the purpose of our investigation, we define a medical equipment innovation as *a medical instrument that represents a significant (non-trivial) departure from previous patterns of diagnosis, treatment, or prevention* (based on Bernstein *et al.*, 1975, p. 86). We will focus on *complex* medical equipment innovations, thus excluding inventory, storage, and consumption articles, as well as all low-priced products.

Market volume

Statistics only offer very rough estimates of the total market volume of medical technological products, which vary widely because of differences in the definitions used. In general, total sales are estimated to be somewhere between 1,000 million guilders (Het Instrument, 1990) and 2,000 million or 3,000 million guilders per year (Willems, 1985, p. 7; Ministry of Economic Affairs, 1986, p. 13).

More detailed sales estimates, that is total sales per specific product category, do not exist since the field of medical technology covers a very broad spectrum of products. Apart from this, many firms operate both within and outside the field of medical technology, while many manufacturing firms realize a significant part of their sales by simply trading in medical products. The matter is further complicated because, due to the small number of sizable manufacturing firms, their anonymity would be affected by the publication of detailed sales estimates.

Number of firms

In the Netherlands there are about 500 firms operating in the field of medical technology. About half of them are trading companies importing medical products. The manufacturing firms comprise Philips Medical Systems (about 2,500 employees in the Netherlands), some twenty-five medium-sized firms and a large number of small ones (Ministry of Economic Affairs, 1986, p. 14). Therefore the number of medium-sized firms *manufacturing complex medical equipment* is very small indeed and both Philips Medical Systems and a number of small firms will be included in the investigation.

Market characteristics

The Dutch market for medical equipment exhibits a number of distinguishing features which are relevant to our research (Willems, 1985, pp. 16–22).

1 As the market for medical technological products is made up of hundreds of smaller sub-markets, each with its own specific characteristics, we will limit the investigation to expensive complex medical equipment.
2 Developing medical equipment innovations involves harmonious cooperation between various complex skills within the organization, such as medical knowledge, technological know-how, and marketing expertise. Where possible, representatives of all relevant disciplines within the organization must be interviewed.
3 As manufacturers compete by means of product differentiation rather than price, a wide range of innovations is available for study.
4 The limited number of potential customers forces Dutch manufacturers to operate internationally, thus influencing the pattern of cooperation.
5 The direct influence of medical equipment on life and death accounts for the existence of extensive regulation (see NEHEM (1987) for a discussion of present and future regulation) and the need for clinical testing before market introduction.
6 Many different persons, such as physicians, engineers, purchasers, advisers, and members of nursing staffs, may be involved in buying medical products, thus complicating matters for the manufacturer. However, since the investigation focuses on user involvement during the development of complex medical instruments, the parties involved will probably be limited to the physicians (Hutton, 1984, p. 162).
7 As regards medical equipment, the focus has shifted from the physical product to the provision of related services, such as maintenance, repair, instruction, and training.

8 The relationship between the customer and the manufacturer is of crucial importance with respect to developing and selling medical products.

9 When the purchase of complex medical equipment is considered, the question of compatibility is often raised. Advanced equipment from one particular manufacturer is in many cases not compatible with that made by a competitor. This lack of compatibility increases the demands on the product development process.

THE DEVELOPMENT, ADOPTION, AND DIFFUSION OF MEDICAL EQUIPMENT INNOVATIONS; SOME THEORETICAL BACKGROUND

In the foregoing section we noted that the Dutch market for medical equipment has a number of special characteristics. This section briefly presents some of the relevant literature on the development, adoption, and diffusion of medical equipment. In addition, the relevance of networks will be discussed.

The development of medical equipment innovations

Although the literature abounds with models describing the process of developing new products (see Chapter 3 for a survey), models dealing with developing medical equipment hardly exist. Roberts provides a general characterization of the process when he states that

> innovation in medical devices results by and large from engineering-based problem-solving by primarily individuals or small firms, that is usually incremental in character, that seldom reflects long periods of basic research, and that does not in general depend upon the recent generation of fundamental new knowledge.
>
> (Roberts, 1989, p. 34)

The most salient feature of the medical equipment development process appears to be the fact that the end user of the equipment often plays an important role in its initial invention and subsequent development. This fact was first reported by von Hippel (1976, pp. 220–1), who studied 111 first-to-market innovations (including many medical instruments) in the United States and found a clearly user-dominated innovation process. More recent studies by Shaw (1986, p. 53) in the UK medical equipment industry and vanden Abeele and Christiaens (1987, p. 52) in Belgian high-tech firms largely corroborate these findings. Shaw studied a sample of thirty-four medical equipment innovations from eleven companies, divided into basic equipment innovations, major improvement innovations, and minor improvement innovations. The principal conclusion from this investigation is that the medical equipment product development process is characterized by a multiple and continuous interaction between the user and the manufacturer.

The studies of von Hippel, together with an early publication of Shaw (1983), led Rothwell (1984, p. 183) to represent the medical instrument product development process as depicted in Figure 6.1. The model clearly shows the intimate involvement of the user in developing medical equipment innovations.

Styles (1984) described some special problems related to the conception, realization, launch, and subsequent support of innovative high-technology health care products.

To develop complex medical equipment innovations that fulfil customer needs and are commercially successful, firms must combine their technological capability with customer requirements. In the Netherlands, however, firms operating in the field of medical technology have been found to be too technologically oriented; marketing expertise seems to be less developed (Willems, 1985, p. 40). One possible reason is that, although subsidies are granted for technological research and development, there are no such subsidies for market research and development. Small firms and individual inven-

Figure 6.1 The medical equipment innovation process

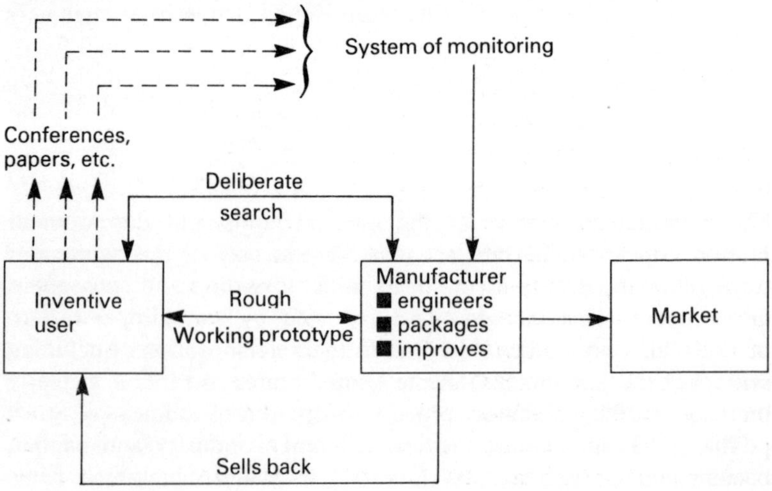

Source: Rothwell (1984), © Elsevier Science Publishers B.V. Reprinted with permission.

tors, in particular, experience problems in translating their ideas into commercial products. Some centres functioning as knowledge brokers try to assist them by scouting for ideas and people, bridging existing gaps, and providing support during the stages of product development. In 1990 a number of such knowledge brokers from various countries (two from the Netherlands, and one from Ireland, Germany, and Denmark) established Euro BioMed, an international network to facilitate technology transfer.

The adoption of medical equipment innovations

Most studies on the adoption of medical equipment by hospitals focus on the involvement of different professional groups during the various stages of the purchasing process. Hutton (1984, p. 161) reviewed hospital purchasing procedures in the countries of the European Community and describes the procurement process as consisting of six stages:

1 identification of need,
2 search for products,
3 evaluation of alternatives,
4 choice of preferred item,
5 budget allocation, and
6 procurement authorization.

A possible seventh stage, performance review, would complete the cycle. The way in which each of the stages is carried out and what professional groups are involved, will largely depend on the type of product. The principal professional groups involved are the users (nursing staff, doctors, and scientists), advisers (hospital physicists, engineers, users in other hospitals), administrators (finance officers concerned with the operation of the whole hospital), and buyers (procurement officers whose expertise is dealing with suppliers and obtaining secure sources of supply at the lowest cost). According to Hutton (1984, p. 162), the decision to purchase sophisticated electronic equipment may be taken by one or two medical specialists. Government-imposed budgets may limit actual purchases; 'selection of the make and model of equipment is made by the user and is seldom challenged but whether the equipment is purchased depends on the availability of finance and committee approval' (Hutton, 1984, p. 167). The fact that a physician, during his formal education, has become familiar with medical equipment from a certain manufacturer has a favourable influence on later adoption decisions. For this reason, manufacturers are often willing to supply university hospitals with equipment free of charge (Bennekom, 1987, p. 59).

Worldwide, a change can be observed from evaluating medical equipment *per se* towards assessing the value of the technological procedure, an evaluation known as technology assessment (Arnstein, 1980; Biggs, 1980; Andreasen, 1984, p. 136). Such a technology assessment could assist hospital managers and medical specialists in choosing from among many alternatives (Stolte, 1984, p. 177) and limit the widespread and uncontrolled diffusion of technology of unproven or restricted value (Staehr Johansen, 1984, p. 146).

The situation in the Netherlands seems to correspond closely to the description given above by Hutton (cf. Willems, 1985, pp. 24–34). A major development influencing the involvement of various professional groups within the hospital in purchasing medical equipment is the implementation of a budgeting system per January 1st 1984. This means that more attention will be paid to the operating costs rather than just the purchase price. Thus, medical specialists are expected to lose part of their influence to financial directors and other administrators. Another consequence of the budgeting system is that hospitals are increasingly leasing rather than purchasing medical equipment (Bennekom, 1987, p. 57). That the imposed limitations of the new budgeting system can result in creative solutions is demonstrated by van der Sluijs and Hogenkamp (1987), who describe how eighteen hospitals in one region cooperated in buying a mobile kidney stone pulverizer. This solution of sharing an expensive piece of mobile equipment was also suggested for computerized axial tomography (CAT) scanners (Barneveld Binkhuysen and van Waes, 1988, p. 137) and realized in November 1988 when a number of regional hospitals purchased the first mobile CAT scanner in the Netherlands.

The diffusion of medical equipment innovations

Regarding the diffusion of medical innovations, most studies relate to pharmaceutical products rather than medical equipment (for example Coleman, Katz and Menzel, 1966; Ryan and Murray, 1977). As regards the diffusion of medical equipment, various investigators have tried to model the process by estimating functions of various shapes. For example, Schmittlein and Mahajan (1982) applied the maximum likelihood estimation procedure to survey data for four pieces of radiological equipment. Wind, Robertson, and Fraser (1982, p. 1) pointed out that this type of single-market forecast may be inappropriate if the market is segmented. A somewhat analogous line of thinking has been presented by Talaysum (1985), who argues that the number and character of prospective users of a new technology change with the passage of time. He illustrates his reasoning by showing how the CAT scanner was adopted over a period of time by different sub-populations of adopters. One group of adopters followed another as the initial product was improved upon, the functional utility extended, and cheaper versions became available. Thus, the ultimate diffusion curve for a technology may be conceived as the aggregation of a time-separated series of smaller diffusion curves.

Based on interviews with almost 300 physicians in the USA, the United Kingdom, and Canada, Greer (1988, p. 17) concludes that the development and introduction of new medical technologies often does not fit with the assumptions of classical diffusion theory. The results of her study led Greer to differentiate between *formed* and *dynamic* technologies. While formed technologies are more or less completed products when they are introduced into the market, dynamic technologies are still emerging, still in part ideas and experiments. This distinction is important, since it determines the innovation's diffusion pattern. Formed technologies can be regarded as defined products and diffuse quickly and predictably. Dynamic medical technologies, on the other hand, develop as they diffuse according to a complicated pattern.

In enumerating the most important factors influencing the diffusion of medical equipment, Baruch draws attention to the specific way in which some factors may play a role. For example, the degree of complexity is an oft-quoted factor influencing diffusion.

> As equipment complexity increases, teaching hospitals readily adopt it, but the rate of diffusion down through the less sophisticated institutions is impeded by lack of expertise. However, once it penetrates around 50 percent of the market, the equipment ... becomes the general-use standard; consequently, an enormous new force acts upon its adoption by other organizations. Frequently these organizations will buy the equipment, even though they cannot initially cope with its complexity.
>
> (Baruch, 1980, p. 46)

A comprehensive survey of the various aspects regarding the diffusion of medical technology is presented by Gordon and Fisher (1975).

The role of networks

Earlier in this chapter we stated as one of the main reasons for selecting medical technology as the field of investigation, the fact that networks seem to play a major role in developing medical equipment innovations. Beneken (1988, p. 3) stressed that, in general, three parties are involved in the development of new medical instruments: a researcher, a manufacturer, and the public health sector (Figure 6.2). If the researcher were employed by the manufacturer the diagram would be less complicated, but the necessity for good communication would remain. Generally, the idea for a new medical instrument originates through an exchange of ideas between an engineer and a physician. If the idea looks promising and sufficient research capacity is available, the problem definition will be translated into a prototype, which will then be evaluated and the results of the evaluation published. Next, the engineer can try to interest a manufacturer in the idea. The manufacturer will analyse the market, build a number of prototypes to test with potential users, and decide

Figure 6.2 The three major parties involved in developing new medical equipment

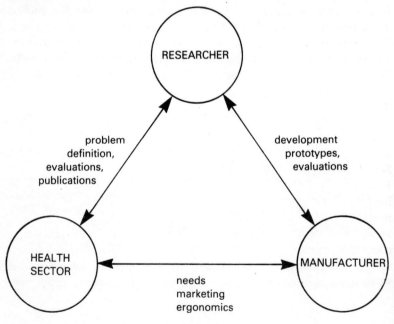

Source: Beneken (1988), © J.E.W. Beneken. Reprinted with permission.

whether or not to start production. Often the prototype needs to be redesigned owing to the results of the market tests.

Frequently, the researcher from Figure 6.2 will work at a university. In the future, cooperation between universities and industrial firms is expected to increase. Due to increasing budgetary restraints, the universities are forced to seek external funds, while ever-shorter product life cycles force industrial firms to speed up product development processes (Snyder and Blevins, 1986, p. 136). By means of cooperation contracts, universities can assist industry in developing new products (Hise, Futrell, and Snyder, 1980; Roberts and Peters, 1982), as well as increase industry R&D expenditures and speed up the transfer and utilization of academic research in industry (Berman, 1990). Cooperation between industrial firms and universities offers advantages to both parties (Dekker, 1986, pp. 8–9). Through cooperation with universities, the manufacturers obtain (1) access to basic and applied research, (2) the opportunity to test prototypes, (3) feedback, such as information for the specification of improved and new products, (4) promotion of a new product among academics, and (5) assistance in recruiting personnel. For their part, through cooperation with industry, the universities obtain (1) clear research objectives, which simplify the comparison of costs and benefits and the acquisition of subsidies, (2) contracts, and thus access to more money and equipment for advanced research, (3) a larger *critical mass*, and thus faster research of higher quality, and (4) recognition by *peers*. Nevertheless, some authors question whether such collaborations will bring the universities financial profit, and fear that academic researchers will be shifted from their social role as suppliers of a collective good, that is scientific and technological knowledge (for example Feller, 1990, p. 335).

Despite these advantages of industry–university cooperation, the literature mentions some distinct problem areas, too (Dietrich and Sen, 1981; Azároff, 1982; Fowler, 1984; Snyder and Blevins, 1986; McDonald and Gieser, 1987; van Dierdonck *et al.*, 1990). The most important potential problems relate to the publication of research results, ownership of patents, overall performance, general orientation, and attitudes. Despite these potential problem areas, the consensus appears to be that industry–university cooperation is workable. In most cases, all of the problems mentioned above can be worked out in advance.

OUTLINE OF THE RESEARCH

All in all, the Dutch market for medical equipment appeared very suitable for conducting our follow-up investigation. For example, the importance of clinical tests allowed us to test and refine the tentative framework for testing prototypes with potential users. Furthermore, the increasing cooperation between industrial firms and universities poses special problems in the development of medical equipment, while the changing influence of physicians and purchasers changes the character of the buying process. The rest of this chapter presents the findings from the in-depth study of seventeen cases concerning the development of complex medical equipment. Chapter 7 integrates the empirical findings with existing theory by presenting the managerial implications.

As with the preliminary investigation, consideration of the objectives of the follow-up investigation led us to conclude that case research would be the most suitable research method (details about the research methodology can be found in Appendix B). A total of seventeen medical equipment innovations, both successful and unsuccessful, developed and marketed by thirteen firms in collaboration with users and third parties, were studied. Table 6.1 shows how the number of firms and innovations is related to firm size. Capsule descriptions of both the firms and the cases investigated are presented in Table 6.2 (more detailed case descriptions can be found in Biemans (1989)). The attempt was made to obtain a sample consisting of firms offering widely varying products to widely varying markets. Thus, even though all the firms and innovations investigated relate to the medical equipment industry, the variation in the data thus

Table 6.1   The number of firms and innovations related to firm size

	Firms		Innovations			
Firm size	*No.*	*%*	*Total*	*Successful*	*Unsuccessful*	*Too early to judge*
Small	5	38	7	3	0	4
Medium	7	54	9	3	3	3
Large	1	8	1	1	0	0
Total	13	100	17	7	3	7

Notes: Small = 50 employees or less
Medium = between 50 and 500 employees
Large = 500 employees or more

Source: Biemans, *Technovation*, Elsevier Advanced Technology (April 1991).

Table 6.2 Capsule descriptions of the firms and cases investigated during the follow-up study

Eye-Tech*	The Netherlands' largest manufacturer of medical equipment based on laser technology; about 125 employees; produces only strategic components and assembles the whole product; very much dependent on export (less than 5% of sales realized in the Netherlands); pursues second-but-better product development strategy; cooperates frequently with universities.	*Case 1* Development of a new product as a reaction to a successful product introduction by a major American competitor; the central elements of the competing product were copied, while an innovative feature was added; close cooperation with local hospital; major problems with production and quality control. *Case 2* Eye-Tech was approached by university researchers who had developed and built an innovative product; the firm started redevelopment work on the original design without conducting market research; after some time the project was terminated because of clearly insufficient market potential.
Spinex*	Independent subsidiary of a company already selling to hospitals; five employees; established in 1986; developed and introduced an ultra-low-temperature freezer, as well as some minor products.	*Case 3* Because of the recent expiration of a patent, Spinex had the opportunity to produce and introduce an ultra-low-temperature freezer; significant problems with the product forced the firm to reformulate the product specifications and start the development cycle anew.
Air*	Specialized in the development, production, and marketing of instruments used in respiratory equipment; about 400 employees in medical equipment division; dependent on original equipment manufacturers for market information; about 90% of total sales realized abroad; develops new products in response to customers' requirements.	*Case 4* In cooperation with a university an innovative piece of medical equipment was developed; an American OEM also contributed; serious communication problems between the university and AIR, mainly because of different starting points and organizational cultures; nevertheless, the project was successful (see this chapter for a detailed description).

Table 6.2 contd.

Applied Laser Technology	Small manufacturer specialized in laser applications; five employees with a predominantly technical background; ALT's main activities involve the development of new products, while it imports and sells some additional products too; proactive innovation strategy.

Case 5
University researchers and physicians from a university hospital jointly developed a microvascular perfusion monitor; ALT was approached to manufacture the product; it took about a year and a half to redevelop the product and get it ready for introduction.

Mijnhardt	Firm specialized in the development, production, and marketing of lung function diagnosis equipment; fifty-five employees; enjoys the reputation of being of good quality: no high tech, but certainly dependable; uses available new technologies to develop new products which offer the user an improved solution with distinct advantages.

Case 6
Mijnhardt combined two existing technologies to develop an innovative version of existing equipment; the firm made good use of marketing during all stages of the product development process; prototypes were extensively tested by various potential users.

Enraf-Nonius	Group of high-technology companies specialized in the development, production, and marketing of scientific, industrial, and medical instrumentation. The world's largest manufacturer of physiotherapy equipment; about 350 employees in the medical equipment division; 70% of total sales realized through export.

Case 7
Developed innovative new product in response to user needs and technological studies; close cooperation with a research institute which solved the technical problems; during external testing problems with the used material became evident, which were subsequently solved by the research organization.

Case 8
Enraf-Nonius started a new development project because (1) some relevant existing user needs were not satisfied by the latest innovation and (2) there were problems with said innovation.

Dahedi

Small manufacturer established in 1986 as a spin-off from a firm producing electronic parts; manufactures several versions of a portable infusion pump; market share of 80% in the Netherlands; eight employees; about half of the pumps are sold abroad.

Case 9

A Dutch specialist had built an innovative portable infusion pump and was looking for a firm to develop an improved version of an innovation; original design improved upon, based on technical considerations and specifications drawn up by physician.

Case 10

During external test, the idea of a miniaturized version occurred; developed in close cooperation with Dutch manufacturer of hybrid circuits.

Case 11

New German safety regulations led to further improvements; programmable infusion pump with duplicated electronics that allow for self-test functions developed in cooperation with German physicians and Dutch suppliers of circuits and software.

Sentrex*

Firm specialized in the design, development, production, and marketing of filters and membranes for industrial use; about 100 employees in the medical equipment division; many strategic reorientations and organizational changes to turn the division into a profitable business; aiming at a proactive product development strategy.

Case 12

Sentrex started to develop a spectro photometer through collaboration with a university hospital; development activities were divided among the partners; serious problems with software resulted in substantial delays; the project was terminated; in the meantime an alternative American product had become available.

Table 6.2 contd.

Ultrolab	Founded in 1984 as a trading concern specialized in medical laboratory equipment; took up production as well to make it less dependent on manufacturers and obtain the opportunity to export; twenty employees; follows the strategy of only selling products that offer unique benefits.	Case 13 Ultrolab came across an engineer at a hospital who had developed an endoscope disinfector; the firm hired the engineer and redeveloped the innovation; the industrial prototype was tested by various users as well as an independent research institute.
Medsound*	Specialized in real-time ultrasound diagnostics; established in 1979 and having twenty employees; approximately 40% of total sales realized abroad; the last couple of years, the firm hired people with specialized training in various fields to upgrade the professional level of the whole firm; proactive product development strategy.	Case 14 Medsound developed a new ultrasound scanner; technical product specifications were drawn up in close collaboration with a German inspection agency; emphasis on design; because of prior negative experiences prototypes were not tested by users.
Vitatron	Dutch manufacturer of pacemakers; about 275 employees; export accounts for 90% of sales; since 1986 subsidiary of Medtronic, the world's largest manufacturer of pacemakers; functions as a relatively independent business; product development strategy is proactive, from purely R&D to a balance with marketing.	Case 15 Vitatron developed the Rhythmyx, a new generation rate-responsive pacemaker as a reaction to user needs; key opinion leaders contributed to the predevelopment stages; the new software was coupled to existing hardware and tested by real patients.
Medlab*	Medium-sized Dutch subsidiary of a large American industrial firm; specialized in the development, production, and marketing of products for use in health care and research labs; in the Netherlands approximately 150 people in R&D and production; the large majority of products are sold abroad; proactive development strategy, with a balance between R&D and marketing.	Case 16 Medlab sponsored experimental research conducted at a university, which led to the development of an anaerobic work station; eventually the cooperation with the university was all but terminated, and Medlab started a joint development project with a competitor; the project was started more than a decade ago and is still not finished.

Philips Medical Systems

One of the world's leaders in advanced high-technology diagnostic and therapeutic systems for the medical profession; approximately 11,000 people worldwide; only a very small minority of its products are sold in the Netherlands; proactive development strategy, with a balance between R&D and marketing.

Case 17

As a kind of spin-off from the Digital Vascular Imaging System, Philips Medical Systems developed the Digital Cardiac Imaging System; a group of three people acted as internal product champions; a prototype was tested extensively by a Dutch university hospital; the system is still being expanded through the development and release of new clinical programmes.

Note: *Both the name of the firm and the product involved have been disguised for reasons of confidentiality.

acquired enhances the significance of the final results. Bearing in mind the structure of the Dutch medical equipment industry, the firms investigated appear to constitute a representative sample.

Chapter guide

The discussion of the results with respect to developing innovative medical equipment within networks, as presented in this chapter, is structured as follows. (1) We start by defining the concept of inter-action which is then analysed according to a number of significant dimensions. Subsequently, some of these dimensions will be used to derive a typology of individual interactive relationships between organizations. (2) This is followed by a discussion of the involvement in product development of manufacturers, users, and various kinds of third parties. (3) The interaction between manufacturers on the one hand, and users and third parties on the other, leads to the concept of networks. Two different classifications of networks are distinguished and the advantages and disadvantages of developing medical equip-ment innovations within complex networks are examined by present-ing a detailed case study (resulting in a third classification of networks). This is followed by a discussion of the most salient short-comings in developing innovative equipment within networks. (4) The chapter ends with some comments on the adoption and diffusion of innovations in the Dutch medical equipment industry.

DEFINING INTERACTION IN THE CONTEXT OF DEVELOPING INNOVATIONS

The results presented in this chapter focus on the interaction between manufacturers and users and/or third parties operating in a network. In the context of developing innovations for industrial markets, the concept of interaction refers to an exchange of values between two parties. Although it is essential that both parties transfer values, these need not be of the same kind. For example, a manufacturer may purchase strategic components from a supplier and thus exchange money for products. Or a manufacturer may be required to write detailed reports in order to be granted a subsidy by the national government and thus exchange information for money. The values transferred in the context of an interactive relationship may belong to one or more of the following four categories (cf. Håkansson, 1982, p. 16).

1 Transfer of products/components or services
   Users and/or third parties may provide a tangible contribution to
   the product development process by delivering specific strategic
   components or even a complete product (which is subsequently
   modified by the manufacturer, for instance by the addition of a
   specially developed component). Furthermore, the manufacturer
   may employ specialized organizations to provide specific services,
   such as testing prototypes, taking care of industrial design, and
   introducing and marketing the innovation.

2 Transfer of information
   During all stages of the product development process the manufacturer may interact with other parties to obtain information. While
   at the outset of the development process the information thus
   obtained will be of a general nature, it will become more specific
   and better defined as the project continues. The information
   provided by other parties may refer to such diverse topics as the
   future needs of a market segment, the technical feasibility of a
   product concept, a possible solution to an existing technological
   problem, and the functioning of a prototype in actual practice.

3 Transfer of financial resources
   Both the national government and scientific foundations may grant
   subsidies for various purposes, such as fostering industry–university cooperation, stimulating the development of innovations in a
   specific area, or assisting small firms in their product development
   efforts. In the same way, a manufacturer may sponsor experimental
   research at a university to stimulate the development of new
   products or new techniques.

4 Transfer of social content
   Social exchange serves the purpose of strengthening an existing
   bond between two parties or helping to establish a new one. A
   manufacturer may supply a major customer who tests the first
   version of a new and complex process installation, with an engineer
   during one day per week. Not just to assist in the operations, train
   the operators, and solve problems, but also explicitly to demonstrate commitment and create trust, both vital ingredients of
   relationship management. However, the development of trust also
   strongly depends on the successful transfer of the other three
   values.

While an interactive relationship implies the mutual exchange of
values between two organizations, the interaction is most successful
when both parties derive benefit from the relationship. Mutual benefit

and concurring objectives are strongly conducive to a positive outcome.

Enraf-Nonius frequently cooperates with The Netherlands Organization for Applied Scientific Research (TNO) in the development of specific components and the testing of new products. The evaluative reports of TNO are used by Enraf-Nonius during market launch as support from an independent research institute, while it gives TNO the opportunity to increase its reputation/prestige in international markets.

A large number of dimensions can be used to describe individual interactive relationships between the various organizations involved in product development networks. We will distinguish between the type, purpose, intensity, duration, and extent of formalization of interaction.

Type of interaction

In Chapter 4 we distinguished between three different *types of interaction* depending on the type of counterpart, that is (1) vertical interaction, which includes all interaction between sellers and buyers, (2) horizontal competitive interaction, encompassing interaction between companies which basically are competitors, and (3) horizontal complementary interaction, which includes cases of interaction between manufacturers of complementary products. However, our investigation argues the necessity to discern a fourth category, namely (4) *diagonal interaction*, which contains all cases of interaction between two partners belonging to two different systems. This distinction is particularly relevant with respect to instances of extensive technical cooperation between the parties involved. The cases of industry–university cooperation that were studied illustrate the point: the inherent differences between the scientific world of the university and the commercial reality of the industrial firm formed the underlying factor accounting for most of the problems and frustrations that occurred during the process of product development.

Purpose of interaction

Depending on the *purpose of interaction*, we can divide individual interactive relationships into two categories. The objective of the interaction can be either to perform or stimulate specific development activities. Two organizations may interact in order to *perform* specific development activities jointly (for example jointly drawing up product specifications) or separately (for example when an industrial supplier lets an original equipment manufacturer (OEM) conduct the external tests). In other instances, interaction between two parties may be initiated to *stimulate* specific development activities, for example through (1) sponsoring of experimental research at a university by an industrial firm, (2) granting of credits by the government to stimulate industry–university cooperation, and (3) granting of subsidies by the government or scientific foundations in order to stimulate industrial firms to develop specific new products or technologies.

Intensity of interaction

Looking at interactive relationships from the manufacturer's viewpoint, a third relevant characteristic is the *intensity of interaction*, which may vary widely. While in some cases the interaction may consist of no more than an *ad hoc* visit in order to gather specific information, other interactions may amount to an extensive cooperation project jointly to develop and market a new product.

Medlab distinguishes three types of cooperation that differ in their degree of intensity: (1) half-yearly contacts with universities and hospitals in order to stay in touch with important developments, (2) sponsoring of research projects through the provision of services and/or the payment of salaries, and (3) intensive collaboration by means of joint research projects.

As regards the intensity of interaction, individual interactive relationships may be classified in six separate categories, running from *use as reference* to *joint performance of activities*.

1 Use as reference
   The diffusion of an innovation can be facilitated by using the names and reputations of users and/or third parties as references during market introduction. Frequently, the organizations used as reference also allow potential buyers to inspect the innovation at their premises.
2 Passive acquisition of resources
   The manufacturer may obtain relevant resources (mostly information) as input to the product development process in an *ad hoc* and passive way. For example, during a visit of a sales represent-

ative, a major customer may mention some significant problems with an existing product and offer suggestions for a solution. Another example involves the manufacturer who is approached by a university researcher with an idea for a new product or a crudely put together home-made device.

3 Active acquisition of resources

In contrast with the previous category, the manufacturer may acquire resources, such as general information or money, by means of a planned process governed by predetermined objectives. The most common example is any kind of market research initiated by the manufacturer, such as the systematic interviewing of a selected group of major customers in order to determine future product requirements. Other examples include a number of visits to major research centres to assess the latest trends in technology, the sponsoring of experimental research at a university, or the application for a subsidy in the context of a stimulation programme from the national government.

4 Response, feedback on specific issues

Key product users and important third parties may also be approached in order to obtain response on specific issues. For example, users may be asked to evaluate a tentative product concept, while a specialized research institute may be approached to assess the technical feasibility of a new product idea.

5 Separate performance of specified activities

Certain clearly defined activities are often conducted by users or third parties instead of by the manufacturer. One of the most obvious examples is the testing of a prototype by a potential user. Others include the industrial design by an outside agency, the production of strategic components by a major supplier, and the introduction and marketing of the innovation by a distributor.

6 Joint performance of specified activities

Finally, the manufacturer may decide to perform certain specified activities jointly with a customer or third party. Examples involve the manufacturer and major customer who jointly develop and test a prototype, and the manufacturer and OEM who jointly formulate the product specifications.

Defined like this, the intensity of interaction can be measured as an ordinal variable consisting of six categories, with increasing intensity representing increasing commitment of the parties involved. Because of the nature of the interaction, the first two categories may be termed *passive interaction*, while the others are examples of *active interaction*.

Some of the categories enumerated above are closely intertwined. Consider the use as a reference of a major customer or university at the time of market introduction. This practice only makes sense when the customer or university in question has been involved in previous product development activities, such as developing and/or testing a prototype (that is 'separate performance of specified activities').

Naturally, there are several gradations within each separate category as well. For example, a firm sponsoring experimental research at a university may increase or decrease the extent of its sponsoring, depending on its strategic objectives.

> Medlab increased its sponsoring of experimental research at a university as the project gained strategic interest and the research started to pay off in the form of newly developed original designs that were of interest to the firm. However, when the development activities at Medlab overtook the progress at the university, the sponsoring was all but terminated.

A firm may maintain minimal contacts with universities for various purposes. Granovetter (1973) has stressed the importance of such weak ties and, describing the various functions and advantages of weak ties, writes about *the strength of weak ties*. While strong ties, that is intensive and comprehensive relationships, may be used to mobilize external resources for the firm's product development, weak ties perform an important function as communication channels. A company can have a large number of weak ties, since they do not demand large resources as strong ties do. Weak ties are mostly used in order to obtain information from different areas. With the help of weak ties a firm can cover very large areas without making large investments of time and money. Therefore weak ties should not be considered substitutive but rather complementary to strong ties. A final important function of weak ties is that they are potential strong ties.

> Together with researchers from a university, AIR developed an innovative respirator. After having concluded the development project, AIR did not totally terminate the sponsoring of experimental research but continued to supply funds, albeit a minimal amount. This provided AIR with direct access both to existing knowledge and new scientific developments.

Duration of interaction

A fourth variable to characterize individual interactive relationships is the *duration of interaction*. Depending on the purpose and intensity of interaction, the duration varies from short (for example a one-hour visit) to long (for example a three-year development contract). The duration of interaction can be measured in two distinct ways: (1) the number of *time periods* or (2) the number of *product development activities*. While both measures are certainly correlated, they need not be identical. Due to technical problems and continual setbacks, the joint development of a prototype by a manufacturer and a major customer may cover a prolonged period of time but only a limited number of product development activities.

A single visit to a customer to see whether there are problems with existing products and a one-hour visit to a university to obtain specific technological information are both examples of interaction of a short duration. An extensive joint development project with a major customer covering several years is positioned towards the other end of the continuum. Another example of a longer-term interactive relationship concerns the firm and the university hospital which have signed a contract according to which the hospital contributes to the development activities of the firm (for example by commenting on new product ideas, evaluating product concepts, testing prototypes, and promoting the product through publications and lectures) in exchange for equipment and salaries of researchers. However, contracts of this kind can usually be terminated from year to year, depending on the strategic interests of the firm and the desired direction of research at the university hospital.

Sentrex, a manufacturer of filters and membranes for industrial use, and the Technical Service Department (TSD) of a university hospital decided to develop an innovative spectro photometer jointly. Whereas the product specifications were formulated by members of the TSD, the actual development of the prototype was split in two. Sentrex would develop the mechanical part, while the hospital would see to the electronics and assembly. Developing the prototype took about two and a half years due to continuous changes in the product specifications. After the prototype was tested on patients the project was discontinued for several reasons. (1) The results were unsatisfactory; the software needed to be modified considerably. (2) The market had changed; increasing competition

> would limit future profits. (3) Due to the required redevelopment efforts, the market launch would be postponed considerably. (4) In the meantime, a similar American product had become available. As a result, Sentrex decided to terminate the cooperation project and import the American product.

Extent of formalization of interaction

In addition to the characteristics discussed above, the *extent of formalization of interaction* may be used to describe individual relationships between organizations. One should take care not to equate the distinction between formal and informal interactions with the difference between very intensive and less intensive forms of interaction. Very close collaborations between two firms involving the joint development of expensive process equipment may initially be based on trust, confidence, and individual commitment, while detailed contracts are only drawn up at a later stage. An obviously less intensive form of interaction, such as the granting of credits by the national government, may require the filling out of comprehensive application forms and the formulation of extensive evaluation reports and thus be very formal indeed! These bureaucratic procedures, combined with a relatively low chance of actually receiving such credits, frequently impede the application for such credits by small firms.

Interrelationships between the factors

The dimensions characterizing individual interactive relationships discussed above are not totally independent. Although universally applicable statements can hardly be made, some general trends can be observed (Table 6.3).

When we compare the type of interaction with all other dimensions involved, we find that most types of interaction aim at performing specific development activities. The goal of stimulating specific development activities is more characteristic of diagonal interactions, where, for instance the government stimulates innovation programmes or an industrial firm sponsors experimental research at a university. The intensity, duration, and extent of formalization of interaction depend very much upon the specific case involved. Nevertheless, the horizontal types of interaction are typically more project oriented and therefore more intensive, covering a longer period of time and tend to

Table 6.3 The relationship between the type of interaction and the purpose, intensity, duration, and extent of formalization of interaction

Dimension of interaction	*Type of interaction*			
	Vertical	*Horizontal competitive*	*Horizontal complementary*	*Diagonal*
Purpose	P	P	P	P/S
Intensity	low–high	high	high	low–high
Duration	low–high	high	high	low–high
Extent of formalization	low–high	high	high	low–high

Note: P = the purpose of the interactive relationship is to perform development activities
S = the purpose of the interactive relationship is to stimulate development activities

be more formalized (that is, based on comprehensive cooperation contracts with respect to clearly defined activities to be performed within the context of one specific project; cf. Håkansson (1987a, p. 7) and the case of AIR presented later in this chapter).

Classification of interactive relationships

The type, purpose, intensity, and extent of formalization are all dimensions that may be used to characterize individual interactions between two organizations during *one stage* of the product development process (that is a limited number of product development activities). For example, during the idea stage, a manufacturer may interact with a number of important customers in order to generate ideas for potential new products. Or, during the testing stage, a manufacturer may interact with a research institute to have his developed prototype tested. However, the cases investigated show that, in reality, an interactive relationship between two organizations need not be limited to one particular stage and may very well cover *several stages* of the development process (that is a large number of product development activities). For example, when a manufacturer selects a major customer jointly to develop, test, and market a new product.

The findings of the investigation suggest a quite complex relationship between the dimensions *intensity* and *duration* of interaction. These two dimensions can be combined to generate a classification of interactive relationships between manufacturers and users and/or third parties (a detailed derivation of the classification is presented in Biemans (1989, pp. 208–10)). Such a classification distinguishes between two major categories: single-level and multiple-level inter-active relationships.

Single-level interactive relationships

The first category consists of single-level interactive relationships between two organizations, that is relationships involving only one level of intensity during one or more product development stages. The single-level interactive relationships are divided into five classes, run-ning from the passive acquisition of resources to the joint performance of activities, embracing comprehensive projects in which a manu-facturer and a major customer jointly generate, develop, test, and market an innovation, for example. The various classes are ranked in order of increasing commitment of the parties involved. Each class is illustrated with some examples from the cases investigated.

1 A single-level interactive relationship consisting of the *passive acquisition of resources* used as input to the product development process.
   (a) A major customer mentions some problems with existing products to a manufacturer's sales representative.
   (b) An important inspection agency informs the manufacturer of its changed evaluation criteria.
2 A single-level interactive relationship involving the *active acquisition of resources* used as input to the product development process.
   (a) A manufacturer periodically visits (for instance twice a year) a major customer or important research institute to stay in touch with noticed significant developments.
   (b) A manufacturer interviews a number of important customers, industry experts, distributors, and competitors to find out about future product requirements.
   (c) A manufacturer applies for and obtains subsidies or credits from the government or scientific foundations.
   (d) A manufacturer sponsors experimental research at a research institute, by (partly) paying the salaries of researchers and/or providing services, equipment, etc. to stimulate the develop-ment of relevant new techniques, products, and/or processes.
3 A single-level interactive relationship in which the manufacturer obtains *response, feedback to specific issues* during the process of product development.

    (a) A manufacturer uses a research institute to test the characteristics of its existing products.

    (b) A manufacturer visits major customers, distributors, industry experts, or important research institutes to obtain response to a concrete new product idea or product concept.

    (c) A manufacturer shows a mock-up (for example an empty box) at a trade show to obtain response from product users to the product concept.

    (d) A manufacturer shows a prototype at a trade show to obtain response from product users.

4 A single-level interactive relationship in which the manufacturer employs other parties for the *separate performance of specified activities* during the process of product development.

    (a) A manufacturer uses customers to test a prototype under actual conditions.

    (b) A manufacturer employs a distributor to launch and market the new product.

    (c) A manufacturer uses a customer to formulate the product concept, and develop and test a prototype.

    (d) A manufacturer contracts a university to solve a specified technical problem and test the solution.

5 A single-level interactive relationship consisting of the *joint performance of specified activities* during the process of product development.

    (a) A manufacturer and major customer jointly formulate a product concept.

    (b) A manufacturer and major customers jointly develop (part of) a prototype.

Multiple-level interactive relationships

The second category of interactive relationships between two organizations consists of relationships involving more than one level of intensity. Numerous individual multiple-level relationships can be constructed by combining different levels of intensity of interaction. We can distinguish between two different kinds of multiple-level interactive relationships.

1 An interactive relationship in which *different levels of intensity* of interaction are realized *at different stages* of the product development process. A number of examples actually encountered during the investigation are enumerated below.

(a) A manufacturer jointly formulates the product concept with an OEM and uses the OEM to test a prototype, formulate the marketing plan, and introduce and market the new product.

(b) A manufacturer and major supplier jointly formulate a product concept, develop and test a prototype, and finalize the design, after which the supplier produces a strategic component.

(c) A manufacturer is approached by a major customer with a new product idea, after which they jointly assess the potential of a new product idea and formulate the product concept, and separately develop and test parts of the prototype.

(d) A manufacturer is approached by university researchers with a home-made device and uses the researchers during the development stage to address specific issues.

2 An interactive relationship in which *different levels of intensity* of interaction are realized *during (at least) one stage* of the product development process. Although this type of multiple-level interactive relationship has not actually been encountered in the course of the investigation it is not theoretically precluded. For example, a manufacturer may employ a major customer to develop a strategic component jointly and develop some other less important product features separately.

INVOLVEMENT OF MANUFACTURERS, USERS, AND THIRD PARTIES IN PRODUCT DEVELOPMENT

Having addressed the issue of how to define interaction and what characteristics to use in describing individual interactive relationships between organizations, we will now turn to the following central questions.

1 During what stages of the product development process may a manufacturer benefit from interaction with other organizations (timing of the interaction)?

2 What kinds of organization are most eligible as collaboration partners (selection of interaction partners)?

Interaction strategies

In answer to these two questions, let us first discuss how the firms investigated *generally* interact with other parties during the process of product development (Table 6.4). For the purpose of this discussion, the product development process will be conceptualized as a series of

Table 6.4 General involvement of interaction partners in the product development process (the percentages refer to the fraction of the total number of firms)

Interaction partners	Number of firms					Involvement in the stages of the product development process						
	Total No.	%	Small	Medium	Large	Idea	Preliminary assessment	Concept	Development	Testing	Trial	Launch
(Potential) users	9	69	1	7	1	+	+	+	+	+++	−	++
Research institutes	5	38	0	4	1	−	−	+	+++	+	−	−
Other partners	1	8	0	1	0	+	+	+	−	−		+
As yet unknown	3	23	3	0	0							

Notes: Small = 50 employees or less
Medium = between 50 and 500 employees
Large = 500 employees or more
− = the interaction partner is not involved
+ = the interaction partner is involved
++ = the interaction partner is strongly involved
+++ = the interaction partner is very strongly involved

seven subsequent stages, that is idea, preliminary assessment, concept, development, testing, trial, and launch (see Chapter 3, Figure 3.5 and Appendix A).

As can be gathered from Table 6.4, in answer to the question which type of partner frequently contributes to the firm's product development efforts, potential product users and research institutes were most often mentioned. Almost three-quarters of the firms investigated reported to interact with users during the development process. Product users were mentioned as predominantly involved in generating product ideas, testing prototypes, and launching the final product. Research institutes (including universities) were mentioned by five firms as important interaction partners. Due to their specialized knowledge, their contribution was reported to be most evident during the actual development of the prototype. The important role ascribed by the firms to product users and research institutes is further illustrated by the fact that only one firm mentioned another important party as being generally involved in the product development process, viz. distributors. Finally, as three of the firms investigated were only recently founded, nothing definite could be stated about their interaction strategies.

Observed interaction

To answer the central questions posed at the beginning of this section in more detail, we will discuss the *actual* contribution of various organizations to the product development process, as studied in seventeen individual cases. We will distinguish between three major parties: the manufacturer, potential users, and a group of organizations termed *third parties*. Users and third parties have been investigated insofar as they contributed substantially to the development activities. Table 6.5 summarizes the involvement of the manufacturer, potential users, and third parties in the product development stages. In the rest of this section we will describe the contribution of the various parties to the product development process. After having discussed both user and third-party involvement, the major differences between manufacturer–user and manufacturer–third party interaction will be analysed.

Manufacturer involvement in product development

In six out of the seventeen cases studied (35 per cent) users and/or third parties dominated the initial stages of the product development process while the manufacturer became the dominant party during the actual development of the prototype. In more than half of the cases investigated (53 per cent) the product development process was initiated by a user or third party. However, as the development process proceeds, manufacturer involvement quickly increases to 100 per cent (Table 6.5).

Regarding the involvement of manufacturers in the process of product development we would like to comment on von Hippel's observations with respect to such *user-dominated* innovation processes. Von Hippel states that in such a process

it is the initial user who perceives the need for the product innovation, conceives of a solution, builds a prototype device, proves the value of the prototype by using it and diffuses detailed information ... to other potential users and to firms which might be interested in manufacturing the device on a commercial basis. Only when all of the above has transpired does the first commercial manufacturer become active in the innovation process. Typically, the manufacturer's contribution is to perform product engineering work on the user's device to improve its reliability, convenience of operation etc. .... [and to] ... manufacture, market and sell the innovative product.

(von Hippel, 1977b, p. 13)

The findings of our investigation do not support these observations. As can be gathered from Table 6.5, while manufacturer involvement was found to be only 47 per cent during the idea stage, it nearly doubles (to 82 per cent) during the subsequent preliminary assessment stage and increases even more (to 94 per cent) during the concept stage. It is during these stages that the manufacturer defines and assesses the value of the new product idea. After having undertaken these critical initial development activities, the manufacturer typically needs to modify the user-developed original design considerably. In specific instances, these modifications may go beyond performing mere product engineering and may entail redefining the product concept and its operating principles.

Looking for new-product opportunities to strengthen its position as a trading concern, Ultrolab came across a member of the Technical Service Department of a hospital. He had developed and built an automatic endoscope disinfector which was actually used in the hospital. The technician was hired by Ultrolab and the prototype was tested by users. As a result of

Table 6.5 Involvement in product development of the manufacturer, potential users, and third parties (the percentages refer to the fraction of the number of cases as stated in the first column)

Stages of the product development process	Number of cases	Involvement of the manufacturer		Involvement of potential users		Involvement of third parties		Involvement of potential users + third parties	
		No.	%	No.	%	No.	%	No.	%
Idea	17	8	47	10	59	7	41	5	29
Preliminary assessment	17	14	82	9	53	6	35	4	24
Concept	17	16	94	12	71	10	59	6	35
Development	17	16	94	7	41	9	53	5	29
Testing	16	16	100	12	75	11	69	7	44
Trial	14	14	100	0	0	3	21	0	0
Launch	13	13	100	6	46	9	69	3	23

Source: Biemans, *Technovation*, Elsevier Advanced Technology (April 1991).

> these evaluations the original prototype had to be modified considerably; redevelopment took about one year.

Furthermore, in four out of the six cases in which users or third parties dominated the initial stages of the product development process, the manufacturer admitted to having spent insufficient resources on these initial development stages. In their opinion, more proficiency during these initial stages could have prevented many problems and shortened the whole development process.

In the literature, the importance of these *predevelopment activities*, consisting of

1 generating and screening ideas,
2 undertaking a preliminary market and technical assessment, and
3 identifying, developing, and testing the concept,

has been stressed as well. These initial stages have been described as the pivotal steps in the product development process since 'it is these early stages where success and failure are largely decided' (Cooper, 1988, p. 237; see also Gupta and Wilemon, 1990, p. 37). Cooper and Kleinschmidt (1986) studied 203 industrial product launches and found that the proficiency with which activities, such as initial screening, preliminary market and technical assessment, and detailed market study were undertaken was strongly correlated with the eventual success of the innovation. As Leiva and Obermayer (1989, pp. 46, 48) put it: 'Do your homework, especially early in the product development cycle ... More work at the definition phase of the project always translates into savings of both time and money as the project nears completion'.

Therefore the differences between von Hippel's findings and the results of our investigation may only be partly explained by differences in sample composition (von Hippel's comments are based on the study of 111 scientific instruments which include many medical instruments). Irrespective of the industry concerned, von Hippel's reasoning should be expected *severely to underestimate the necessary involvement of a manufacturer in the initial stages of the process of product development.* For, even when a manufacturer is approached by a user with a home-made device that has been built, tested, and used in practice, the manufacturer needs to carry out the critical initial stages of the product development process (see also Chapter 7).

User involvement in product development

The second major party of interest in the context of developing innovations for industrial markets consists of the potential users of the innovation. We speak of *potential* users, since the product is still under development and has not been introduced yet. Nevertheless, sometimes the product/prototype is actually used by a customer.

> An innovative and expensive piece of medical equipment (such as Magnetic Resonance Imaging equipment), developed by Philips Medical Systems may be used by a hospital for two years. During the first six months the basic equipment is tested, while the remaining period is used to test newly developed clinical programs and minor additions to the basic hardware.

Therefore, the terms *potential users* and *users* will be used interchangeably. In this chapter the term *users* will refer to the people/organizations using the innovative medical equipment. In the vast majority of the cases the users are medical specialists working in a hospital.

> The only exceptions concern Enraf-Nonius and Medsound. In the Netherlands, many of the physiotherapists using Enraf-Nonius equipment work in a hospital. The majority, however, work in the private sector, that is in a group practice consisting of from two up to twenty persons. In other countries a different structure and different trends may exist. The physiotherapists working in the private sector are clearly different from the ones working at hospitals: the former are more oriented towards costs and benefits of equipment rather than ways of treatment and can make quicker decisions regarding the purchase of new equipment. A similar situation exists for the users of Medsound.

By involving potential users in the process of product development, the manufacturer may develop a product that better fits user needs, shorten the duration of the total development project, and accelerate market acceptance of the product.

As has been found by numerous researchers (see Chapter 4), users may be involved in many stages of the product development process. The results of our own investigation support these observations. Table 6.5 indicates that potential users were found to contribute to all but one stage of the product development process (namely the trial stage, which consists of finalization of the design, trial production, and finalization of the marketing plan). Their contributions consisted of

1 suggesting a new product idea (either directly or indirectly by criticizing existing products),
2 providing general information on user requirements,
3 commenting on formulated new product concepts,
4 assisting in the development of prototypes,
5 testing developed prototypes, and
6 assisting in the marketing of the innovation.

Predevelopment stages

The cases investigated show varying ways of user involvement at the predevelopment stages (that is, the idea, preliminary assessment, and concept stages). In 59 per cent of the cases, potential users were involved in idea generation through the formulation of problems encountered with existing products, the suggestion of concrete improvements, or the generation of a new product idea. In 53 per cent of the cases, potential users were somehow involved in the preliminary assessment stage, while in 71 per cent of the cases they were involved in the concept stage either by defining or testing the product concept. (However, these numbers include the one case in which the manufacturer was not involved in the predevelopment stages.) From a manufacturer's viewpoint, user involvement during the predevelopment stages in these cases was frequently less than optimal. Taking a closer look at the individual cases reveals that this sub-optimal situation was typically caused by

1 a limited number of users involved, (*quantitative user selection*) and
2 the absence or arbitrariness of the selection criteria (*qualitative user selection*).

Table 6.6 shows that, in the majority of the cases investigated (that is ten out of sixteen) only a limited number of potential users (or none at all) were involved in the critical predevelopment stages by the manufacturer. At the same time, in only eight cases (Table 6.7) potential users were selected on the basis of such well-considered criteria as the available expertise or representativeness.

Table 6.6 The number of users involved in the manufacturer's predevelopment activities (quantitative user involvement)

	Number of users			
Firm size	None	One	≤ Five	≥ Six
Small	2	2	1	2
Medium	0	4	1	3
Large	0	0	0	1
Total	2	6	2	6

Notes: Small = 50 employees or less
Medium = between 50 and 500 employees
Large = 500 employees or more

Table 6.7 Criteria used for selecting users during the predevelopment activities (qualitative user involvement)

	Selection criteria		
Firm size	No selection	Arbitrary	Considered
Small	2	1	2
Medium	2	1	5
Large	0	0	1
Total	4	2	8

Notes: Small = 50 employees or less
Medium = between 50 and 500 employees
Large = 500 employees or more

The experiences of Eye-Tech demonstrate that a user's level of expertise may be difficult to assess beforehand and only be determined through actual interaction. In developing an innovative piece of equipment used by ophthalmologists, Eye-Tech decided to collaborate with a physician at the local university hospital. The collaboration aimed to determine the user's interest in the product concept, access the knowledge available at the hospital, and establish a bilateral flow of information. The user's contribution was not limited to purely medical issues, but concerned medical technological aspects as well. After some time it became obvious that Eye-Tech had overestimated the

> user's expertise. Switching to another user during the development process could have prevented many of the ensuing problems.

In four cases it was the user who took the initiative for the first contact (and no real selection took place), while in the remaining two cases the manufacturer selected the potential user(s) because of present knowledge in a related field, existing relationships, or chance contacts.

Development stage

The involvement of users in the actual development of a prototype (41 per cent of the cases) typically consisted of assisting in the actual development activities or in providing feedback to developers in the industrial firm and answering specific questions. In some instances the original design of the new product was developed by a user.

The fact that the original design of innovative medical equipment is developed by a university linked with a hospital is generally considered by industry to be a major advantage. Thus the innovation can be developed by engineers with ready access to a clinical environment. The direct and intensive dialogue between engineers and physicians is assumed to result in a high-quality product. During the actual development stage, new improved versions of the original design can continuously be tested by physicians on real patients. Both the physicians and the engineers are motivated to cooperate closely, since the tests may be used to generate scientific research results and publications and thus to increase the prestige of the institute, the department, and the individual scientists. Nevertheless, developing an original design within a clinical environment has some potential disadvantages as well. When an original design is developed within a university linked with a university hospital, *actual user involvement* in the development activities *is none the less often quite limited.* This *User Involvement Paradox* can be explained as follows. Although the original design may be developed through an intensive dialogue between engineers and physicians, typically only a few physicians are actually involved in the development activities. Therefore industrial firms should address the question whether the results thus obtained are representative of the market segment in question.

> Eye-Tech was approached by university researchers who had developed, built, and tested a prototype. During the negoti-

ations with Eye-Tech the enthusiasm of the university research-ers was picked up by a member of the board of directors, who subsequently promoted the project internally. After having spent considerable resources on the project, Eye-Tech discovered that the innovation was only of interest to a very limited group of customers, and thus represented insufficient potential for profit. The development activities were discontin-ued and the project terminated.

In other cases, the project still has some potential. In the case of Ultrolab, for instance, the evaluation led to significant changes in product specifications and to new development acti-vities initiated by the manufacturer in order to satisfy the requirements of a wider market.

Theoretically, the initially limited involvement of users can be corrected by having other hospitals test the original design as well. In practice, however, this ideal situation is not easily realized.

In the case of AIR, problems arose since the physicians held on to all existing units of the developed original design in order to experiment and publish profusely. Thus they were able to main-tain a monopoly on publications and it became virtually impos-sible to test the various versions of the original design in other (university) hospitals. This situation also interfered with an efficient transfer of the original design from the university to AIR.

Testing stage

The external testing stage is of crucial importance to medical equip-ment innovations. Because of the possible direct influence on the patient's health, every new piece of equipment that is intended for clinical use, first needs clinical assessment and trial. Therefore it is not surprising that the majority of the firms investigated involved users in product development by having them test a developed prototype (75 per cent of the cases). Only about half of the firms investigated employed comprehensive clinical evaluation protocols or evaluation forms. Potential users to test new equipment were mostly selected because of their assumed medical expertise, an existing relationship, and their position in the market. In a minority of cases the geo-graphical proximity was mentioned as an additional selection criterion (see also the section on shortcomings during the product development process).

Launch stage

In six cases, users were found to be involved in the launch of the innovation. This finding is consistent with the fact that *commercial potentialities* were very frequently mentioned as a criterion for selecting users to test a newly developed prototype. Nevertheless, many firms neglected fully to capitalize on the available opportunities with respect to employing users during market introduction. The most frequently used mechanisms for involving users in marketing the innovation were having them

1 demonstrate the new equipment to other potential users,
2 function as references,
3 present scientific papers at both national and international conferences, and
4 promote the product among colleagues.

> Sometimes users go far beyond the mechanisms mentioned above and take active part in distributing the innovation. In one case, a physician who had tested a prototype actually set up a business to market the innovation in his country.

Third-party involvement in product development

Various kinds of third party were found to be involved in the product development process. The third parties encountered during the investigation included distributors, universities (quite often linked with a university hospital), research institutes (for example The Netherlands Organization for Applied Scientific Research (TNO), an organization consisting of thirty-five specialized institutes), government agencies (various ministries), scientific foundations (for example The Technology Foundation (STW), a government organization established to finance research projects), competitors, suppliers, original equipment manufacturers, consultants, and inspection agencies (for example the German Technischer Überwachungsverein).

The principal contributions of third parties to the product development process consisted of

1 influencing cooperation strategies,

2 funding user and manufacturer research,
3 providing market information,
4 providing engineering skills and specific technological knowledge,
5 providing specific services, such as industrial design,
6 testing developed prototypes,
7 producing strategic components,
8 carrying out specific marketing-related activities, such as having the prototype tested by customers and introducing the product, and
9 assisting in the diffusion of the innovation.

One of the cases illustrates how a third party may strongly influence cooperation strategies by limiting the available alternatives. The case concerned a university and a university hospital which jointly developed and built a prototype. After having tested it successfully, a grant of application was submitted to The Technology Foundation (STW). According to the subsidy arrangement, the university would develop the technical aspects, while the hospital would focus on the application aspects, and a *Dutch* firm had to be found to manufacture and market the product. The last requirement made it impossible to cooperate with a certain foreign manufacturer, who would be the most logical cooperation partner.

Excepting the studies of Mantel and Rosegger (1987), who studied the role of third parties in the diffusion of innovations, and Shaw (1988) who drew attention to some of the mechanisms mentioned above, third-party involvement in the process of product development has received little attention. Our investigation indicates that this overlooked aspect of innovation may be critical to the successful development of new products for industrial markets: third parties performed key activities for more than half (64 per cent) of the products that were actually launched on the market. These critical activities consisted of developing the original design, formulating the product concept, solving major technical problems, developing, testing and producing strategic components, and launching and marketing the final product.

Predevelopment stages

Unlike users, third parties were found to participate actively in all stages of the product development process (see table 6.5). They contributed to the predevelopment activities by generating and screening new product ideas (41 per cent of the cases), providing both commercial and technical information (35 per cent of the cases), and generating and evaluating new product concepts (59 per cent of the cases). Although distributors, universities, and research institutes were the third parties most frequently employed during these stages, other less obvious and often overlooked third parties may provide significant information too.

One manager commented on the use of competitors during the preliminary assessment and concept stages: 'Because of existing personal relationships and by using subtle interview techniques, competitors can be induced to provide significant market and technical information'.

Development and testing stages

Third parties were also found to contribute substantially to the development (53 per cent of the cases) and testing (69 per cent of the cases) activities. Regarding these stages of the product development process, their contribution usually consisted of supplying highly specialized technological expertise, developing clearly defined parts of the new product, solving specified technical problems, and performing specific technological tests. Third-party involvement at the testing stage includes the case of a university that develops an original design and tests it before transferring it to an industrial firm.

In four of the cases investigated a university contributed substantially to the development of a functioning prototype, while in another case an industrial firm cooperated with a university in formulating the product concept. In addition, there were numerous instances of cooperation with universities in order to develop parts of the product, to test prototypes, to solve technological problems, etc.. The cases of industry–university cooperation point to some major causes of coordination problems (which are discussed in the section on shortcomings during the product development process).

Trial stage

In three of the cases investigated, third parties were involved in the trial stage of the product development process. In two cases this refers to a major supplier manufacturing part of the product and thus carrying out the trial production as well. A third case involves an original equipment manufacturer who markets the innovation and therefore formulated the final marketing plan too.

Launch stage

Finally, in nine cases (69 per cent) third parties were involved in the launch stage by

1 assisting the manufacturer in marketing the innovation (in seven cases), or
2 manufacturing strategic components of the product (in two cases involving one small technology-oriented firm).

Differences between manufacturer–user and manufacturer–third-party interaction

Although the data in Table 6.5 indicate that both users and third parties contribute substantially to the process of product development, the percentages provide only a quantitative indication of their involvement in the product development process. Moreover, the percentages demonstrate that in 53 per cent of the cases the new product idea is generated and evaluated by users and/or third parties, while in a number of cases (18 per cent) they perform the preliminary assessment as well. In one case the manufacturer was not even involved at the concept stage either. In these cases the predevelopment stages are undertaken by a user or third party *before a potential manufacturer is even approached.* Thus, the percentages offer only limited (quantitative) information about the *involvement* of manufacturers, users, and third parties during the stages of the product development process and fail to furnish information regarding the *interaction* between the manufacturer on the one hand, and users and/or third parties on the other. The numbers in Table 6.5 indicate that there is no significant difference between the quantitative involvement of users and third parties during the product development process. (Even only a mild correction for continuity results in a Chi-square of 3.512 at six degrees of freedom, this being well below the critical value and thus leading to rejection of the hypothesis that differences exist.) Nevertheless, there is a great difference between manufacturer–user interaction and manufacturer–third-party interaction during product development. The difference can be illustrated by taking a closer look at how the *intensity of interaction* (providing qualitative information) varies during the stages of the product development process.

The intensity of the interaction can be measured along the continuum presented earlier in this chapter. For each case the intensity of all major individual interactive relationships was subjectively assessed by the researcher for each relevant stage of the development process. The results of this analysis are summarized in Figure 6.3, which presents the occurrence in percentages of each level of intensity of interaction at each product development stage. As is demonstrated by the percentages, the intensity of interaction varies dramatically, depending on the stage of the product development process and the counterpart involved. The intensity of manufacturer–user interaction tends to increase during the predevelopment stages: during concept generation and testing, the number of cases with 'no interaction' had dropped to 33 per cent, while typically the intensity of interaction had increased substantially. The intensity of manufacturer–user interaction tends to decrease considerably during the actual development stage (the number of cases with 'no interaction' has nearly doubled). Finally, manufacturer–user interaction is characterized by a peak of 67 per cent at a relatively high level of intensity ('separate performance of activities') during the testing stage and another peak of 38 per cent at a relatively low level of intensity ('use as reference') during the launch stage. The intensity of manufacturer–third-party interaction, on the other hand, tends to increase steadily during the stages of the product development process, only finally to decrease during the trial and launch stages.

The two observed patterns of intensity of interaction should be interpreted differently. While the pattern of manufacturer–third party interaction is just the chance result of a number of different underlying patterns, the pattern of manufacturer–user interaction is of a more general nature. Manufacturers tend to interact with a particular third party (for example a supplier) because of its specific contribution (for example some specific critical knowledge or service). The interaction is determined by the nature of the situation and tends to be incidental, non-recurrent, and based on dependence. A small firm may lack some specific technological know-how and depend on a supplier or university. A medium-sized firm entering a new market may depend on a distributor for market information and access. Thus the nature of the situation strongly determines (1) the type of interaction partner, (2) the stages of the product development process to which the partner will contribute, and (3) the intensity of interaction. The interaction with potential users is quite different. Manufacturers

Figure 6.3 The occurrence of intensity of interaction (expressed as a percentage) during the process of product development

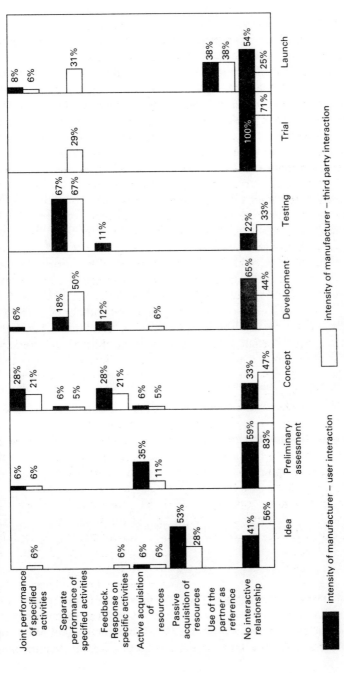

intensity of manufacturer – user interaction

intensity of manufacturer – third party interaction

Source: Biemans, *Technovation*, Elsevier Advanced Technology (April 1991).

are familiar with their target markets and frequently maintain close personal relationships with a number of major customers. As a result, users can be asked to contribute to the concept, development, or testing stage. However, the identity of the users actually employed typically varies with the stage of the product development process. For instance, a firm may interview a relatively large number of potential users during the concept stage, while only one user may be involved in the actual development activities and a selected few in testing the prototype.

PRODUCT DEVELOPMENT WITHIN NETWORKS

In the preceding section we discussed the involvement of both users and third parties in product development processes and focused on the interaction between manufacturers on the one hand, and potential users or various third parties on the other. However, our findings indicate that only four out of the seventeen medical equipment innovations investigated (24 per cent) were developed through a network in its simplest form, that is to say, a single interactive relationship between a manufacturer and a user or third party. Three-quarters (76 per cent) of the innovations studied were developed within networks consisting of a number of different organizations linked together by individual interactive relationships of varying strength, nature, and duration. The relevance of networks is further illustrated by the last column of Table 6.5, which indicates that manufacturers frequently employ *both users and third parties* during the various product development stages.

Simple and complex networks

Thus medical equipment innovations are developed within networks of varying complexity. At the one extreme we found *simple networks* consisting of a single interactive relationship between the manufacturer and a user, university, or inspection agency, while at the other extreme we discovered *complex networks* in which the manufacturer interacted, for example with a university linked with a university hospital, the government, users, and an original equipment manufacturer (OEM). The simple networks were found to suffice when

1 the product development process was uncomplicated, or
2 the manufacturer possessed most of the necessary know-how (and, for instance needed a user only for some specific application knowledge).

Complex networks, on the other hand, were established when

1 the development process involved a very complex innovation,
2 the manufacturer lacked knowledge or expertise with respect to some relevant areas,
3 unanticipated problems arose during product development which necessitated the hiring of specialized organizations, or
4 the manufacturer wanted early market launch to pre-empt the competition.

Based on the occurrence of specific interactive relationships, the various networks can be divided into three categories (see Table 6.8): (1) networks dominated by manufacturer–user interaction, (2) networks dominated by manufacturer–third party interaction, and (3) mixed networks consisting of a manufacturer having major relationships with both users and third parties. The four simple networks investigated were equally distributed over the first two categories.

In the rest of this section we will explore some of the advantages, intricacies, and pitfalls of developing innovations within networks. These will first be demonstrated by describing and analysing the case of AIR in detail, since this case concerns the development of a medical equipment innovation through interaction between a number of essentially different organizations (a manufacturer, a university linked with a university hospital, and an OEM) and illustrates many of the aspects involved. Next, we discuss the most salient short-comings of developing innovations within networks that were noted during our investigation.

Table 6.8 The occurrence of three types of network related to firm size

	Type of network		
Firm size	*Network dominated by manufacturer–user interaction*	*Network dominated by manufacturer–third-party interaction*	*'mixed' network*
Small	2	3	2
Medium	3	2	4
Large	1	0	0
Total	6	5	6

Notes: Small = 50 employees or less
Medium = between 50 and 500 employees
Large = 500 employees or more

Source: Biemans, *Technovation*, Elsevier Advanced Technology (April 1991).

Product development within complex networks; a case study*

Applied Instruments for Respiration (AIR) is a worldwide operating manufacturer, specialized in the development, manufacture, and marketing of instruments used in respirators. Since AIR has specialized in the production of component instruments, rather than entire respirators, AIR's customers are original equipment manufacturers (OEMs) who use AIR's advanced instruments as components of artificial respiration and monitoring systems. This implies that AIR is very dependent on the market information relayed by the OEMs. For example, product specifications are largely formulated by the OEM because of its direct knowledge with respect to user requirements (thus, the OEM is always known at the outset of the product development process). The process of product development at AIR does not finish with a comprehensive market introduction. Individual contracts are entered into with OEMs who carry out the market launch.

A number of years ago a competitor introduced an innovative respirator. However, users experienced major problems with the new product. AIR significantly improved the existing product through the development of an advanced micro-electronic component. This component is built into existing respirators bought from an outside supplier. Subsequently, the modified respirator is sold to an American OEM who integrates it into artificial respiration and monitoring systems used in operating-rooms in hospitals (Figure 6.4). Thus, by the addition of the advanced micro-electronic component, the performance of the whole system is greatly enhanced. Thanks to the implemented technology, AIR has a competitive edge and, although competition will follow, competitors are not expected to introduce similar products in the very near future.

Figure 6.4 The innovation in relation to the whole system

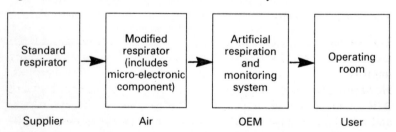

*It should be noted that the names of all organizations mentioned in this case study, as well as the nature of the innovation itself, have been disguised for reasons of confidentiality.

Source: Biemans, *Technovation*, Elsevier Advanced Technology (April 1991).

The product development process

For the sake of clarity, we will divide the process of product development into three separate parts (Figure 6.5). The first part, starting with idea generation and ending with the construction and testing of the original design, is conducted by the Dutch University (DU). The second part, performed by AIR, starts with the development of an industrial prototype and ends with the production of the ultimate product. Finally, the third part, conducted in parallel with the first two parts, consists of the contributions of the OEM to the product development process.

Initiative for the cooperation

The cooperation between AIR and the DU was initiated because of a third party: the government, which aimed at stimulating industry–university cooperation through the granting of credits. AIR's management had discovered an interesting market segment and was searching for a university to provide existing basic knowledge in order to develop and manufacture me-too products. The DU was considered a suitable collaboration partner since (1) the DU possessed the desired expertise and (2) was linked with a university hospital so that a clinical environment was immediately available. The department of Experimental Respiratory Techniques (ERT) of the DU, on the other hand, wanted to develop an innovative product and was looking for an industrial partner to provide the necessary funds. Eventually, a contract was drawn up: AIR would sponsor experimental research to be conducted by the DU and in return would obtain the desired technological know-how. Furthermore, AIR would have first claim on any new product developed as a result of the experimental research.

The Dutch University

The Department of Experimental Respiratory Techniques of the Dutch University looked at the development of a significantly improved version of the existing product as an ideal project. However, due to the supposed limited size of the market segment AIR's management did not express interest in this specific application and would rather have the DU concentrate on more traditional applications. Thanks to the persistence of the university researchers, the development project was eventually approved by AIR. These differences between the objectives and expectations of AIR and the DU

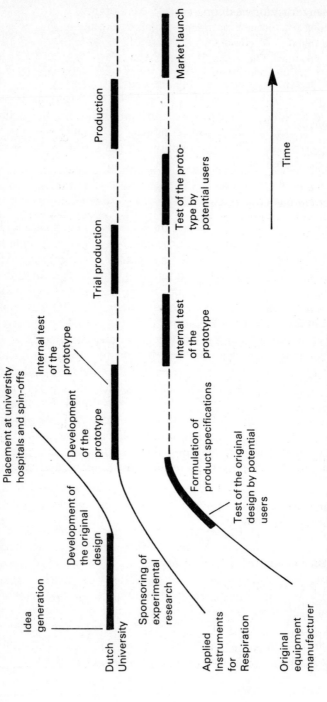

Figure 6.5 The contributions of the three major parties to the product development process

Source: Biemans, *Technovation*, Elsevier Advanced Technology (April 1991).

led to many frustrations during product development.

The idea for the new product originated with the engineers at the DU as a reaction to complaints expressed by users with respect to an existing product. The product specifications were drawn up in the course of an intensive dialogue between engineers of the DU and physicians of the university hospital. The requirements formulated by the users were combined with the technological possibilities and development of the original design commenced. After almost two years, an original design had been developed which, compared with the existing product, represented a significant improvement. It was tested both by the engineers (internal technical test) and on patients. During the next six months it was demonstrated at various national and international congresses to obtain response from users. The first reactions were positive and the DU was contacted by an OEM who expressed interest in marketing the product. Since the DU lacked both the ability and the interest in manufacturing the product, the OEM was referred to AIR. Only when AIR was confronted with this potential customer was enthusiasm for the project displayed.

Applied Instruments for Respiration

The user was involved in the development process through the close collaboration between physicians and engineers in developing the original design. The development activities at Applied Instruments for Respiration were based on user requirements too, since the OEM provided most of the product specifications. The OEM's knowledge of the market was very important in guiding product development at AIR. Theoretically, AIR could turn this knowledge into profit by selling to other OEMs as well. Therefore, the contract stipulated that for a period of one year after first delivery, AIR was not allowed to sell to other OEMs. The development activities at AIR took more than one year since several important aspects of the developed original design needed to be modified.

The original equipment manufacturer

Initially, the original equipment manufacturer had started a similar development project. However, when it learned of AIR's development activities, it decided to terminate its own development project and cooperate with AIR. A separate project would take too much time and, through cooperating with AIR and demanding exclusivity during a specified period, the OEM could obtain a lead on potential competitors. The OEM was involved in the product development process in five different ways.

1 The OEM tested some units of the original design with users in the United States. Thus a more universal response was obtained, while the information acquired could be used to draw up the product specifications.
2 In collaboration with AIR, the OEM formulated the product specifications.
3 The OEM duplicated the internal (technical) tests performed by AIR with the prototype. In addition, the OEM conducted a number of specialized technical tests which AIR could not conduct itself.
4 The OEM conducted the external tests because of its existing relationships with users. The prototype was sent to the OEM in the United States, who subsequently sent it to customers all over the world. The test results were used by AIR to finalize the design.
5 Obviously, the OEM carried out the last stages of the product development process, that is introducing and marketing the product.

Advantages and disadvantages

The case description demonstrates that the innovation was developed through cooperation between many different parties, the most important parties being a university linked with a university hospital, an industrial supplier of component instruments, and a supplier of whole systems. This resulted in overlaps, duplications, simultaneous developments, and spin-offs. For example, while AIR sponsored the development of the original design, the OEM had started a comparable development project. At a later time, the DU placed the original design at other university hospitals' disposal for scientific research which resulted in various spin-offs. The whole network is presented in Figure 6.6.

Developing a new product through close cooperation between a number of different organizations linked together to form a comprehensive network offers obvious *advantages* to the parties involved.

1 The contribution to the product development process of every party involved can be limited to its own specialized activities. For example, because of its existing direct relationships with users, the OEM is best suited to conduct the external tests.
2 Deficiencies caused by one party at an early stage of the develop-

Figure 6.6 The complete network

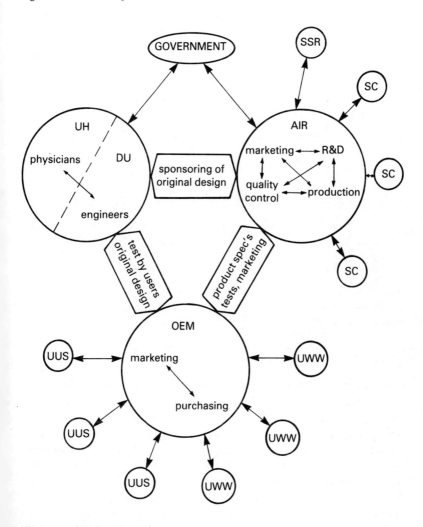

UH = university hospital
DU = Dutch University
AIR = Applied Instruments for Respiration
OEM = original equipment manufacturer
SSR = supplier of standard respirator
SC = supplier of component
UUS = user United States
UWW= user worldwide

Source: Biemans, *Technovation*, Elsevier Advanced Technology (April 1991).

ment process can be corrected by another party at a later stage. For example, the substantial involvement of users in developing the industrial prototype (by means of the comprehensive product specifications based on market information supplied by the OEM) compensated for the limited involvement of users in developing the original design.

However, the case of AIR exemplifies some major *disadvantages* of product development within complex networks as well.

1 Overrating of each other's capabilities may result in friction and misunderstanding between the partners.
2 The limited involvement of users in developing the original design may slow down the development of the industrial prototype.
3 Further delays may be caused by inefficiently conducted activities (for example the external tests).
4 Involvement of various parties in product development may lead to duplication of some activities; for example, developing and testing both an original design and an industrial prototype.

These disadvantages could have been prevented or reduced through more intensive cooperation and open communication between all parties involved.

Internal versus external networks

Analysis of the cases investigated leads us to conclude that networks should be considered at two different levels. While each of the major parties involved in the product development process is part of a large *external network*, every one of them has its own *internal network* as well. An illustration is provided by the network depicted in figure 6.6. The successful development of the original design within the DU necessitated close cooperation between engineers from the department of Experimental Respiratory Techniques and physicians at the university hospital. The successful translation of the original design into an industrial new product by AIR was made possible through effective communication and coordination between the departments of marketing, R&D, production, and quality control. Finally, the purchasing and marketing departments of the original equipment manufacturer had to coordinate their activities. The distinction between external and internal networks is crucial, since *the functioning of each of the internal networks directly influences the efficiency and efficacy of the external network*. Thus, the old saying 'a chain is no stronger than its weakest link' proves to be relevant to the management of innovation processes as well.

> This is also demonstrated by the case of Sentrex, where the geographical distance between the marketing department on the one hand, and the departments of R&D, production, and quality control on the other, formed a serious impediment for the successful development of new products.

Shortcomings during product development within networks

Although practically every case investigated has its own idiosyncratic problems, comparison of all individual cases uncovers a number of general problem areas regarding the development of medical equipment innovations within networks. In this section we will present the most salient of these deficiencies, concerning:

1 integration of marketing and R&D,
2 performance of the predevelopment activities,
3 resources allocated to the actual development activities,
4 testing prototypes with users,
5 timing of the market launch,
6 use of the names and reputations of users during market launch,
7 cooperation between industrial firms and universities, and
8 specific problems of small firms.

Integration of marketing and R&D

When asked about their firm's general product development strategy, only two of the managers interviewed responded by characterizing it as being a *balanced mixture of R&D and marketing* (Table 6.9). Five of the thirteen firms investigated maintained that they based their new product development predominantly on *future-oriented R&D* activities. Three of these firms were quite small in size, very much technology oriented and lacked any formal marketing department. In one of them the marketing activities were undertaken by engineers with some commercial knowledge, while in the two other firms marketing activities were practically absent. The remaining two medium-sized firms were in transition from basing the development of new products on research and development activities alone to founding it on a careful balance between directed research and development activities and a clearly formulated marketing strategy. Finally, almost half of the

Table 6.9 The general product development strategy related to firm size

Firm size	Product development strategy		
	Future oriented R&D	*Marketing*	*Balanced strategy*
Small	3	2	0
Medium	2	4	1
Large	0	0	1
Total	5	6	2

Notes: Small = 50 employees or less
Medium = between 50 and 500 employees
Large = 500 employees or more

firms let *marketing considerations* guide their product development activities. However, only a minority of them employed a formal marketing plan to guide the product development process. Instead, most firms relied on an explicitly stated market introduction strategy. In general, the firms studied showed a growing awareness of the need to integrate marketing with the product development activities. However, at present this objective has been realized by only a small minority.

It should be stressed that the strategy of having product development guided by a balanced mixture of marketing and R&D (in the sense of paying equal attention to both factors) should not automatically be considered the ideal one. Individual cases illustrate that the best strategy strongly depends on the situation involved.

Mijnhardt is the only Dutch firm specialized in the development, production, and marketing of lung function diagnosis equipment. As technological developments have slowed considerably in this particular industry, Mijnhardt has adopted the strategy of combining available technologies to develop new products that offer the user an improved solution with distinct advantages. Marketing is clearly involved in all stages of the product development process: potential users comment on new-product ideas, well-known specialists criticize initial prototypes, and several groups of widely different users test prototypes under actual user conditions.

Performance of predevelopment activities

The findings of our investigation into the development of innovations in the Dutch medical equipment industry lend partial support to Cooper's conclusion with respect to the predevelopment activities, that 'it is these early stages ... that often receive the least management attention and resources, and are so often found lacking in industrial firms' new product processes' (Cooper, 1988, p. 241). According to our results, in only one of the cases investigated was the manufacturer not involved in the predevelopment stages. However, in many of the remaining cases, the manufacturer was actively involved in these early stages but carried out the activities inadequately. A closer look at the cases reveals that the inadequate performance of the predevelopment activities takes many forms.

Not undertaking preliminary assessment

As mentioned above, in one case the manufacturer was not involved in the predevelopment activities.

> Eye-Tech was approached by university researchers with a functioning original design. Enthusiasm on the part of a director carried the firm directly, that is to say, without performing a preliminary assessment, into actual product development. Only after quite some resources had been spent on redeveloping the prototype, was a market assessment undertaken and it was discovered that a broader (and profitable!) market did not exist for this particular innovation.

The case of Eye-Tech serves to illustrate the importance of undertaking a comprehensive preliminary assessment. Execution of this stage is essential in order to check the product's characteristics against general user requirements. Other firms, that were approached by users or third parties with a new product (idea), generally found that the developed original design (or product concept) needed to be considerably modified in order to satisfy more universal user requirements.

Involving only one type of cooperation partner

The majority of the firms took insufficient advantage of the different types of cooperation partners who were available. Thus, for example, in six of the cases studied the firms confined themselves to acquiring information from their major customers and neglected to use other potential sources of relevant information, such as distributors (who typically possess a broader view of the market), industry experts (who can provide information regarding general trends in technology and the market), inspection agencies (which can assist in drawing up product specifications), research institutes (which have information with respect to new technological developments), and competitors (who can provide first-hand information about product specifications and production techniques).

Because of previous negative experiences with involving users in the product development process, Medsound decided to change its strategy. The firm hired a limited number of knowledgeable users to assist in the development process and focuses on inter-action with third parties. For instance, in developing the innovation investigated Medsound closely cooperated with a German inspection agency (the Technischer Überwachungs-verein). The interaction was limited to this one particular agency, because (1) it made high demands on new products and (2) interaction with additional inspection agencies would have been too expensive.

Involving a limited number of cooperation partners

In addition to limiting themselves to just one type of cooperation partner, mostly major customers, during the predevelopment activi-ties, in three cases the firm made the mistake of relying on just one customer. In four other cases firms were satisfied with incorporating user requirements in their product specifications through a dialogue with one particular user, but supplemented it by interacting with one or two third parties, such as universities, a research institute, a competitor, and an original equipment manufacturer.

Neglecting to apply well-considered selection criteria

As can be seen from Table 6.7, in only eight cases was the selection of users (chosen to generate and screen new product ideas, provide user information, and generate and evaluate product concepts) based on such well-considered criteria as representativeness and the available expertise. In two of the cases studied, users were selected on the basis of rather arbitrary criteria, while in another four cases the manufacturer was approached by a user and neglected to interact with other potential users during the predevelopment stages. Typically, the selection of research institutes and other third parties was based on such objective criteria as the available know-how.

Performing the predevelopment activities superficially

About a quarter of the firms investigated combined many of the deficiencies noted above in quickly and superficially carrying out the predevelopment activities (Table 6.10). Typically, this course of action was rationalized by saying 'We have been selling on this particular market for years; we know how many customers there are and know exactly what they want'. Thus, the predevelopment activities can be characterized as having been performed only perfunctorily in four cases, reasonably in five cases, and well in seven cases.

Inadequate performance of the predevelopment activities may result in problems during later stages of the product development process. In most cases this meant that the actual development activities took much longer than expected, leading to increased development costs, a prolonged product development process, and a postponed market launch, thus giving competitors ample opportunity to catch up with their own development activities (cf. Leiva and Obermayer, 1989, p. 48).

Allocation of resources to the actual development activities

Typically, the firms studied tended to underestimate the time, money, and resources needed for the actual development activities, that is the employment of technological resources, such as R&D, engineering,

Table 6.10 Performance of the predevelopment activities related to firm size

| | *Performance of predevelopment activities* | | |
Firm size	*Perfunctory*	*Reasonable*	*Well*
Small	2	3	2
Medium	2	2	4
Large	0	0	1
Total	4	5	7

Notes: Small = 50 employees or less
Medium = between 50 and 500 employees
Large = 500 employees or more

and industrial design, to the transformation of product specifications (the product concept) into a prototype. The majority of the managers interviewed admitted that the actual development activities had taken longer than planned. In general, they stated that both the experienced risks and the total costs involved were considerably larger than anticipated. Product development processes (from idea generation till market introduction) that took up to twice as long as planned proved to be the rule rather than the exception.

Also in the case of a manufacturer who is approached by university researchers who developed and built an original design, adequate resources must be allocated to the redevelopment activities. The findings of our investigation clearly show that in these cases the developed device typically needs to be considerably modified before it is suitable for large-scale industrial production and satisfies more universal user requirements.

In cooperation with a physician of the Groningen University Hospital, a number of researchers from the University of Twente developed a prototype of a measuring instrument for use in obstetrics and proved its value through use in practice. Applied Laser Technology, a small manufacturer specialized in laser applications, was asked to manufacture and market the innovation. Because of various technical problems it took about a year and a half to redevelop the product and get it ready for market introduction.

Testing prototypes with users; validation and elaboration of the tentative framework

The majority of the firms investigated (69 per cent, see table 6.4) reported to interact predominantly with potential users during the process of product development. The interaction was mentioned as occurring particularly during the testing and launch stages, as would be expected, since users who have tested the prototype can be employed for promotional purposes during market launch. This general strategy is reflected by the fact that in 75 per cent of the cases studied the manufacturer employed users to test a newly developed prototype (Table 6.5); this number closely corresponds with the 70 per cent found by both Cooper and Kleinschmidt (1986, p. 79) and Moore (1987, p. 14). While the firm's in-house tests mainly concern the innovation's technical aspects, particularly its technical functioning and electrical safety, the clinical tests with users serve a totally different purpose. These are generally undertaken as a last check on the match between the product characteristics and user requirements and to discover any problems that may arise in actual use of the product in a clinical environment. Despite the manifest importance of undertaking clinical tests, in many of the cases investigated the firm paid insufficient attention to this critical stage of the product development process. The results suggest a series of eleven critical activities (cf. the tentative model presented in Chapter 5).

Activity 1: Planning

Four of the thirteen innovations that actually reached the market were introduced without ever having been clinically tested by potential users. In all cases the firms in question displayed an excessive amount of confidence in their own technical abilities and the functioning of the product. Based on the initial positive results of the in-house tests, two products were modified slightly and subsequently introduced. A clinical evaluation was not thought to be necessary. In another case, a firm started production directly on the basis of product specifications formulated by a distributor. After having been confronted with subsequent failure in the market, the firm had to start from scratch and formulate new product specifications. Eventually, the prototype was tested by a user, but this concerned only the product's safety rather than its functioning in a clinical environment. Finally, the fourth case concerns Medsound which decided against testing prototypes with users as a matter of principle. The decision was based on prior negative experiences with gynaecologists who were afraid to injure their patients by using unsafe new products and tested a new prototype only superficially on themselves. Although, by skipping the clinical evaluation stage, a firm may manage to stay ahead of the competition, it is at the same time running the risk of launching an imperfect product.

Activity 2: Timing

In two other cases the firms involved launched the new product prematurely owing to pressure of time. In one case this was due to an important trade show while, in the other case, an impending annual sales meeting rushed the firm into an untimely market introduction. Typically, at the outset of the project, the products had been scheduled for introduction during the trade show or sales meeting, but the actual development activities took longer than was anticipated. In order to achieve the scheduled introduction date (market launch between two important trade shows or sales meetings was generally considered useless), the clinical testing stage was carried out prematurely and/or carelessly. This resulted in the initiation of redevelopment activities, modification of the product, strained relationships with distributors and customers, loss of credibility in the market, and a postponed market launch.

Activity 3: Determining the number of users

Although undertaking clinical evaluations may be an important determinant of the product's eventual success, its influence largely depends on both the number and quality of the users involved. Table 6.11 shows that, in six cases, the firms employed more than three users to test the developed prototype, the large majority of these firms being of medium size. In four cases the prototype was tested by only one user. Sometimes this limited quantitative user involvement can hardly be avoided.

In developing its very expensive and complex medical equipment, Philips Medical Systems often feels compelled to use just one site to test a prototype. The high investments and the essential intensive interaction with the user prevents the use of more than one beta site.

Table 6.11 The number of users involved in clinical evaluation related to firm size

| Firm size | Number of users | | |
	One	Two or three	⩾ Four
Small	2	1	1
Medium	1	1	5
Large	1	0	0
Total	4	2	6

Notes: Small = 50 employees or less
Medium = between 50 and 500 employees
Large = 500 employees or more

Table 6.12 Criteria used for selecting test users related to firm size

		Selection critera			
Firm size	Not selected	Knowledge	Commercial potentialities	Existing relationship	Geographical proximity	Representativeness
Small	1	2	3	1	0	1
Medium	1	6	3	5	1	0
Large	0	1	0	1	1	0
Total	2	9	6	7	2	1

Notes: Small = 50 employees or less
Medium = between 50 and 500 employees
Large = 500 employees or more

Activity 4: Selection of users

The firms investigated reported a wide variety of criteria for selecting users to test newly developed prototypes (table 6.12). In nine cases (75 per cent of the cases where users tested a prototype) the *reputed know-how* of the medical specialist or hospital in question was reported to be a major selection criterion. An *existing relationship* was mentioned seven times as a selection criterion. Often a specific university hospital with a positive attitude towards the manufacturer and its products was habitually employed to test new prototypes. The *perceived commercial potentialities* were mentioned in only half of the cases as an important reason in selecting users to test prototypes. In these cases the choice was generally based on the reputation of the specific physician (or institute) involved, and the willingness to test prototypes, publish the results, present the findings at national and international conferences, and promote the new product with colleagues. This figure of 50 per cent should be regarded as being low, due to the obvious link between the testing and launch stages. In two cases the 'selection' was based on a *chance contact*, that is the manufacturer was approached by a user with a new product idea, after which the manufacturer commenced development activities and employed the same user for testing the prototype. Because of the need for intensive interaction, culminating in frequent visits to the customer, *geographical proximity* of the user was considered to be a great advantage by the manufacturer in two other cases. Finally, in only one case the manufacturer mentioned the *representativeness* of the user for the specific market segment as strongly influencing the selection of user sites.

Activity 5: Formulation of objectives

Nearly all the firms employed users to test their prototypes with the explicit objective of testing the new product under actual conditions in a clinical environment.

The one exception concerns Spinex, a small-sized manufacturer of an innovative ultra-low-temperature freezer, who asked a hospital's technical department to test the electrical safety of the innovation (thus changing the character of the beta test and making it a simple technical test).

Activity 6: Instruction

Without exception, the firms provided the users with instructions as to the innovation's operation. In one case the complex nature of the prototype demanded extensive training of the physicians and nurses who would have to use the equipment.

> The importance of instruction is further illustrated by the case of Medsound mentioned above: by improving the instruction of the physicians and registration of the test results (by determining the desired format of the needed information and informing the physicians of it) Medsound could use gynaecologists to evaluate prototypes meaningfully.

Activity 7: Execution

In two of the cases investigated the execution of the clinical evaluations also left something to be desired. Eye-Tech had an important hospital clinically evaluate a prototype while (the slightly modified) units of the trial production were already available. In the case of AIR, due to the involvement of an OEM who had direct relationships with users, the clinical evaluations were undertaken somewhat inefficiently. For example, AIR would ship the product to the OEM in the USA, who would then send it to a German user to have it tested. After completion of the test, the results would be sent back to the OEM and finally relayed to AIR again. This resulted in delays and possibly in distorted information as well.

Activity 8: Support and control

In a limited number of cases the managers interviewed commented on the need to visit the user frequently during the execution of the clinical evaluation.

> In the case of Philips Medical Systems (selling very complex and expensive medical equipment), an engineer was present at the user site one day per week to instruct the operators, answer questions, solve problems, obtain first-hand information, demonstrate new software, and check the equipment's functioning and the way it is used.

Activities 9 and 10: Registration and evaluation

Despite the importance of clinical evaluations and the need for detailed and structured information, in only half of the cases investigated did the manufacturer affirm the need for and existence of comprehensive formalized evaluation protocols (Table 6.13). In specific situations, such as the case of Vitatron which manufactures pacemakers, quite elaborate evaluation protocols are demanded by the government because of the involved potential dangers to the patient. In the other 50 per cent of the cases the firm relied on oral information from the user. It should be noted that three-quarters of the small firms testing prototypes with users relied on oral information. One manager (of a small firm with no existing relationships in the field of medical technology) justified it by saying 'You cannot ask them to fill out comprehensive forms; you should be glad that they are willing even to talk to you!'

Activity 11: Follow-up

Considering the criteria used in selecting potential users to test prototypes, the most obvious kind of follow-up to the clinical evaluation stage is having the same users assist in launching the innovation. The involvement of reputable physicians or institutes in the launching stage lends additional credibility to the manufacturer's claims and confirms the user's reputation in the medical field. Nevertheless, only 60 per cent of the innovations clinically evaluated by users were subsequently launched by the manufacturer with the assistance of these users (see also the section entitled 'Employing users as references during market introduction').

Table 6.13 The mode of evaluating clinical test results related to firm size

	Mode of evaluation	
Firm size	*Oral evaluation*	*Evaluation protocol*
Small	3	1
Medium	3	4
Large	0	1
Total	6	6

Notes: Small = 50 employees or less
Medium = between 50 and 500 employees
Large = 500 employees or more

The framework firmly embeds the external testing stage in the process of product development. Planning and timing of the tests are carried out in advance, while the follow-up links the external tests to the market introduction. Awareness of these interrelationships between the various stages of the development process enables managers to plan and carry out the external tests efficiently while fully capitalizing on its opportunities.

The general conclusion is that successful beta testing consists of paying attention to a large number of critical activities. Numerous examples from actual practice illustrate how relationships with major customers may be impaired because of mistakes made during external testing. However, careful design of this critical stage of the development process provides the manager with a veritable wealth of essential information.

Mijnhardt, a manufacturer of lung function diagnosis equipment, had a prototype tested extensively by four groups of potential users: (1) a barracks, with military athletes in top condition to test the functioning at the upper end, (2) a hospital, with real patients to obtain clinical information, (3) a business firm, that intended to measure large numbers of employees, to test the durability and user friendliness of the device, and (4) healthy young children to test the prototype's functioning at the bottom end. Furthermore, at the time of the investigation additional tests were planned with very young sick patients to test the product under even more extreme circumstances.

The evidence demonstrates that manufacturer–user relationships in the context of testing newly developed prototypes frequently display symptoms of ossification. Once relationships are established and strengthened by good personal contacts, they tend to function during a number of successive development projects. Long-term relationships with a limited number of high-quality physicians/ hospitals are established in which the very existence of a relationship, rather than the characteristics of the project, determines the co-operation. Needless to say, this need not represent the ideal situation: a well-functioning personal relationship is no guarantee for good results (in this case: high-quality information).

The experiences and activities of the firms investigated largely support the tentative model for testing prototypes with potential product users as formulated in Chapter 5. All the steps distinguished in the original model were identified during the follow-up investigation in the medical equipment industry. Apart from this, the cases investigated point to the need to discern two additional steps, that is 'planning the external testing stage' and 'determining the number of users to test the prototype'.

Timing of market launch

The timing of the market introduction has often been cited in the literature on product development as an important determinant of the innovation's success. As regards complex medical equipment, the right time to introduce a new product may be strongly determined by a limited number of annually organized (inter)national *trade shows*. These trade shows are very important to the manufacturer, since they attract a significant number of potential users, who come to acquaint themselves with the latest technological developments. For this reason, many firms commented on the need to be present at certain selected trade shows, while launching a new product between two important trade shows may be considered less effective and require substantial additional support of promotional effort. In four of the cases studied, an annual trade show or sales meeting greatly influenced the scheduling of the product development efforts. In three of these cases the resulting tight schedule led to an untimely showing of the product at either a trade show or sales meeting.

In response to a new-product introduction by a major competitor, Eye-Tech developed an improved version of the product with distinct user benefits. The developed prototype was tested in-house, demonstrated at an important annual trade show for end users, and tested by a local hospital. Based on the positive results, the product was subsequently launched during an annual sales meeting and clinically tested by a number of hospitals in the Netherlands and abroad. After modifying some details of the product's design, the first production run of twenty-five units was started. One of these units was tested by an evaluation centre in Germany. While the first orders generated by the enthusiastic dealers arrived, some essential defects were uncovered by the German centre. This necessitated (1) stopping delivery, (2) taking back and modifying all units already delivered, and (3) discouraging further demand generated by the dealers.

Firms may shorten the duration of the total product development process by consciously skipping the clinical evaluation stage, as was done in four of the cases investigated (31 per cent of the innovations that were actually launched). The clinical evaluations were skipped because of (1) confidence in the technical abilities of the firm, (2) confidence in the functioning of the product, and (3) lack of confidence in the ability of physicians to evaluate prototypes meaningfully. In one case the product failed in the market and the firm started reformulating the product specifications anew.

Nowadays, in addition to the hardware, complex medical equipment increasingly contains the software needed to control and direct the product's operation. The case of Philips Medical Systems illustrates how this may suggest another way to advance the time of market launch, namely by means of a *basic package introduction*. According to this strategy, the firm develops and introduces the hardware and the basic software, consisting of (1) the operating software and (2) software to perform the innovation's most basic functions, that is the 'basic package'. Additional software (various clinical programs) can be developed after launching the basic package and can be introduced in a number of subsequent releases. The most significant advantage is obvious. The hardware plus the accompanying basic software can be introduced relatively early, resulting in market penetration at an early stage, a competitive advantage, and confirmation of the firm's innovative image (leading to a prominent position in the minds of leading physicians). However, this strategy entails some potential disadvantages, too. Although most of the software is launched in future releases, it must be compatible with the previously introduced hardware and therefore be specified quite early in the development process, which calls for detailed planning and coordination. Despite these efforts, the firm may run into problems in developing the clinical programs that were already announced at the time of launching the basic package. Delayed introduction of announced releases may give the customer the impression that the manufacturer does not live up to his promises, thus impairing the firm's reputation. In addition, certain clinical programs found to be of interest to physicians, but that were not foreseen at the time of designing the basic package, may prove to be incompatible with the hardware of the basic package. Therefore, the development of such programs may have to be postponed until it is time (that is until it has become profitable) to develop and introduce a second, updated version of the hardware.

Employing users as references during market launch

It was noted before that the firms investigated interacted predominantly with potential users during the testing and launch stages. This reflects a conscious strategy, as users who have tested a prototype can be employed for promotional purposes during market launch. For this reason, these users may be referred to as *launching customers* and some manufacturers do speak of *luminary sites* when selecting users to test prototypes.

In addition to potential users, manufacturers sometimes have specialized research institutes test their newly developed prototypes. Often these tests by external organizations are necessary to obtain a needed 'sign of approval', but naturally these test results may also be used for promotional purposes during market launch. An example (mentioned previously) concerns Enraf-Nonius, which uses the evaluative reports of The Netherlands Organization for Applied Scientific Research (TNO) during market launch as support from an independent research institute.

As has been shown previously (see Table 6.12), the 'reputed know-how', an 'existing relationship', and the perceived 'commercial potentialities' were by far most frequently mentioned as criteria in selecting test users. This particular combination of criteria appears to point to the regular use during market launch of reputable physicians or institutes which, mostly due to their repeatedly proven medical expertise, occupy central positions in the medical community. However, the results of our investigation do not fully support this observation. The findings show that ten of the thirteen innovations that actually reached the market were clinically evaluated by users, while just six of these (that is 60 per cent) were introduced with the help of these users. This number is surprisingly low, even more so, as informal communication and opinion leadership have often been said to be of great importance in institutional markets (Webster, 1971, p. 187; Schiffman and Gaccione, 1974). Apparently, manufacturers do consider the commercial potentialities in selecting test users, but fail to capitalize on the opportunities thus generated during market launch. This is further illustrated by the fact that those manufacturers who do employ users during market introduction, only do so marginally. Typically, they employ users only by using the name of the physician or institute involved in promotional material and during sales presentations (for example by including such remarks as 'extensively tested and approved by ...'). However, test users may be employed in a variety of ways during market launch:

1 having the physician or institute demonstrate the new equipment to other potential buyers;
2 having the test user publish scientific articles about the innovation (especially articles that compare the innovation's performance with that of competing products are suitable for promotional purposes);
3 stimulating the test user to deliver talks or present papers at trade shows and scientific conferences;
4 employing the test user to distribute the innovation.

AIR, a medium-sized manufacturer of instruments used in respiratory equipment, collaborated with researchers of a university in developing an innovation. After the development project was finished representatives from both parties gave a joint presentation during an important national trade show. Rather than using the time for an extensive discussion of the product's unique features, they focused on the problems encountered in the course of the project and the measures taken to solve them.

Industry–university cooperation

In four out of the seventeen cases studied university researchers developed the original design or contributed substantially to the development of the prototype. In three of them, both university researchers and physicians from a university hospital were involved in the development project through intensive interaction. In addition, there were numerous instances where industrial firms interacted with universities in order to have the latter develop parts of the product, test prototypes, or solve technological problems. Due to the essentially different nature of industrial firms and universities, such cooperation was frequently accompanied by a number of problems. While these are partly of a general nature, some of them are specific to industry–university cooperation. The collective experiences of the firms involved led to the formulation of the following recommendations.

State the objective of the cooperation, the expectations, and the criteria for evaluation

At the outset of the cooperation project, both partners should unequivocally state their objectives, their expectations, and the criteria they will use to evaluate the cooperation, since they need not concur.

These three aspects are perfectly illustrated by the case of AIR.

(1) *Objectives* The university cooperated with industry to obtain funds for conducting experimental research in exchange for existing knowledge. AIR, on the other hand, was looking for the basic technological know-how required to develop and manufacture me-too products.

(3) *Expectations* The university expected to use the funds to develop a new diagnostic method of interest to the academic community. AIR expected the university to assist during the start-up of production and to conduct clinical tests with prototypes.

(2) *Criteria for evaluation* The university would consider the cooperation with AIR to be successful if it led to more scientific publications, increased project efficiency, faster clinical experience, improved diagnostics, and enhanced status and competitive scientific position. AIR, on the other hand, would characterize the cooperation as being successful if it resulted in a shortened start-up period, lowered costs, higher product quality, critical external quality assessment, and inexpensive access to a 'brain tank'.

These differences led to lack of commitment, unclear agreements, and delays and inefficiencies during the development process.

Make clear-cut agreements

In order to prevent frustrations and misunderstandings, at the outset of the cooperation project the parties involved should make clear-cut agreements about publication of the research results by the university researchers, the activities to be carried out by each party, and the accompanying time schedule. Specific attention should be paid to the division of responsibilities; ideally, the final responsibility and authority should rest with one person. In the case of AIR, the divergent objectives and expectations were partly responsible for the absence of such clear-cut agreements.

Start the cooperation at an early stage of development

In two cases university researchers were found to contact industrial firms only after the original design had already been developed. This resulted either in costly delays since the original design had to be modified considerably, or in termination of the development project since the innovation's market potential was found to be unattractive.

Conduct market research to evaluate a developed original design

When an industrial firm is contacted by a university that has developed an original design, the firm should conduct substantial market research in order to evaluate the innovation's commercial attractiveness. Such a market study is necessary to determine general user requirements and estimate market potential. The market study should be supplemented by an evaluation of the technological requirements and opportunities. In two cases the firms neglected to conduct such a preliminary assessment. In one of them enthusiasm for the project was not based on the results of an extensive market study, but rather on the interest displayed by an original equipment manufacturer.

Allocate sufficient time, money, and resources to the redevelopment activities

In general, the industrial firms investigated tended seriously to underestimate the time, money, and resources needed to transform the original design developed by university researchers into a commercially viable industrial product. For instance, initially Applied Laser Technology hardly spent any time on redevelopment of the original design and introduced it too early at a trade show. Typically, the small-scale production techniques used by a university in a laboratory proved to be unsuitable for large-scale industrial production.

Show commitment to the cooperation project

When an industrial firm cooperates with a university to obtain a developed and tested original design, both parties should display commitment to the project. For example, from the manufacturer's perspective, approving a university research programme and providing part of the necessary funds is not sufficient for a fruitful collaboration. Instead, the firm needs to participate in the development activities in order to demonstrate commitment and ascertain that its own objectives are being met.

Develop and maintain good personal relationships

Even when sufficient resources are allocated to a cooperation project and the necessary agreements are put down in writing, the collaboration may still fail. As success ultimately depends very much on the people involved, great care should be taken to establish close and well-functioning personal relationships (see also van Dierdonck *et al.*, 1990, p. 564). In the case of Medlab, the sub-optimal personal relationship between the representatives of two parties hindered effective collaboration.

Demonstrate and accommodate for flexibility

An intensive and long-term cooperation project requires flexibility of the partners involved. For example, the contract should accommodate for enough flexibility, so that changed circumstances (such as market conditions or strategic considerations) can be met by the appropriate actions. Examples are provided by Eye-Tech, which terminated an advanced development project when a profitable market was found to be non-existent, and Medlab, which terminated a collaboration project as soon as the partner in question was expected to be unable to supply additional relevant information.

An issue that warrants special attention in the context of intensive industry–university cooperation is the *transfer of the original design* from the university researchers to the industrial firm. Due to mutual misunderstanding and overrating/underrating, this transfer may be a major source of friction between both parties. Typically, the university researchers expect the developed original design to be only slightly modified before start-up of production and underestimate the extent of development needed to be undertaken by the industrial firm. The firms, on the other hand, typically overestimate the capabilities of the universities by expecting them to develop industrial prototypes. These problems may be significantly reduced if industrial firms and universities establish open communication and cooperate more closely during product development.

Take, for example the joint development project at AIR and the Dutch University. Instead of limiting itself to sponsoring experimental research at the DU, AIR could have assisted in the development of the original design (thus incorporating the requirements of the industrial firm at an early stage of development). Next, the DU could assist AIR in translating the original design into an industrial prototype (thus applying the knowledge and experience acquired through developing the original design). Such a set-up would not only prevent many frustrations and misunderstandings, but would also shorten the duration of the development project and reduce total development costs.

In all instances of joint development, close attention should be paid to project management, that is the division of tasks and responsibilities, documentation, and drawing up clear-cut agreements and procedures. If project managers are appointed at both the university and the industrial firm, the communication and coordination at the interpersonal level assume the utmost importance. Trust, openness, and commitment become the key concepts determining the eventual success of the cooperation.

It should be noted that, while communication problems caused by different cultures appear to be at the heart of the problem, their existence may depend on the size of the industrial firm. If a medium-sized firm cooperates with a university, communication problems are generally to be expected. If, on the other hand, the industry–university cooperation concerns a large-sized firm, serious communication problems are less likely because the R&D cultures at both organizations are rather similar (Riedle, 1989, p. 220). Finally, in the case of small firms, the widely differing R&D cultures tend to foster communication problems. In addition, it should be noted that experience with industry–university linkages is expected to reduce the cultural differences which may exist between both worlds (van Dierdonck *et al.*, 1990, p. 563).

Specific problems of small firms

More than one-third of the firms investigated (five out of thirteen) are characterized as being small, that is having fifty employees or less. Although these firms for the most part encountered the same problems as the somewhat larger firms, due to their small size they experienced some specific problems, too. These additional problems relate to the functional interdependence, availability of cash, and existence of marketing expertise and realistic GO/NO GO decisions.

Strong functional interdependence

In all of the small firms, various problem areas, such as finance, organization, product development, marketing, and production, were found to be strongly intertwined. Thus the marketing decisions, problems, and activities could not be considered separately from the overall running of the company.

Applied Laser Technology redeveloped an original design built by researchers at a university in cooperation with a physician at a university hospital. After having spent about one year on redevelopment (during which numerous problems were solved), a prototype was ready for production. However, at that time ALT did not possess enough funds to start production. Partly because of this limitation, the firm started redevelopment activities again and over the next eight months improved the design. After this substantial delay the prototype was tested worldwide at five different sites and the product was finally introduced on various markets abroad. Thus, the deteriorated financial position determined the outcome of fundamental marketing-related decisions during product development.

Limited cash funds

Typically, the limited cash available in small companies had major effects on their own activities and dealings with other organizations.

1 Two very small firms (five or six employees) reported they were heavily dependent on subsidies. One of them even went so far as to mention the grant of a subsidy as a major criterion in selecting and initiating new product development projects.
2 Functioning and promising prototypes, developed by university researchers, cannot be paid for with a lump sum. Instead, the university has to be satisfied with a certain percentage of future sales, thus severely limiting their bargaining position.
3 Each of the small firms investigated mentioned that they could afford only one or two development projects at a time. Although this simplifies the management of the product development

process, it makes the company's continuation strongly dependent upon the success of just a few products.

No real marketing expertise

All of the five small firms investigated did not possess any real marketing knowledge. Typically, no special marketing department existed and the marketing function was fulfilled by the general director of the firm or an engineer with limited commercial training. The very small firms were strongly technology oriented and relied on their distributors for the relevant marketing information.

No realistic GO/NO GO decisions

Each of the managers interviewed at small firms maintained that, in their situation, the product development process did not contain very many realistic GO/NO GO decisions. After having passed a certain stage of the product development process, a NO GO decision would be equivalent to discontinuing the firm. However, in the case of Philips Medical Systems (the one large firm studied), a relatively small group of people became convinced of the feasibility of a comprehensive development project, managed to persuade top management in favour of the project, and functioned as internal product champions. Despite the existence of extensive official review procedures, a NO GO decision was unlikely to be made.

THE ADOPTION AND DIFFUSION OF COMPLEX MEDICAL EQUIPMENT

The investigation concerned the development of complex medical equipment within networks. Of special interest was the way manufacturers interact with potential product users during the product development process. Nevertheless, some basic understanding of how these users (mostly hospitals) evaluate and purchase medical equipment, was often found to be essential in understanding the contribution of potential users to the product development activities. Thus the firms that are successfully developing innovations within networks are those that manage to link individual value chains into a synergistic whole (Biemans and Shaw, 1990). While we did not systematically interview a representative sample of product users, we did gain some basic understanding in the course of our investigation.

The adoption of complex medical equipment

About ten years ago, the way hospitals bought complex medical equipment was quite uncomplicated. The relevant physician was clearly the most important person involved in the buying decision. As the members of the nursing staff often had to operate the new equipment, they were generally consulted by the physician. Therefore, manufacturers of medical equipment used to focus their sales effort on personal contact with the physicians, stressing the medical benefits of the new equipment. These visits by sales representatives were supplemented by advertisements in the relevant trade journals and presentations at the most important (international) trade shows. As the physicians were traditionally quite impressed by any new product representing a technological advance and there were no serious limits to the hospitals' expenditures, innovative medical equipment used to be readily adopted by the medical community. The adoption by hospitals of complex medical equipment was thus reduced to a purchasing decision made by a single individual and often based on non-rational motives. Thus, hospital buying behaviour was quite different from the purchasing behaviour of industrial firms.

The implementation of a budgeting system as from 1 January 1984 has started to change hospital buying behaviour considerably. As the budgeting system places an absolute limit to hospitals' expenditures, hospitals are increasingly focusing on the costs involved. In general, the emerging picture is the following.

1 Purchasing decisions are being made by buying committees instead of single individuals.
2 These buying committees do not consist of only physicians and members of the nursing staff, but typically include a purchasing agent, a member of the technical services department, a financial director, and an engineer specialized in medical technology as well.
3 All the people involved in the purchasing decision use different criteria in evaluating innovative medical equipment. While a physician may still focus on the innovation's medical benefits, the technical services department will stress the serviceability of the product and its electrical safety, and a financial director will emphasize the operating costs in addition to the purchase price.
4 The physician is clearly losing influence to the purchasing department, the financial director, and the members of the technical services department.

Thus, the way hospitals purchase complex medical equipment is undergoing considerable change (Figure 6.7). About ten years ago, the decision to buy a new piece of medical equipment in effect used to be made by an individual physician, whose decision was largely based on emotional–psychological motives (for example peer pressure or status considerations) without being influenced by organizational guidelines or restrictions. Nowadays, the decision to purchase innovative medical equipment is made by a group of people, who base their decision on mostly rational (often economic) motives guided by organizational requirements and objectives. While these two situations are presented as two very opposite extremes, it illustrates the major point to be made. In the Netherlands, hospital buying behaviour is becoming more and more similar to the purchasing behaviour of industrial firms. Although hospitals still consider the medical benefits of new equipment, they increasingly emphasize the costs involved. Therefore, new medical equipment which offers improved medical benefits at higher costs stands less chance of being adopted than new equipment which performs an existing medical function more efficiently and/or at a lower price.

Naturally, the change depicted above did not occur overnight. In fact, most hospitals are still in transition. The position of an individual hospital strongly depends on its size and position in the medical community. While the larger university hospitals have generally come a long way in adopting many aspects of organizational buying behaviour, small regional hospitals may still employ powerful physicians who dominate purchasing decisions. In addition, young physicians are more likely to adapt to the new procedures than older physicians who are really losing their traditional influence. Also, limited budgets may only foster intensive lobbying by powerful

Figure 6.7   Changes in hospital buying behaviour

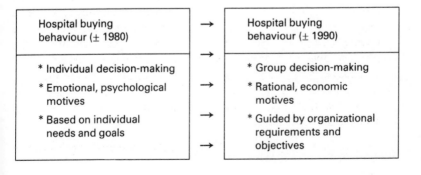

physicians; thus only limiting the number of requests for new equipment that can be granted, rather than resulting in cost-efficient buying behaviour.

The diffusion of complex medical equipment

In discussing the diffusion of medical equipment, people often distinguish between university hospitals and regional hospitals. The manufacturers were asked their opinion about possible differences between both types of hospital concerning

1 the parties involved in the buying process,
2 the time required to decide to purchase the equipment,
3 the evaluation criteria employed, and
4 the time interval between the time of market introduction and that of adoption.

Due to the limited information provided, the issue of the diffusion of new medical equipment remains unclear. Most manufacturers do not have sufficient insight into diffusion processes, while one of them sells its equipment through distributors and possesses only limited market information. Of the nine manufacturers who responded and were able to comment on these specific issues, four stated that as far as their products were concerned there were no differences between university hospitals and regional hospitals as regards the criteria mentioned above. The remaining managers concluded that some general differences did exist.

1 Four managers characterized university hospitals as employing an elaborate decision-making unit, usually including engineers and financial directors. In regional hospitals the buying process is said to be dominated by the actual product user.
2 Two managers consider university hospitals to be slower and more bureaucratic in their decision-making.
3 Only one manager stated that there were differences in the evaluation criteria. University hospitals evaluate new equipment on the level of technology incorporated, while regional hospitals stress economic criteria.
4 Two managers concluded that university hospitals tend to adopt innovative equipment earlier than regional hospitals.

Surprisingly, the differences between university hospitals and regional hospitals are not considered to be very great. Nevertheless, manufacturers typically prefer to involve university hospitals in their product development processes. This is because university hospitals are generally more interested in and knowledgeable about new technologies and have extended facilities for testing new equipment (and often for comparing it with existing products). Despite all this, manufacturers generally need to develop equipment of interest to both university and regional hospitals. The strong emphasis on cooperation with university hospitals may still be justified by stressing the innovative image of university hospitals. Because of this image, product acceptance by university hospitals has a positive effect on, and is therefore necessary for acceptance by regional hospitals.

This chapter has discussed the major results of the follow-up investigation, involving the in-depth study of seventeen cases of developing innovative medical equipment. The next and final chapter presents the total investigation's managerial implications.

7 Managerial implications

Science is a collection of successful recipes.

(Paul Valéry, 1871–1945)

This book discusses many of the intricacies involved in developing innovations within networks. In addition to an integrative survey of existing theory, it presents the results of an in-depth empirical investigation. The study was specifically designed to investigate how manufacturers of products for industrial markets interact with both users and various third parties during the development of complex innovations. The investigation was conducted with two major objectives in mind:

1 to provide industrial marketing management with practical guidelines to improve the interaction with both users and third parties and thus to enhance the quality of the industrial product development process, and
2 to contribute to existing theory with respect to developing complex innovations within networks.

The findings presented in Chapters 5 and 6 contribute a number of theoretical concepts to existing theory as regards interaction and networks. However, because of the objectives and practical character of the investigation, most of the findings lead directly to implementable recommendations to industrial marketing management. This final chapter structures the managerial implications around a number of major themes:

1 the concepts of interaction and networks,
2 the role of the manufacturer in product development,
3 interaction between the manufacturer and potential users,
4 interaction between the manufacturer and various third parties, and
5 the functioning of firms within networks.

The chapter closes by presenting The Five Cs of Innovation Management, which integrate our main conclusions.

THE CONCEPTS OF INTERACTION AND NETWORKS

Our investigation resulted in a better understanding of the central concepts of interaction and networks. These conceptual contributions relate to the elements of interaction, the dimensions characterizing individual interactive relationships, the distinction between active and passive interaction, and the classification of both interactive relationships and networks. The proposed scheme for classifying individual interactive relationships can be used to construct the Interaction Potential Evaluation matrix, a managerial tool for manufacturers to evaluate potential relationships meaningfully.

Interaction defined

Interaction was defined as *the mutual exchange of values which may belong to one or more of the following categories: (1) products/ components or services, (2) information, (3) financial resources, and (4) social content.* While in a specific individual interactive relationship all four types of values may be involved, this need not necessarily be the case. For example, a manufacturer may trade information with a major customer. However, most interactive relationships somehow (should) involve three or all four kinds of value. When this fact is ignored or forgotten, a manufacturer may, for instance, exchange services for money without paying attention to the transfer of information or social exchange. This may result in unnecessary misunderstandings and personal relationships which do not function optimally.

The fact that interaction involves the *mutual* exchange of values indicates the need for harmony which may be obtained through timely and detailed communication. Interactive relationships are most successful when both parties benefit from the relationship. While a shared goal is frequently mentioned as an important ingredient for success, this is not a universal law. Two organizations may pursue different objectives and still enter into a highly effective and efficient collaboration, so long as they state and accommodate for their deviating goals.

The dimensions used to characterize interactive relationships serve to pinpoint some of the most relevant aspects to be considered before starting such a relationship and when estimating the chances of success. For example, the dimension 'duration of the interaction' must be carefully considered and might even be laid down in a contract. For extensive collaborative projects, a contract with no real time limit, but terminable by any partner from year to year, is not advisable, since it (1) strongly depends on specific incidental situations and (2) undermines mutual trust, commitment, and the development of structural relationships. A better alternative would be to have the contract automatically continue from year to year with a substantial term of notice (for example two years).

It should also be noted that the dimensions may change over time. For example, a manufacturer may provide a university with money to conduct exploratory research, representing interaction with a low level of intensity (weak tie). If the university researchers should come up with some concrete idea of interest to the firm, both parties may initiate a joint development project, that is a relationship with a high level of intensity (strong tie). Thus, a weak tie represents a potential strong one. Because of the relatively low costs involved, a manufacturer can maintain a large number of such weak ties and thus keep in touch with the major technological developments.

The distinction between active and passive interaction serves to alert management to the existence of passive forms of interaction. Although these forms of interaction are termed passive, management can actively employ them and improve their handling of them. Passive interaction consists of (1) using a partner as a reference and (2) the passive acquisition of resources.

1 Potential users who have tested a prototype frequently become actual buyers of the product. Management should seriously consider the possibility of using such customers as references and having them demonstrate the innovation to prospective buyers.
2 As regards the passive acquisition of resources, management should establish an optimal receptiveness in the firm and its employees. That is, sales managers should be easily accessible to customers, customers with complaints should be phoned back without delay (the customer may have problems with the product, but possibly he has some suggestions to improve it as well!), sales representatives should be receptive to any suggestions from customers and seriously analyse them, etc.

The Interaction Potential Evaluation matrix

The findings of the investigation show how relationships can be grouped in a number of distinct categories. Although many alternative classification schemes are conceivable, the one presented in chapter 6 helps a manager to consider the benefits and investments related to various types of interactive relationship by focusing on the two major dimensions 'duration' and 'intensity' of interaction. When these two dimensions are combined with the potential interaction partners to be considered (as is done in the examples given in chapter 6), the resulting framework becomes an important tool in evaluating the potential of various relationships and reducing the chance of overlooking promising ones. The importance of such a strategic planning instrument was emphasized by Håkansson (1990, p. 378) when he stated that 'Each company ought ... to analyse, design and evaluate its cooperation profile'. An example may illustrate the use of the Interaction Potential Evaluation (IPE) matrix. Consider the manufacturer who is thinking of cooperating with potential users. For this purpose he takes the standard IPE matrix, constructed by combining the product development stages (that is the duration of interaction) and the levels of intensity of interaction (Figure 7.1). Then, for every column (or development stage) he considers the various intensities of interaction with potential users. In this way, each individual cell of the matrix is analysed in terms of opportunities, benefits, and investments. This procedure may be conducted with one type of cooperation partner (for example potential users) or a specific cooperation partner (for example major customer X) in mind. The analysis should be repeated for all potential cooperation partners, while accounting for possible 'interaction effects' between distinct relationships. For instance, cooperation with one major competitor may exclude another competitor from consideration. Håkansson (1990, p. 379) warned that if a planning model, such as the IPE matrix, 'is overly simple or rigid, it may well do more harm than good'. Therefore we would like to stress that the matrix is just a general framework. Every firm should modify and refine the dimensions to fit its own needs and specific market situation. Thus the IPE matrix becomes a flexible tool, which can assist in obtaining a balanced portfolio of relationships that acknowledges the idiosyncratic strengths and benefits of individual relationships.

Chapter 6 characterized networks according to (1) their complexity, (2) the major cooperation partners, and (3) the environment of the interactive relationships. The managerial implications of these classification schemes are discussed in the section about the functioning of organizations within networks.

Figure 7.1 The Interaction Potential Evaluation matrix

(Type of) cooperation Partner:	Idea	Preliminary assessment	Concept	Development	Testing	Trial	Launch
				Stages of the product development process			
1. Use as reference							
2. Passive acquisition of resources							
3. Active acquisition of resources							
4. Response, feedback on specific issues							
5. Separate development of specified activity							
6. Joint development of specified activity							

INTENSITY

THE ROLE OF THE MANUFACTURER IN PRODUCT DEVELOPMENT

Many of the findings presented in the previous chapters have important implications for manufacturers. However, in this section we will focus on two critical issues that significantly contribute to the success of product development: the integration of marketing and product development, and the performance of the predevelopment activities.

Integrating marketing and product development

Manufacturers of industrial products are predominantly technology oriented, while marketing is treated only as a secondary function. This is illustrated by the fact that, although the majority of the manufacturers reported that they generally interact with users during product development, such interaction was found to be poorly conducted in the actual cases investigated. The secondary position of marketing is also reflected by the lack of integration of marketing with the product development process. Nevertheless, both previous research reported in literature and our own investigation have proved marketing to be an essential ingredient of successful product development.

Obviously, marketing should be given its legitimate position within the organization. For many manufacturers this means that they should rely on experienced marketing managers, rather than sales managers bearing the title, but lacking the expertise. Naturally, this advice only makes sense for medium- or large-sized firms, as many of the small ones lack the financial resources to employ experienced marketers and need to rely on the marketing knowledge that 'just happens to be present' (for instance, because the director has some commercial training or experience) or can be acquired incidentally from external sources (such as marketing consulting firms). Acquiring the necessary marketing expertise is a prerequisite for integrating marketing with the product development process. While this integration may be achieved in many ways (as is shown throughout this book) it is best started by realizing that marketing should be involved in all product development stages. Often this involvement can be accomplished effectively in very simple ways. For instance, Philips Medical Systems had an extensive user manual drawn up before even the actual development of the prototype began! This obliged the people involved to consider the product specifications both carefully and in detail, leading to better specifications, reduced problems during actual development, improved internal communication, shorter duration of the development process, and therefore reduced development costs and early market launch.

Predevelopment activities: laying the foundation of success

While manufacturers typically performed the predevelopment activities inadequately, the recipe for improvement is quite obvious. In all situations, the manufacturer should undertake the predevelopment activities and undertake them well by carefully considering the following three basic questions. Competitive advantage can be gained through the creative use of available options.

1 What type of cooperation partners should be involved?
   Frequently, manufacturers make the mistake of relying solely on major customers for their information. Much specific information can be provided by other potential cooperation partners, such as distributors (broad view of the market), industry experts (general technological and market trends), inspection agencies (product specifications), research institutes (new technological developments), and competitors (product specifications and production techniques). As each partner offers different information, the choice of a partner may depend on the specific predevelopment stage. For example, a firm may use distributors and potential users to evaluate a new idea and employ a research institute in evaluating the technical aspects of a product concept.

2 How many cooperation partners should be involved?
   For each category of potential cooperation partners the manufacturer must determine the optimal number to cooperate with. The optimal number strongly depends on the category involved. For example, in the whole world there may be only two or three renowned industry experts (often termed *gurus*) as regards the specific medical sub-discipline involved, but thousands of potential users of the new product.

3 How should the cooperation partners be selected?
   In selecting cooperation partners, the manufacturer should determine the partner's representativeness, knowledge, objectivity, willingness to cooperate, market position, ability to keep confidential information, and ties to major competitors. For example, because of close contacts with a major competitor, a key user may be questioned in a roundabout way so as not to divulge the exact nature of a new-product idea.

When approached by a user or university researcher with a home-made device, a manufacturer should not limit his contribution to the product development process to carrying out minor engineering just to improve the product, and subsequently producing and marketing it. In these situations it is of the utmost importance for the manufacturer to assess the product concept and its commercial potential carefully, that is, he must:

1 identify the potential users of the product,
2 formulate the user requirements,
3 determine whether the new product meets a significant user need,
4 assess the market potential,
5 analyse the competitive market situation,
6 determine and evaluate the necessary investments and inherent risks,
7 evaluate the new product's fit with the firm's existing products,
8 define the product concept in terms of user benefits,
9 define the technical aspects of the product concept, and
10 test the product concept with a representative group of potential users, distributors, and industry experts.

Firms ignoring this basic truth run the risks of increasing development costs, a prolonged development process, a postponed market launch, and large investments in a project with no commercial future.

INTERACTION BETWEEN THE MANUFACTURER AND POTENTIAL USERS

The conclusion that potential users may contribute to nearly all stages of the product development process serves to make management aware of the many forms of manufacturer–user interaction. For example, many firms limit their interaction with potential users to having them comment on product concepts and test newly developed prototypes. By not involving them in such stages as the development and launch stages, manufacturers fail to make optimal use of the full potential of users. In the context of manufacturer–user interaction, three specific stages of the development process (in addition to the predevelopment activities, discussed in the previous section) deserve careful attention from management. Specific attention will be given to the influence of changing hospital buying behaviour on manufacturer–user relationships in developing medical equipment innovations.

Developing a prototype

In general, potential users were not extensively involved in the actual development of prototypes. This was particularly true in the case of medical equipment innovations. The physician's expertise lies in a specific medical (sub)discipline rather than in the latest technology. Therefore physicians are best suited to formulating problems with existing products, suggesting ideas for new products, evaluating new product concepts, and testing newly developed prototypes. During the actual development of the technologically complex prototype their contribution is, by necessity, limited to reacting on questions and requests from the manufacturer's engineers about highly specific medical (technology) issues. As these engineers are unfamiliar with this medical knowledge, the manufacturer should carefully select physicians (based on their reputation in the field) and build up a good personal relationship. Only when the physician is working in a large hospital, with a major technical services department, the potential user is likely to provide a more substantial contribution.

Potential users may be more closely involved in the actual development stage when an original design is developed by engineers of a university linked with a university hospital. In these instances there will be close cooperation between the engineers of the university and the physicians of the hospital. Thus the original design will actually be developed within a clinical environment. While this should be encouraged by the manufacturer, he should make sure that (1) he is involved in formulating the specifications for the original design, (2) there is a good relationship between the engineers and the physicians, (3) the original design will also be tested by physicians at other hospitals, and (4) the original design will be transferred to the firm in time, thus again emphasizing the need for detailed and timely communication.

External testing

Having a prototype tested by potential users under actual working conditions is a very critical stage in the development process that should be performed with care. This stage can be broken down into a series of activities which all need to be considered carefully. Chapter 6 describes in great detail a general framework for testing prototypes with potential users, containing all these individual activities and decisions, while a tentative version of the framework, together with many practical considerations, can be found in chapter 5. The managerial implications of the framework are numerous. However, the detailed analysis of each separate activity provides the manager with sufficient directions for improvement. (An integral description of the framework is presented in Biemans (1990)).

Market launch

Although the large majority of manufacturers of medical equipment employed potential users to test their prototypes, only about half of them employed them during market introduction and subsequent diffusion of the product. This is very surprising considering (1) the logical link between both activities and (2) the importance of word-of-mouth communication in hospital buying behaviour. The names and reputations of the physicians who tested the prototype, together with their positive experiences with the product, are powerful instruments in convincing prospective buyers of the innovation's benefits. However, this highly effective strategy presupposes that (1) renowned physicians can be identified in the medical discipline in question, (2) at least one of them is willing to test the prototype, (3) experiences with the new product are positive, and (4) the physician is willing to have the firm use his name and reputation for promotional purposes. In the ideal case, the physician will even present papers, write articles about the product, and demonstrate it to colleagues. When it concerns a relatively small and simple piece of medical equipment, which can be sent by mail, the renowned physicians may be identified globally. If, on the other hand, the equipment is bulky, expensive, and requires frequent checking by an engineer, the manufacturer must identify a local renowned physician (that is, from the perspective of a Dutch manufacturer, someone in the Netherlands, Germany, or Belgium, preferably as close as possible).

Changing hospital buying behaviour

The Dutch medical equipment industry is going through a number of changes having major implications for the firms' marketing practices. Due to implemented budgeting procedures and an accompanying growing cost awareness in hospitals, hospital buying behaviour is becoming more and more like that of industrial firms. Whereas the decision to buy a new medical instrument typically used to be made by the physician, such decisions are nowadays being made by a buying committee. Such a committee may consist of a physician, nursing staff, an administrator, a purchasing manager, and a representative of the technical services department. Several of the large hospitals even employ an expert on medical technology who is able to evaluate the various alternative technologies offered by the manufacturers. In the smaller hospitals, however, the physician may still be the major decision maker. These changes concerning the principal decision makers are accompanied by changes in the buying motives employed. These developments have important implications for the way manufacturers interact with potential customers.

1 As hospitals are increasingly in the possession of technological expertise in addition to medical know-how, they may be more intensively involved in product development processes (for instance during the concept and the actual development stages).
2 During market introduction, manufacturers should interact with all relevant persons involved in the purchasing decision. Instead of approaching only the physicians, manufacturers also need to establish and maintain good relationships with purchasing managers, administrators, and engineers.
3 In introducing new medical equipment, manufacturers should match the communication channels and selling propositions to the targeted decision makers. For example, while physicians can still be approached through sales representatives and advertisements in trade journals stressing the medical benefits of the innovation, an administrator should be confronted with calculations emphasizing the new product's cost effectiveness.

INTERACTION BETWEEN THE MANUFACTURER AND VARIOUS THIRD PARTIES

Many different organizations, termed third parties, contribute a wide range of activities to the product development process. While potential users are basically employed to provide user information, the involvement of third parties includes such activities as influencing cooperation strategies, funding research, providing information, and producing components.

Creative interaction with third parties

Both (1) the wide variety of organizations and (2) the broad range of activities they contribute to the product development process, draw management's attention to forms of interaction which are frequently forgotten. For example, manufacturers often question potential users of the product during the predevelopment stages. However, at these stages important information may also be provided by third parties such as universities, or even competitors. While competitors are hardly employed during the predevelopment stages (for reasons of confidentiality), they can be a reliable source of first-hand information as regards certain products and specific production techniques. To use this source of information effectively, managers in the manufacturing firm need to establish and maintain good personal relationships with their counterparts in the firm's major competitors. Thus, instead of (or in addition to) a formal network of competitors, the establishment of an informal network consisting of personal relationships between colleagues should be encouraged.

Third-party involvement: three typical examples

To illustrate the wide variety of situations encountered, this section briefly discusses three examples of third-party involvement: assisting in the development of a prototype, producing strategic components, and assisting in marketing the innovation.

Prototype development

Third parties were found to contribute substantially to the actual development of prototypes. These third parties were mostly universities, specialized research institutes, and suppliers, who possess very specialized advanced technological knowledge needed by the firm. Some of the firms developing innovative medical equipment depend on outside sources for specific technological knowledge. In some cases, it is a medium-sized firm in the need of some very specific knowledge from a specialized research institute. In other cases, it is a small firm which does not possess all the technical expertise to develop the new product. Both cases do not pose special problems to management. Research institutes are well publicized and easy of access. In addition, each firm can check with the universities and specialized suppliers as to the availability of the necessary know-how. By using some kind of snowballing interview technique, that is asking each person for other references, potential cooperation partners are easily identified.

Although industrial firms and universities are increasingly cooperating in the development of new products, this kind of interaction is frequently accompanied by a number of special problems, most of them caused by the inherent differences between both partners. For example, while (1) an industrial firm often expects a university to develop an industrial prototype and (2) a university often expects a firm to start manufacturing its original design as it is, neither of these viewpoints is very realistic. The basic remedy for improving industry–university cooperation is detailed and timely communication, that is, at the start of the cooperation project, all relevant aspects must be discussed and agreed upon by both parties. The discussion on product development within networks in Chapter 6 includes a list of eight important factors to bear in mind when considering cooperation with a university in developing an innovation.

Producing strategic components

Third parties may be involved in the development process through the production of strategic components. This situation often occurs when a (small) firm has a supplier developing and producing a part of the new product. In these situations the manufacturer must (1) select a high-quality supplier to develop the component, (2) formulate the specifications together with the supplier so as to use both knowledge areas optimally, (3) carefully control the development of the component (deviations from the original specifications must be discussed), and (4) test the component both separately and as part of the complete product.

Marketing

If the developed prototype is tested by an external research organization, its name and reputation can be used during market introduction. Sometimes, a small firm may lack any marketing expertise and use an established distributor to market the innovation. In this situation, the firm needs to take care of the maintenance and repair, as well as the technical training of the operators.

THE FUNCTIONING OF ORGANIZATIONS WITHIN NETWORKS

Manufacturers were found to interact with both potential users and various third parties in developing complex innovations. This section discusses interaction strategies, alternative classifications of networks, and the potential disadvantages of developing innovations within networks.

Interaction strategies

As has been stated before, a manufacturer wanting to develop a complex piece of medical equipment needs to evaluate cooperation with a number of potential partners (for example by using the Interaction Potential Evaluation matrix presented earlier in this chapter). The choice of cooperation partner and the desired level of intensity of interaction depends on the stage of the development process. For example, one manufacturer of innovative medical equipment decided that distributors, rather than physicians, are best suited to assess the potential of new product ideas. Because physicians are generally in favour of any new product representing a technological advance, they were thought to be useless in assessing the value of an abstract product concept (nevertheless, they may still provide relevant information during these predevelopment stages!). However, physicians are the obvious choice when it comes to testing and criticizing a concrete prototype, not only because of their access to a clinical environment, but also because the Dutch physicians can be characterized as being very critical of new equipment.

Alternative classifications of networks

Networks can be classified according to (1) the network's complexity, (2) the nature of the major cooperation partners, and (3) the environment of the interactive relationship.

When a firm interacts with just one partner (a simple network), management can direct all its attention to managing that relationship. On the other hand, when a firm collaborates with a number of partners (a complex network), management is confronted with the task of managing a portfolio of relationships, some of which may be influencing each other. Individual relationships need to be evaluated in terms of investments, benefits, and potential interaction effects. The potential disadvantages of developing innovations within a complex network are discussed further on.

Whether the network is dominated by interaction with users or third parties strongly influences the content and intensity of the interactive relationships. As both types of interaction have been discussed elsewhere in this chapter, we will not elaborate on them further.

The distinction between internal and external networks is of critical importance to every organization that is part of the total network. As the effectiveness and efficiency of the total external network is determined by the functioning of all internal networks, each organization involved must take care of its internal network. That is, each organization must ensure that all the relevant parties within the organization are involved and that good communication exists between them.

Developing innovations within networks: potential disadvantages and how to deal with them

Developing innovations through cooperation with external partners offers a firm numerous substantial benefits, as has been discussed extensively in Chapter 4. Developing an innovation within a *complex network* has the additional benefits of specialization and correction of deficiencies, thus suggesting a highly efficient and effective operation. However, as illustrated by the case of AIR (presented in chapter 6), the involvement of many parties in product development may lead to friction, delays, and unnecessary duplication of activities.

The other side of the coin

However, it is not just product development within complex networks that confronts a firm with potential disadvantages. Along with the many benefits that may be obtained, every mode of cooperation with an external partner involves various costs as well. Let us take a closer look at this other side of the coin.

Increased dependency

Cooperation implies that certain specified activities are no longer done by the manufacturer himself but carried out by an external partner instead. Therefore every type of cooperation is accompanied by an increased level of dependency, which in the case of substantial differences in input may be detrimental to the weaker partner. The level of dependency and its related economic effects depend on the cooperation mode selected (Hagedoorn, 1990). Kanter (1989, pp. 133–40) describes in detail how Digital Equipment Corporation increasingly cooperated with a selected group of suppliers. The consequential increased dependency was amply made up for by the numerous benefits involved.

Increased costs of coordination

Involving a number of external parties in the development of new products requires the people responsible for integration to commit increasing amounts of time to communication and coordination. Most of the time will be spent on writing progress reports, attending formal meetings and review sessions, but the required presence at informal joint lunches and other similar social gatherings may take up much time as well. The coordination becomes especially complicated when the partners involved represent different corporate cultures (Riedle, 1989, p. 223).

Changed personnel management

Successful management of strategic partnerships places new demands on personnel management. Long-term comprehensive joint development projects necessitate new incentive and compensation systems that reward long-term group performance rather than direct individual results, and emphasize creativity and freedom to use personal talents instead of salaries, bonuses, and promotion (cf. Olson, 1990, p. 43). As Nevens, Summe, and Uttal (1990, p. 161) noted, successful firms stress coordination, not functional skill. In addition, long-term complex projects of strategic importance may bring a firm to reduce personnel mobility by asking key personnel to commit themselves for the life of the project. At the same time, selection procedures in hiring new personnel should emphasize cooperative behaviour rather than an aggressive attitude. Existing employees may find the shift from competition to cooperation (where lifelong competitors are suddenly referred to as colleagues!), and the accompanying shift in required skills, extremely confusing and the source of much frustration and reduced performance.

Access to confidential information and proprietary skills

In the course of a joint development project the partner may get access to certain information of a confidential nature, as well as proprietary skills. While, frequently, such sharing of information and skills is critical to the project's eventual success and an open atmosphere has the side benefit of creating a mutual feeling of trust and commitment, firms may want to take precautionary measures. For instance, Lyons, Krachenberg, and Henke (1990, p. 32) note that industrial buyers looking for cooperation partners are using increasingly explicit supplier evaluation programmes, thereby gaining access to all aspects of the supplier's operations (including financial information!) (see also Burt, 1989, p. 130). In the case of collaboration with external partners, the firms may want to control trading of information at operational levels, since this is where the day-to day interactions occur.

Loss of critical knowledge and skills

Joint product development implies that a carefully defined series of activities are no longer performed in-house but carried out by an external partner. If increased cooperation with external partners results in a gradual shift from development to production, the resulting loss of critical knowledge and skills has serious implications for the firm's strategic position. Hamel *et al.* (1989, p. 137) call this phenomenon 'the ratchet effect'. However, such a strategic shift has also important implications for many of the present suppliers. The announcement, made at the end of October 1990, that another 40,000 jobs needed to disappear at Philips created great unrest in the market. The loss of jobs and the consequential tendency to enter into strategic partnerships with external partners makes the firm strongly dependent on a limited number of highly qualified suppliers. The director of Neways Electronics (one of Philips' many suppliers) reacted on the announcement by expressing his worry that in the future Philips will probably be unable to supply critical knowledge and expertise (*NRC Handelsblad*, 1990d).

Dominance by the partner

Increased dependency may be accompanied by a fear of being dominated by the cooperation partner in question. The risk of dominance and exploitation is always present, but especially in the case of unequal contributions by the partners should one beware of the pursuit of power and control. In the case of international alliances the selection of the country that serves as 'home' to the alliance influences the danger of dominance and control (Hamel *et al.*, 1989, p. 138).

Lack of commitment

The potential synergistic benefits of joint product development may be completely nullified by lack of commitment at one or more co-operation partners. While most direct personal contacts exist at operational levels, top management support and strategic vision is crucial for the project's success. The vital commitment should not just be expressed in pretty declarations of intent and empty slogans, but result in visible investments in the relationship. However, it should be noted that insufficient commitment does not always result from unwillingness or lack of interest. An unexpected strategic shift at one of the partners may cause the collaboration to be terminated. For example, the partnership of Siemens and RCA was ended abruptly when RCA informed Siemens that it was no longer in the computer business in a surprise phone call: 'Okay, we were just in a board meeting and we decided to get out of computers' (Alster, 1986).

The remedy: prevention is better than cure

As is implicit in the description of the various potential disadvantages of cooperation, they come in three basic categories. (1) Some potential disadvantages are inherent in cooperation with external partners and the firm just has to learn to live with them (for instance, increased dependency, increased costs of coordination, and changed personnel management). Evaluation of these organizational effects of co-operation is at the heart of making decisions about strategic partnerships. (2) Other disadvantages are only relevant in certain specific situations, for example at Philips the loss of critical knowledge and skills due to a strategic shift from development to production is closely tied to the firm's economic performance, corporate business strategy, and changing management culture. (3) Finally, the effects of many potential disadvantages may be easily minimized through innovation management tailored to the contingencies of the situation. Frequently, effective communication proves to be the key to success. For instance, in the case of AIR much of the friction, frustrations, misunderstandings, delays, and unnecessary duplication of activities could have been prevented through detailed and timely communication, carefully drawing up agreements, and having partners interact freely during the development process. The managerial guidelines to improve industry–university cooperation, presented in chapter 6, can be employed to prevent the enormous cultural differences between the scientific world of the university and the practical reality of the industrial firm from resulting in frustration and failure.

Typically, a successful cooperation strategy consists of three basic elements, that is selection of a suitable partner, formulation of clear-cut agreements (getting the project on its way), and management of the on-going relationship.

Quite obviously many problems can be prevented by carefully selecting future cooperation partners. According to Hagedoorn (1990, p. 22) one should aim at *similarity balanced by comple-*

mentarity, with similarity referring to the firm's size, resources, and economic performance. However, of more importance is the required complementarity offered by the cooperation partner; the creative combination of complementary activities, knowledge, and skills realizes the desired synergy. The literature about strategic partnerships offers many models to evaluate potential cooperation partners (see for example Souder and Nassar, 1990b). In practice, however, firms are clearly struggling with this critical question. Should one cooperate with the market leader or prefer the number two (who 'tries harder') as a partner? Under different circumstances a firm might clearly favour cooperation with a small firm, where direct contact with the director/owner or someone else in an influential position is expected to guarantee a prosperous partnership. To avoid these difficult decisions, firms are frequently found to choose their cooperation partner because of an already existing relationship. While existing good personal relationships without a doubt assure a successful start of a new joint development project, the effect on the ultimate project's outcome is much less obvious. Whatever strategy is followed, the selection of a suitable cooperation partner is only the first step. Much harder is the subsequent identification and motivation of the right person within the organization.

After having selected the best partner from among the many alternatives available, detailed agreements concerning a large number of issues need to be arrived at. In addition to clarifying the basis of the collaboration (division of tasks, link with responsibilities, reasons for entering the partnership, goals to pursue, life of the project, contributions to be made, divisions of costs and benefits, etc.), the agreements should install control mechanisms to ensure successful management of the cooperation project (such as interorganizational decision-making, motivation of personnel, resolution of conflicts, and informal communication processes).

From the very moment the project is on its way, effective management of communication (both formal and informal) and recognition of the critical role played by individuals become essential ingredients for success. The observations and managerial implications presented in this book may help to increase both the likelihood of success and its results.

THE FIVE Cs OF INNOVATION MANAGEMENT

This chapter discussed the major managerial implications. The most relevant observations with respect to the integration of marketing and innovation management are summarized in the checklist presented in appendix A. While these implications are of interest to all firms developing innovations for industrial markets, they are relevant to small firms in particular. The very small firms, consisting of up to ten employees, are typically very much technology oriented and do not have the resources to hire experienced marketers. In many cases they have just started and are unfamiliar with the markets in which they are operating. Moreover, the success of these firms strongly depends on the success of one or two innovative products. A longitudinal study of five new product failures by small Indian firms led Sarin and Kapur (1990) to conclude that they lacked the resources, competence, and interest to manage the required marketing task in successfully developing and introducing new products. Therefore, they advise these firms to concentrate on small innovative steps, rather than major break-throughs. However, we would like to argue that small firms are very capable of learning basic marketing principles and applying them to their specific situation. Therefore these firms stand to benefit the most from reading the conclusions and implications presented in this book, applying them to their own business, and acting on them.

This final chapter concludes with presenting The Five Cs of Innovation Management, a managerial concept which integrates the major conclusions into one simple framework. Based on the results of empirical investigations into innovation processes, numerous academics have demonstrated the need for cooperation within networks and commended its beneficial consequences. However, the investigation discussed in this book demonstrates many potential problems and pitfalls that may confront a firm functioning within a network. The findings can be summarized by The Five Cs of Innovation Management (see Figure 7.2). This managerial concept captures the following train of thought.

Particularly in industrial markets, a number of trends can be observed. Technological developments have accelerated to a level where product life cycles have shortened considerably. This implies that a manufacturer must continually and actively be searching for innovative products to succeed the existing ones, while the time available to reap the benefits has been significantly reduced. In addition, industrial new products are becoming increasingly complex and their development necessitates the combination of different areas of knowledge. This growing complexity fuels a demand for standardization. To further complicate matters, competition is growing and becoming more and more global. New products need to be aimed at

Figure 7.2 The five Cs of innovation management

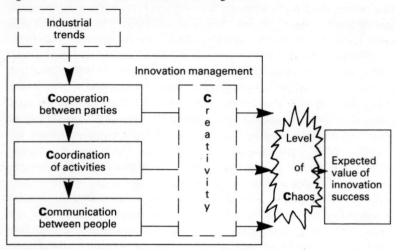

Source: Biemans (1990), © Basil Blackwell Ltd. Reprinted with permission.

international markets, which may not always be easily accessible to the manufacturer. Typically, these trends combine to make new product development an expensive and high-risk endeavour.

More often than not, one or more of these factors forces a manufacturer to develop industrial innovations through *COOPERATION* with other organizations, such as users, competitors, research institutes, suppliers, and distributors. One author stressed the critical relevance of this observation by entitling his article 'Innovation is spelled cooperation' (Norris, 1985). New product development is no longer considered to be the sole province of the manufacturer. Instead, many parties may contribute in various ways to the product development process. This has the obvious advantage that each party can do what it does best. For example, a selected group of potential users may supply the necessary application knowledge, a university may incorporate the latest technological know-how, and a specialized agency may be hired to provide the industrial design. In addition to this external cooperation, management needs to organize for internal cooperation by setting up multi-disciplinary project teams that take the new product from its inception to market launch (Takeuchi and Nonaka, 1986, p. 138). Recent publications emphasize that these project teams are increasingly likely to include supplier representatives as well (Burt, 1989, p. 131; Nonaka, 1990, p. 32; Lyons, Krachenberg, and Henke, 1990, p. 30).

The benefits of cooperation may only be enjoyed when the parties involved establish effective and efficient *COORDINATION* of the various activities to be undertaken. Key activities need to be divided among the partners involved and the accompanying responsibilities must be assigned to the right people. However, subdividing the problem like this should not preclude parties from providing creative contributions to areas outside their assigned tasks (cf. Nonaka's (1990, p. 28) concept of information redundancy). Having a product champion at a high level in the firm may facilitate coordination and prove to be very beneficial in supplying the necessary commitment. Firms may employ several mechanisms to achieve coordination of activities, for instance, periodic job rotation, joint customer visits, physical proximity of work places, project teams, seminars, regular joint review meetings, social interactions, and joint development contracts. State-of-the-art information systems may be instrumental in achieving the desired level of coordination, both externally and internally (Henderson, 1990). Effective cooperation is guided by clear agreements, commitment, and trust. A formal contract should be regarded as a document that reflects this mutual agreement and understanding, rather than an instrument to control and correct a partner (cf. Ohmae, 1989, pp. 149–50).

While activities need to be coordinated, the outcome of the innovation process is largely determined by the people involved. Effective and efficient coordination can only be achieved when the cooperation partners involved create and maintain an atmosphere that encourages good and timely *COMMUNICATION*, not just externally (with cooperation partners) but internally (at a departmental, functional, and personal level) as well. In both cases, personal relationships prove to be a major mechanism for creating effective linkages, both in day-to-day execution of the partnership and from a long-term perspective. In the case of cooperation with external partners, these personal relationships need to exist at all levels of the organization. Henderson (1990, p. 12) cites one manager as saying: 'It is often the personal relationships built between organizations that enable you to manage across the rough spots'. However, it should be noted that interaction with external cooperation partners is a means by which strategic information may be disseminated as well as gathered. This calls for employee loyalty, greater self-discipline, and even greater emphasis on individual responsibility for relationships and for communications (cf. Drucker, 1988, p. 47; Hamel *et al.*, 1989, p. 138).

Whereas many investigators have attempted to formulate recommendations concerning the management of innovation processes, we need to mention that some authors question the value of such guidelines. According to them, innovation processes are not rational and ordered, but to a large extent better described by *CHAOS.* For example, Quinn (1985, p. 83) argued in an article that 'Innovation tends to be individually motivated, opportunistic, customer responsive, tumultuous, nonlinear, and interactive in its development. Managers can plan overall directions and goals, but surprises are likely to abound'. However, the article's revealing title 'Managing innovation: controlled chaos' captures the essence of our argument: even though innovation processes are very much characterized by chaos, in the sense of surprises and unexpected changes, they can still be controlled *to a certain extent.* The three Cs of cooperation, co-ordination, and communication are key elements in successfully developing innovations through reduction of the level of chaos. A reduced level of chaos serves to increase the expected value of innovation success at a project level, which is a product of (1) the probability of developing and introducing a successful innovation, and (2) the returns in terms of money, competitive advantage, reputation, etc.. However, this should not be taken to imply that in the ideal situation chaos is eliminated entirely. Nonaka (1988, pp. 61–2) acknowledges the beneficial potential of a certain level of chaos by arguing that a firm may use chaos as a catalyst for the creation of innovative solutions. Indeed, this very idea led Tom Peters (1987) to entitle his latest bestseller 'Thriving on Chaos'. Hamel *et al.* (1989, p. 134) emphasize that occasional conflict, rather than harmony, may be the best evidence of mutually beneficial collaboration.

The extent to which the three Cs of cooperation, coordination, and communication are able to reduce the level of chaos may be significantly enhanced through creative use of management practices. Thus, the fifth C of *CREATIVITY* serves as a critical intermediary variable. Successful innovations are not achieved through routine adherence to prescribed detailed procedures, schedules, and measures. Instead, a firm should strive to enhance its competitive advantage by applying creative management to devise innovative solutions. Experimentation and the principle of trial and error have proved to indicate the right direction on the route to success. A sense of urgency may help to achieve the desired effect. As Paul Cook, founder and CEO of Raychem Corporation acknowledges, 'People need a fair amount of pressure to have creative ideas' (Taylor, 1990, p. 98). The importance of creativity is also acknowledged by Bradbury who states that

Innovation is ... a *creatively* initiated process which is then developed and progressed to a definable goal by the application of further *creativity* allied to logical analysis and work organization in which the *creative* element continuously introduces 'change' as a 'horizontal shift' in the logical progression of the chain. (Emphasis added)

(Bradbury, 1989, p. 14)

Sometimes the element of creativity is recognized by firms as an essential element of their development strategy. For instance, Mitsch (1990, p. 18) mentions how 3M has a company policy that encourages researchers to use 15 per cent of their time on projects of their own choosing.

The presented concept of The Five Cs of Innovation Management acknowledges that cooperation with other parties may be essential in developing innovations. However, cooperation with external parties is nothing like the purely beneficial strategy it is often made out to be. Instead, it may pose numerous unexpected problems and requires a lot of serious effort and commitment of the people involved to make it work.

Appendix A
Critical issues to be considered when involving potential users and various third parties in product development processes

In chapter 6 we frequently referred to stages of the product development process, which were derived from a model presented by Cooper (1983b). Most researchers postulate models that are quite similar; nevertheless, large differences in both the number and nature of the stages distinguished still exist. Therefore this appendix starts by defining and describing each stage of the product development process. The main part of the appendix, however, consists of a checklist enumerating the most critical issues to be considered when interacting with potential users and third parties during product development.

Table A.1 The stages and activities of the product development process

Development stages	Activities	Description
1. Idea	Idea generation	An idea results when technological possibilities are matched with an expected market demand.
	Screening	First evaluation of the idea; the initial decision to commit resources.
2. Preliminary assessment	Preliminary market assessment	Conducting a quick market study, using in-house information, secondary data, and outside sources.
	Preliminary technical assessment	Assessing the idea's technical viability.

3. Concept	Concept identification	Identifying a market need and the way to meet it. Formulating the basic design.
	Concept development	Translating the market requirements into an operational concept.
	Concept test	Conducting a market study to test market acceptance of the concept.
4. Development	Development of prototype	Employing various resources to develop a prototype.
	Development of marketing plan	Formulating a general marketing plan, based on the concept stage.
5. Testing	In-house tests (Internal or alpha tests)	Testing the technical functioning of the prototype.
	Tests with users (external or beta tests)	Testing of the prototype under working conditions by real customers.
6. Trial	Pilot production	Testing the production method that will be used for full-scale production.
	Finalization of marketing plan	Formulating the final marketing plan.
	Business analysis	Undertaking a pre-commercialization business analysis.
7. Launch	Full production	Starting up full production.
	Market launch	Introducing the product into the market.

1 IDEA STAGE

1a Defining a new product idea

A new product idea may be actively generated by the firm through
- establishing and maintaining contact with innovative users,
- periodically scanning technological developments at leading universities,
- periodically interviewing selected distributors,
- establishing and maintaining good relationships with leading figures in the field (for example retired physicians, industry experts, gurus), and
- continuously scanning the relevant (technological) literature.

1b Screening new product ideas

At this early stage, both new product ideas generated by the firm and new product ideas suggested by users or third parties undergo their first evaluation by being checked against a limited number of criteria. Although the evaluation involves only a tentative decision to proceed to the next stage, a representative user, distributor, university, or industry expert with whom the firm maintains a good relationship may be employed to comment on the value of the new product idea.

2 PRELIMINARY ASSESSMENT STAGE

2a Preliminary market assessment

The preliminary market assessment, undertaken to determine user requirements and estimate market potential, can be conducted by interviewing

– major potential users (who may provide information about user requirements),
– distributors (who possess a relatively broad view of the market (segment)), and
– industry experts (who possess information about general trends regarding developments in the market).

The critical decisions to be made at this stage relate to

– the types of cooperation partners to involve,
– the number of cooperation partners to involve,
– the criteria to use in selecting cooperation partners, and
– the general extension of undertaking the preliminary market assessment (depending on the uncertainties and risks involved, as related, for instance to the newness of the product, the information available, etc.).

2b Preliminary technical assessment

As a complement to the preliminary market assessment, the manufacturer needs to undertake a preliminary technical assessment to cover the technical aspects of the innovation. Contributions to this stage may be made by

– research institutes (which possess information regarding existing technologies, as well as the latest and future technological developments),

- competitors (who have first-hand information about products and production techniques),
- industry experts (who possess information about general technological trends), and
- sister organizations, subsidiaries, and holding companies (which may possess specialized technical knowledge or may be able to provide critical product components or manpower at a competitive price).

3 CONCEPT STAGE

3a Concept identification

The various parties mentioned under 2A and 2B may also be involved in identifying, developing, and testing the concept. Therefore we will only point out some special potential problems.

In identifying, and also in testing the product concept, the manufacturer must beware of the classic mistake of relying solely on the information provided by innovative users. While these users are typically very interested and willing to cooperate, their wishes and demands may not be representative of the market in general. The information provided by them should therefore be checked against a broader group of users.

Sometimes, (for example to obtain very objective information) it may be desirable to question users who have a good relationship with one of the major competitors. These users should be asked about their needs and expectations, without disclosing the exact nature of the product concept.

3b Concept development

All kinds of organizations (potential users, distributors, sister organizations, competitors, research institutes, inspection agencies) and individuals (for example, industry experts) may provide input to this stage. The manufacturer should exercise caution in his selection of partners and ensure the confidentiality of information.

3c Concept test

The product concept should be tested with a representative group of potential users. As the manufacturer is now forced to disclose the exact nature of the new product, he may follow three strategies in keeping the concept a secret:

- skipping this concept test and trusting the information acquired earlier,
- having the concept tested exclusively by users with whom he has a good relationship, or
- maintaining confidentiality by having all users sign a contract.

4 DEVELOPMENT STAGE

4a Development of prototype

Potential users and research institutes can, in particular, contribute to the actual development of the prototype. Users possess the necessary application knowledge, while research institutes may have highly specialized technological know-how. Suppliers may contribute to the development stage by developing a (key) component of the product. In all cases, the manufacturer must

- select the cooperation partner (quality, image),
- define the contribution of both parties (demarcation of tasks), and
- formulate detailed agreements (contributions, responsibilities, deadlines, quality levels, costs).

4b Development of marketing plan

During the development stage, a marketing plan should be developed in addition to a prototype. The marketing plan is usually formulated by the manufacturer, except for those cases where the manufacturing firm employs an outside organization (such as an OEM or a distributor) to perform the marketing function. The marketing plan should address issues such as

- identification of the target customers,
- organization of the internal communication (informing and instructing the sales representatives),
- date of market introduction,
- how the new product will be launched (for example by means of a trade show),
- identification of the (groups of) people to be reached within the buying organizations,
- communication channels to be used,
- selling propositions to be employed,
- price level and strategy to be followed,

- expected reactions from competitors and suggested ways to prevent them, or react to them, and
- provision of information, instructions, training and promotional material to distributors.

5 TESTING STAGE

5a In-house tests

Although the in-house tests are undertaken by the manufacturer to test the technical functioning of the prototype, users or third parties may be indirectly involved.

- For example, users may be consulted to build a testing system that matches real-life conditions as closely as possible.
- Alternatively, research institutes may be called in to devise ingenious testing systems for testing prototypes under extreme conditions.

5b Test with users

When employing potential users to test a newly developed prototype the firm's most critical decisions relate to

- the time during the product development process when the tests will be performed (timing),
- the number of potential users to be testing the prototype,
- the criteria to be used in selecting potential users,
- the formulation of the test objectives,
- the instruction of potential users regarding the operation of the prototype and the performance of the tests,
- the execution of the test,
- the support and control provided by the firm,
- the registration of the test results (comprehensive evaluation protocols versus oral inquiry), and
- the evaluation of the test results.

The potential users who have tested the prototype may be employed during the launch stage to facilitate market acceptance (and thus diffusion) of the innovation. The pursuit of this strategy should be reflected in the criteria employed in selecting the potential users to test the prototype.

6 TRIAL STAGE

6a Finalization of design/pilot production

After finalization of the design, pilot production is generally under-taken by the manufacturer himself. Interaction at this stage may only occur if a supplier manufactures a strategic component. However, this can be handled, as with any other supplier, by agreements on quality control, rejects, delivery schedules, price discounts, etc.

6b Finalization of marketing plan/test market

At this stage, the final marketing plan is formulated. This plan contains a detailed market introduction strategy based on the more general marketing plan and addresses all issues in detail. Most of the promotional material to be used during market introduction should be ready about this time. Test markets are usually not feasible for complex industrial products.

6c Pre-commercialization business analysis

The pre-commercialization business analysis has also been found not to fit the situation of complex industrial innovations too well. For small firms, in particular, this activity is unrealistic at this point in the process.

7. LAUNCH STAGE

7a Full production

Apart maybe from some components, the manufacturer will see to production. With its suppliers, the manufacturer has to make agree-ments about such issues as

- quality levels,
- delivery schedules,
- handling of rejects,
- prices, and
- guaranteed future delivery.

7b Market launch

Both potential users and external research organizations, who tested the prototype, may be employed during the launch stage to accelerate market acceptance of the innovation. Involvement may take the form of

- using the names, reputations, and test results during sales presentations,
- using the names, reputations, and test results in promotional material,
- having the users demonstrate the innovation to prospective buyers,
- having the persons involved in the testing publish scientific publications about the results,
- having the users deliver talks or present papers at trade shows and scientific conferences, and
- having a user distribute the innovation.

Appendix B
Some methodological considerations

A large number of different research methods can be used in addressing a specific research question. The research methodology selected has important consequences for the interpretation of the results obtained, while the choice of the research methodology depends largely on the characteristics of the problem to be investigated. This appendix explains why we used case research and describes the main elements of the research methodology employed (additional details, as well as the questionnaires, can be found in Biemans (1989)).

According to Bonoma (1985, pp. 201–2) there are two important criteria to be taken into consideration when selecting a research method: the purpose of the research and the phenomena of interest. Similar criteria are given by Yin (1989, p. 16). For our investigation, we considered *case research* (defined by Bonoma (1985, p. 199) as the 'qualitative and field-based construction of case studies') to be the preferred research method for the following reasons.

1 The research aimed at describing the functioning of firm within networks and generating practical guidelines for management.
2 The existing body of theory is fairly limited.
3 The processes involved needed to be studied within their natural setting.
4 The information sought was largely qualitative and not amenable to quantification.
5 The events studied were both contemporary and outside the control of the researcher.

Both the exploratory study and follow-up investigation were conducted along the following lines.

Based on newspaper clippings, an export catalogue, expert interviews, and chance contacts the *samples* of firms were selected.

Typically, either a *marketing manager, R&D functionary, business unit manager or director* was contacted and, after being briefed on the nature and objectives of the study, asked to take part in the investigation. In specific cases a number of interviews with various persons had to be conducted in order to identify and reach the person most closely involved with the most recent innovation project.

Next, the basic information was gathered by means of *semi-structured in-depth personal interviews* with one or more persons at the manufacturer (such as managing directors, business unit managers, production employees, R&D managers, and sales representatives), the people most closely involved with the project acting as coordinator and being interviewed more than once. Each interview took between two and four hours. Interviewees were asked to (1) provide general information concerning the firm, its products and target markets, (2) describe in general the process of product development at their company, and (3) to give a detailed description of a recent and appropriate innovation project. Specific questions included the following. What is the most recent innovation? What are the benefits it offers to users? How is the firm's competitive position regarding the innovation? What are the stages that make up the process of product development? During which stages did the firm interact with other organizations? Which problems did occur during the development process and which measures were taken to solve them? The results of the interviews were written down in *comprehensive reports* and reviewed with the interviewees, thus inviting them to correct errors of fact and supply additional information. The information thus obtained was supplemented by (1) the incidental study of documents (for example schematic representations of the product development process, written-down review procedures, market introduction brochures, product information leaflets, articles, and books) and physical artefacts (for example the innovation, mock-ups, test models, and simulation devices) and (2) direct observation (for example of the testing of developed software, discussions between the manufacturer and major customers, and the functioning of prototypes at test sites).

In two cases during the exploratory study it was necessary to interview *competitors and/or industry experts* to gain insight into the market structure, the competitive position of the firm, the products offered by major competitors, and the current technological and market developments.

Subsequently, the *potential users and third parties*, insofar as they contributed substantially to the product development process, were interviewed in order to obtain additional information and cross-check the information provided by the manufacturer. Typically, one interview of two hours, supplemented by a limited number of phone conversations, proved to be sufficient to obtain the needed information. Because of existing relationships, the users in particular, and many of the third parties as well, were contacted through the manufacturer.

Based on all interview reports, *comprehensive case descriptions* were drawn up. Discrepancies between the information obtained from different sources were generally eliminated by conducting one follow-up interview (where necessary, cross-checked by telephone). These descriptions, including an analysis in the form of summary conclusions, were eventually reviewed by the manufacturers.

The comprehensive procedure outlined above was followed in all five firms of the preliminary study, as well as seven of the thirteen firms investigated during the follow-up investigation, sometimes resulting in conducting as many as ten in-depth interviews involving eleven different persons. In the remaining six firms (five of which were small and one of medium size), however, the managers operated under extreme time pressure and had only a limited amount of time available. In these cases, the desired information had to be gathered by means of only one personal interview, complemented by a few follow-up enquiries by telephone to obtain additional information. However, this presented no special problems because (1) all these cases were studied near the end of our investigation, (2) the innovation processes in question were relatively simple, and (3) we benefited from the experiences gained previously.

References

Abernathy, W.J. (1982), Competitive Decline in U.S. Innovation: The Management Factor, *Research Management*, September, pp. 34–41.

Abratt, R. (1986), Industrial Buying in High-Tech Markets, *Industrial Marketing Management*, Vol. 15, pp. 293–8.

Abu-Ismail, F.A.F. (1976), *Predicting the Adoption and Diffusion of Industrial Product Innovations*, PhD Thesis, University of Strathclyde, Department of Marketing, Glasgow.

Ackermans, M. (1987), Inkoop in Gezondheidszorg: Nog Veel Wantrouwen bij Relatie Inkoper-Leverancier (Purchasing in the Health Sector: Still Much Distrust in Purchaser–Supplier Relationship), *Tijdschrift voor Inkoop & Logistiek*, Vol. 3, No. 5, pp. 4–7.

Agarwala-Rogers, R. (1978), Re-Invention: The Reshaping of Innovations in Adoption, in: *Organizational Buying Behavior*, T.V. Bonoma and G. Zaltman (eds), American Marketing Association, Chicago, pp. 138–44.

Alster, N. (1986), Dealbusters: Why Partnerships Fail, *Electronic Business*, 1 April, pp. 70–5.

Ammer, D.S. (1974), Is Your Purchasing Department a Good Buy?, *Harvard Business Review*, March–April, pp. 36–159.

Andreasen, P.B. (1984), The Users' Need for Information on the Product, in: *The Health Service Market in Europe – Hospital Equipment*, R. Rapparini (ed.), Proceedings of an International Symposium, Luxemburg, 17–19 October, Elsevier Science Publishers B.V., Amsterdam, pp. 136–42.

Arguëlles, J.-M., L. Miravitlles, and P. Nueno (1990), Technological Strategy: Formulation, Method and Implementation, *European Business Journal*, Vol. 2, No. 1, pp. 42–52.

Arnstein, S.R. (1980), Technology Assessment: Opportunities and Obstacles, in: *The Management of Technology in Health and Medical Care*, C.A. Caceres (ed.), Artech House, Dedham, MA., pp. 175–97.

Avard, S., V. Catto, and M. Davidson (1982), Technological Innovation – Key to Productivity, *Research Management*, July, pp. 33–41.

Azároff, L.V. (1982), Industry–University Collaboration: How to Make it Work, *Research Management*, May, pp. 31–4.

Bahrami, H. and S. Evans (1989), Strategy Making in High-Technology Firms: The Empiricist Mode, *California Management Review*, Winter, pp. 107–28.

Balachandra, R. (1984), Critical Signals for Making Go/No Go Decisions in

New Product Development, *Journal of Product Innovation Management*, Vol. 2, pp. 92–100.

Banting, P.M. (1978), Unsuccessful Innovation in the Industrial Market, *Journal of Marketing*, Vol. 42, January, pp. 99–100.

Barath, R. and P.S. Hugstad (1977), Professionalism and the Behavior of Procurement Managers, *Industrial Marketing Management*, Vol. 6, pp. 297–306.

Barclay, I. and M.H. Benson (1987), Improving the Chances of New Product Success, in *Innovation: Adaptation and Growth*, R. Rothwell and J. Bessant (eds), Elsevier Science Publishers B.V., Amsterdam, pp. 103–12.

Barnes, J. and W.B. Ayars (1977), Reducing New Product Risk Through Understanding Buyer Behavior, *Industrial Marketing Management*, Vol. 6, pp. 189–92.

Barneveld Binkhuysen, F.H. and P.F.G.M. van Waes (1988), De Mobiele Computertomograaf (The Mobile Computerized Axial Tomograph), *Medisch Contact*, Nr. 5, 5 February, pp. 137–8.

Baruch. J. (1980), The Transfer of Medical Technology, in *The Management of Technology in Health and Medical Care*, C.A. Caceres (ed.), Artech House, Dedham, MA., pp. 45–50.

Becker, S. and T.L. Whisler (1967), The Innovative Organization: A Selective View of Current Theory and Research, *The Journal of Business*, Vol. 40, No. 4, pp. 462–9.

Beije, P.R. (1989), *Innovatie en Informatie-Overdracht in Interorganisatorische Netwerken – Gedrag van Actoren en Resultaat van Meso-Economische Groepen* (Innovation and Information-Transfer in Interorganizational Networks – Behaviour of Actors and Result of Meso-Economic Groups), PhD Thesis, Erasmus University, Faculty of Economics, Rotterdam, The Netherlands.

Bellizzi, J.A. (1979), Product Type and the Relative Influence of Buyers in Commercial Construction, *Industrial Marketing Management*, Vol. 8, pp. 213–20.

Bellizzi, J.A. (1981), Organizational Size and Buying Influences, *Industrial Marketing Management*, Vol. 10, pp. 17–21.

Bellizzi, J.A. and C.K. Walter (1980), Purchasing Agents Influence in the Buying Process, *Industrial Marketing Management*, Vol. 9, pp. 137–41.

Beneken, J.E.W. (1988), *De Problematiek van Communicatie binnen de Medische Technologie* (The Problems of Communication in Medical Technology), Paper presented at the World Trade Center Electronics Seminar on Medical Instrumentation and Communication, 14 September, Eindhoven, The Netherlands.

Bennekom, A. (1987), Medische Apparatuur is te Duur (Medical Instruments are too Expensive), *Intermediair*, Vol. 23, No. 40, 2 October, pp. 57–63.

Berkowitz, M. (1986), New Product Adoption by the Buying Organization: Who Are the Real Influencers?, *Industrial Marketing Management*, Vol. 15, pp. 33–43.

Berman, E.V. (1990), The Economic Impact of Industry-Funded University R&D, *Research Policy*, Vol. 19, pp. 349–55.

Bernstein, L.M., V.H. Beaven, J.R. Kimberly, and M.K. Moch (1975), Attributes of Innovations in Medical Technology and the Diffusion Process, in *The Diffusion of Medical Technology – Policy and Research*

Planning Perspectives, G. Gordon and G.L. Fisher (eds), Ballinger Publishing Company, Cambridge, MA, pp. 79–114.

Berry, L.L. (1980), Services Marketing is Different, *Business Magazine*, May–June, reprinted in *Services Marketing* (1984) C.H. Lovelock, Prentice-Hall, Englewood Cliffs, NJ, pp. 29–37.

Biemans, W.G. (1989), *Developing Innovations within Networks – With an Application to the Dutch Medical Equipment Industry*, PhD Thesis, Eindhoven University of Technology, Faculty of Industrial Engineering, Eindhoven, October.

Biemans, W.G. (1990), Manufacturer–User Relationships in Testing Newly Developed Prototypes, in *Research Developments in International Industrial Marketing and Purchasing*, R. Fiocca and I. Snehota (eds), Proceedings of the 6th IMP Conference, SDA Bocconi, Area Marketing, 24–5 September, Milan, pp. 132–50.

Biemans, W.G. and M.J. Brand (1989), Recente Trends in Onderzoek naar Industriële Marketing (Recent Trends in Research into Industrial Marketing), *Tijdschrift voor Marketing*, November, pp. 21–5.

Biemans, W.G. and B. Shaw (1990), Managing Innovation from a Value Chain Perspective; A Comparative Analysis in the Dutch and UK Medical Equipment Industries, in *Research Developments in International Industrial Marketing and Purchasing*, R. Fiocca and I. Snehota (eds), Proceedings of the 6th IMP Conference, SDA Bocconi, Area Marketing, 24–5 September, Milan, pp. 151–82.

Biemans, W.G. and R. de Vries (1987a), Het Markttesten van Industriële Innovaties (Testing Industrial Innovations with Customers), *Tijdschrift voor Marketing*, Vol. 21, March, pp. 24–9.

Biemans, W.G. and R. de Vries (1987b), Aanschaf van een Nieuwe Industriële Verpakking: Uitsluitend een Zaak voor Inkoop? (Purchasing a New Industrial Packaging: Exclusively the Business of the Purchasing Department?), *Tijdschrift voor Inkoop & Logistiek*, Vol. 21, November, pp. 32–7.

Biemans, W.G. and R. de Vries (1988), Supplier–Customer Relationships in Developing a Technological Process Innovation, in *Research Developments in International Marketing*, P.W. Turnbull and S.J. Paliwoda (eds), Proceedings of the 4th IMP Conference, University of Manchester, Institute of Science and Technology, 7–9 September, pp. 33–48.

Biggs, T.C. (1980), The Need for Methodology to Evaluate Clinical Technologies, in *The Management of Technology in Health and Medical Care*, C.A. Caceres (ed.), Artech House, Dedham, MA., pp. 169–74.

Boag, D.A. and B.L. Rinholm (1989), New Product Management Practices of Small High Technology Firms, *Journal of Product Innovation Management*, Vol. 6, No. 2, pp. 109–22.

Böcker, F. and H. Gierl (1988), Die Diffusion Neuer Produkte – Eine Kritische Bestandsaufnahme (The Diffusion of New Products – A Critical Review), *Zeitschrift für betriebswirtschaftliche Forschung*, Vol. 40, No. 1, pp. 32–48.

Boekema, F.W.M. and D.J.F. Kamann (1989), *Sociaal-Economische Netwerken* (Social-Economic Networks), Wolters-Noordhoff, Groningen, The Netherlands.

Bonoma, T.V. (1982), Major Sales: Who Really Does the Buying?, *Harvard*

Business Review, May–June, pp. 111–19.

Bonoma, T.V. (1985), Case Research in Marketing: Opportunities, Problems and a Process, *Journal of Marketing Research*, Vol. XXII, May, pp. 199–208.

Bonoma, T.V. and W.J. Johnston (1978), The Social Psychology of Industrial Buying and Selling, *Industrial Marketing Management*, Vol. 17, pp. 213–24.

Bonoma, T.V. and G. Zaltman (eds) (1978), *Organizational Buying Behavior*, American Marketing Association, Chicago, Ill.

Boorsma, M.A. and G.C. van Kooten (1989), *Role of Attitudes and Other Factors in the Adoption of Technological Innovations: Empirical Evidence from the Netherlands*, University of Groningen, School of Management and Organization, Research Report 89-06, Groningen, The Netherlands.

Booz, Allen and Hamilton (1968), *Management of New Products*, Booz, Allen & Hamilton Inc., New York, NY.

Booz, Allen and Hamilton (1982), *New Products Management for the 1980s*, Booz, Allen & Hamilton Inc., New York, NY.

Bradbury, J.A.A. (1989), *Product Innovation; Idea to Exploitation*, John Wiley, Chichester.

Braun, A. (1980), Interdependence Between Social and Technical Innovation, in *Current Innovation – Policy, Management and Research Options*, B.-A. Vedin (ed.), Almqvist & Wiksell International, Stockholm, pp. 115–20.

Briscoe, G. (1973), Some Observations on New Industrial Product Failures, *Industrial Marketing Management*, Vol. 2, pp. 151–62.

Bronikowski, K. (1990), Speeding New Products to Market, *The Journal of Business Strategy*, September/October, pp. 34–7.

Brown, L.A. (1981), *Innovation Diffusion: A New Perspective*, Methuen, New York, NY.

Brownlie, D.T. (1987), The Strategic Management of Technology: A New Wave of Market-led Pragmatism or a Return to Product Orientation?, *European Journal of Marketing*, Vol. 21, No. 9, pp. 45–65.

Buijs, J.A. (1984), *Innovatie en Interventie* (Innovation and Intervention), Kluwer, Deventer.

Buise, H. (1990), *Technology Transfer in the Dutch Electronic Industry: Analysis of Interorganizational Networks Supporting Small and Medium Sized Enterprises*, Erasmus University, Department of Institutional and Industrial Economics, Rotterdam, January.

Burt, D.N. (1989), Managing Suppliers up to Speed, *Harvard Business Review*, July–August, pp. 127–35.

Business Week (1990), Apple's New Strategy.

Cadbury, N.D. (1975), When, Where and How to Test Market, *Harvard Business Review*, May–June, pp. 96–105.

Campbell, N.C.G. (1985), Buyer/Seller Relationships in Japan and Germany: An Interaction Approach, *European Journal of Marketing*, Vol. 19, No. 3, pp. 57–66.

Campbell, N.C.G. and M.T. Cunningham (1985), Managing Customer Relationships. The Challenge of Deploying Scarce Managerial Resources, *International Journal of Research in Marketing*, Vol. 2, pp. 255–62.

Capon, N. and R. Glazer (1987), Marketing and Technology: A Strategic

Coalignment, *Journal of Marketing*, Vol. 51, July, pp. 1–14.

Carrière (1990), United Mist Niet de Bus (United Does Not Miss the Bus), 15 September, p. 11.

Chakrabarti, A.K. (1974), The Role of Champion in Product Innovation, *California Management Review*, Winter, pp. 58–62.

Chakrabarti, A.K., S. Feinman, and W. Fuentevilla (1982), Targeting Technical Information to Organizational Positions, *Industrial Marketing Management*, Vol. 11, pp. 195–203.

Chakrabarti, A.K. and J. Hauschildt (1989), The Division of Labour in Innovation Management, *R&D Management*, Vol. 19, No. 2, pp. 161–71.

Clifford, D.K., Jr, and R.E. Cavanagh (1985), *The Winning Performance: How America's High-Growth Midsize Companies Succeed*, Bantam Books, New York, NY.

Cohn, S.F. (1981), Adopting Innovations in a Technology Push Industry, *Research Management*, September, pp. 26–31.

Coleman, J.S., E. Katz, and H. Menzel (1966), *Medical Innovation: A Diffusion Study*, The Bobbs-Merrill Company, Indianapolis.

Commandeur, H.R. and P. Taal (1989), *Ontwikkeling van Industriële Netwerken* (Development of Industrial Networks), Research Paper 4, Erasmus University, Faculty of Economics, Rotterdam, The Netherlands.

Cook, D.E. (1970), *A Review of Some Methodological Aspects of Diffusion Research*, M.Sc. Dissertation, University of Bradford.

Cook, K.S. and R.M. Emerson (1978), Power, Equity and Commitment in Exchange Networks, *American Sociological Review*, Vol. 43, October, pp. 721–39.

Cooper, R.G. (1976), Introducing Successful New Industrial Products, *European Journal of Marketing*, Vol. 10, pp. 299–329.

Cooper. R.G. (1979a), The Dimensions of Industrial New Product Success and Failure, *Journal of Marketing*, Vol. 43, Summer, pp. 93–103.

Cooper, R.G. (1979b), Identifying Industrial New Product Success: Project NewProd, *Industrial Marketing Management*, Vol. 8, pp. 124–35.

Cooper, R.G. (1980), *Project NewProd: What Makes a New Product a Winner?*, Quebec Industrial Innovation Centre, Montreal, Canada.

Cooper, R.G. (1982), New Product Success in Industrial Firms, *Industrial Marketing Management*, Vol. 11, pp. 215–23.

Cooper, R.G. (1983a), The New Product Process: An Empirically-Based Classification Scheme, *R&D Management*, Vol. 13, No. 1, pp. 1–13.

Cooper, R.G. (1983b), A Process Model for Industrial New Product Development, *IEEE Transactions on Engineering Management*, Vol. EM-30, No. 1, February, pp. 2–11.

Cooper, R.G. (1984), The Performance Impact of Product Innovation Strategies, *European Journal of Marketing*, Vol. 18, No. 5, pp. 5–54.

Cooper, R.G. (1988), Predevelopment Activities Determine New Product Success, *Industrial Marketing Management*, Vol. 17, pp. 237–47.

Cooper, R.G. and E.J. Kleinschmidt (1986), An Investigation into the New Product Process: Steps, Deficiencies, and Impact, *Journal of Product Innovation Management*, Vol. 3, pp. 71–85.

Cooper, R.G. and E.J. Kleinschmidt (1987a), Success Factors in Product Innovation, *Industrial Marketing Management*, Vol. 16, pp. 215–23.

Cooper, R.G. and E.J. Kleinschmidt (1987b), New Products: What Separates

Winners from Losers?, *Journal of Product Innovation Management*, Vol. 4, pp. 169–84.

Cooper, R.G. and R.A. More (1979), Modular Risk Management: An Applied Example, *R&D Management*, Vol. 9, No. 2, pp. 93–9.

Corsten, H. and O. Lang (1988), Innovation Practice in Small and Medium-Sized Enterprises: An Empirical Survey of the Member States of the European Community, *Technovation*, Vol. 7, pp. 143–54.

Cowell, D.W. and K.J. Blois (1977), Conducting Market Research for High Technology Products, *Industrial Marketing Management*, Vol. 6, pp. 329–36.

Crawford, C.M. (1977), Marketing Research and the New Product Failure Rate, *Journal of Marketing*, April, pp. 51–61.

Crawford, C.M. (1979a), New Product Failure Rates – Facts and Fallacies, *Research Management*, September, pp. 9–13.

Crawford, C.M. (1979b), *The Rate and Causes of New Product Failure: An Intensive Literature Review*, The Third Annual Fall Conference of the Product Development & Management Association, November, Washington, DC.

Crawford, C.M. (1980), Defining the Charter for Product Innovation, *Sloan Management Review*, Fall, pp. 3–12.

Crawford, C.M. (1983), *New Products Management*, Richard Irwin, Homewood, Ill.

Crawford, C.M. (1987), New Product Failure Rates: A Reprise, *Research Management*, July–August, pp. 20–4.

Crow, L.E. and J.D. Lindquist (1985), Impact of Organizational and Buyer Characteristics on the Buying Center, *Industrial Marketing Management*, Vol. 14, pp. 49–58.

Cyert, R.M. and J.G. March (1963), *A Behavioral Theory of the Firm*, Prentice-Hall, Englewood Cliffs, NJ.

Czepiel, J.A. (1974), Word-of-Mouth Processes in the Diffusion of a Major Technological Innovation, *Journal of Marketing Research*, Vol. XI, pp. 172–80.

Dalton, G.W. (1968), *The Distribution of Authority in Formal Organization*, Harvard University Division of Research, Boston, MA.

Davidow, W.H. (1986), *Marketing High Technology*, The Free Press, New York, NY.

Day, R.L. and P.A. Herbig (1990), How the Diffusion of Industrial Innovations is Different from New Retail Products, *Industrial Marketing Management*, Vol. 19, pp. 261–6.

de Brentani, U. (1989), Success and Failure in New Industrial Services, *Journal of Product Innovation Management*, Vol. 6, pp. 239–58.

Dekker, W. (1986), 'Transfer' – *Het Belang van de Overdracht van Kennis tussen Universiteit en Bedrijfsleven* ('Transfer' – The Importance of the Transference of Knowledge between University and Industry), Address during the Business Day 86 of Leyden, University Hospital, University of Leyden, 20 November.

Dickson, D. (1988), Eureka!, *Technology Review*, August/September, pp. 27–33.

Dietrich, J.J. and R.K. Sen (1981), Making Industry–University–Government Collaboration Work, *Research Management*, September, pp. 23–5.

Docter, H.J. and C.T.M. Stokman (1987), *Diffusie van Innovaties: Met Kennis Meer Kans* (Diffusion of Innovations: Knowledge Breeds Prospects), Economisch Instituut voor het Midden- en Kleinbedrijf, December, Zoetermeer.

Doyle, P., A.G. Woodside, and P. Michell (1979), Organizations Buying in New Task and Rebuy Situations, *Industrial Marketing Management*, Vol. 8, pp. 7–11.

Drucker, P.F. (1954), *The Practice of Management*, Harper & Row, New York, NY.

Drucker, P.F. (1985), *Innovation and Entrepreneurship: Practice and Principles*, Harper & Row Publishers, New York, NY.

Drucker, P.F. (1988), The Coming of the New Organization, *Harvard Business Review*, January–February, pp. 45–53.

Duffy, J. and J. Kelly (1989), United Front is Faster, *Management Today*, November, pp. 131–9.

During, W.E. (1984), *Innovatieproblematiek in Kleine Industriële Bedrijven* (Innovation Problems in Small Industrial Firms), PhD Thesis, Twente University, Department of Management Studies, Enschede, The Netherlands.

During, W.E. (1986), Project Management and Management of Innovation in Small Industrial Firms, *Technovation*, Vol. 4, pp. 269–78.

Dwyer, F.R., P.H. Schurr, and S. Oh (1987), Developing Buyer–Seller Relationships, *Journal of Marketing*, Vol. 51, April, pp. 11–27.

Easton, G. (1989), Industrial Networks – A Review, in *Research in Marketing: An International Perspective*, D.T. Wilson, S.-L. Han, and G.W. Holler (eds), Proceedings of the 5th IMP Conference, Penn State University, Institute for the Study of Business Markets, 5–7 September, pp. 161–82.

Easton, G. and A. Lundgren (1988), Changes in Industrial Networks as Flows Through Nodes, in *Research Developments in International Marketing*, P.W. Turnbull and S.J. Paliwoda (eds), Proceedings of the 4th IMP Conference, University of Manchester, Institute of Science and Technology, 7–9 September, pp. 181–97.

Erickson, R.A. and A.C. Gross (1980), Generalizing Industrial Buying: A Longitudinal Study, *Industrial Marketing Management*, Vol. 9, pp. 253–65.

Erickson, T.J., J.F. Magee, P.A. Roussel, and K.N. Saad (1990), Managing Technology as a Business Strategy, *Sloan Management Review*, Spring, pp. 73–78.

Ettlie, J.E. (1986), Implementing Manufacturing Technologies: Lessons from Experience, in *Managing Technological Innovation*, D.D. Davis and Associates (eds), Jossey-Bass Publishers, San Francisco, pp. 72–104.

Ettlie, J.E. and A.H. Rubenstein (1987), Firm Size and Product Innovation, *Journal of Product Innovation Management*, Vol. 4, pp. 89–108.

Feller, I. (1990), Universities as Engines of R&D-Based Economic Growth: They Think They Can, *Research Policy*, Vol. 19, pp. 335–48.

FEM (1987), De Ondergewaardeerde Inkoper (The Underrated Purchaser), 4 April, pp. 31–3.

Fiocca, R. and I. Snehota (eds) (1990), *Research Developments in International Industrial Marketing and Purchasing*, Proceedings of the 6th IMP

Conference, SDA Bocconi, Area Marketing, 24–25 September, Milan.

Fombrun, C.J. (1982), Strategies for Network Research in Organizations, *Academy of Management Review*, Vol. 7, No. 2, pp. 280–291.

Ford, D. (1980), The Development of Buyer–Seller Relationships in Industrial Markets, *European Journal of Marketing*, Vol. 14, No. 5/6, pp. 339–53.

Ford, D. (1984), Buyer–Seller Relationships in International Industrial Markets, *Industrial Marketing Management*, Vol. 13, pp. 101–12.

Ford, D. (1989), One More Time, What Buyer–Seller Relationships are all About, in *Research in Marketing: An International Perspective*, D.T. Wilson, S.-L. Han, and G.W. Holler (eds), Proceedings of the 5th IMP Conference, Penn State University, Institute for the Study of Business Markets, 5–7 September, pp. 814–36.

Fortune (1987), Speeding New Ideas to Market, 2 March, pp. 54–7.

Fortune (1989), How Managers Can Succeed through Speed, 13 February, pp. 30–5.

Fortune (1990), Turning R&D into Real Products, 2 July, pp. 64–9.

Foster, D.W. (1972), *Planning Products and Markets*, Longman, Harlow.

Foster, R.N. (1986), *Innovation; The Attacker's Advantage*, Macmillan, London.

Fowler, D.R. (1984), University–Industry Research Relationships, *Research Management*, January–February, pp. 35–41.

Foxall, G.R. (1979), Farmers Tractor Purchase Decisions: A Study of Interpersonal Communication in Industrial Buying Behaviour, *European Journal of Marketing*, Vol. 13, No. 8, pp. 299–308.

Foxall, G.R. (1980), Adoption of a Discontinuous PDM Innovation in Agriculture: Rough-Terrain Forklift Trucks, *European Journal of Marketing*, Vol. 14, No. 1, pp. 75–82.

Foxall, G.R. (1984), *Corporate Innovation: Marketing and Strategy*, Croom Helm, London.

Foxall, G.R. (1986), A Conceptual Extension of the Customer-Active Paradigm, *Technovation*, Vol. 4, pp. 17–27.

Foxall, G.R. (1989), User Initiated Product Innovations, *Industrial Marketing Management*, Vol. 18, pp. 95–104.

Foxall, G.R. and B. Johnston (1987), Strategies of User-Initiated Product Innovation, *Technovation*, Vol. 6, pp. 87–102.

Foxall, G.R. and J.D. Tierney (1984), From CAP1 to CAP2: User-Initiated Innovation from the User's Point of View, *Management Decision*, Vol. 22, No. 5, pp. 3–15.

Frey, B.E. (1986), Innovation through Joint Venture – A Case Study, in *The Art and Science of Innovation Management*, H. Hübner (ed.), Elsevier Science Publishers B.V., Amsterdam, pp. 285–95.

Gadde, L.-E. and L.-G. Mattsson (1987), Stability and Change in Network Relationships, *International Journal of Research in Marketing*, Vol. 4, pp. 29–41.

Gatignon, H. and T.S. Robertson (1989), Technology Diffusion: An Empirical Test of Competitive Effects, *Journal of Marketing*, Vol. 53, January, pp. 35–49.

Gelderman, C.J. and P.S.H Leeflang (1988), Marketing van Diensten (Marketing of Services), in *Probleemvelden in Marketing* (Problem Areas in Marketing), Vol. II of Probleemgebied Marketing, een Management-benadering (Problem Field Marketing, a Management Approach), P.S.H. Leeflang (ed.), Stenfert Kroese, Leiden, The Netherlands, pp. 89–109.

Gemünden, H.G. (1985), 'Promotors' – Key Persons for the Development and Marketing of Innovative Industrial Products, in *Industrial Marketing – A German–American Perspective*, K. Backhaus and D.T. Wilson (eds), Springer, Berlin, pp. 134–66.

Gisser, P. (1973), New Products are a Gamble, But the Risk can be Reduced, *Industrial Marketing*, May, pp. 28–32.

Giunipero, L.C. (1984), Purchasing's Role in Computer Buying: A Comparative Study, *Industrial Marketing Management*, Vol. 13, pp. 241–8.

Giunipero, L. and G. Zenz (1982), Impact of Purchasing Trends on Industrial Marketers, *Industrial Marketing Management*, Vol. 11, pp. 17–23.

Gobeli, D.H. and D.J. Brown (1987), Analyzing Product Innovations, *Research Management*, July–August, pp. 25–31.

Gordon, G. and G.L. Fisher (eds) (1975), *The Diffusion of Medical Technology – Policy and Research Planning Perspectives*, Ballinger Publishing Company, Cambridge, MA.

Granovetter, M.S. (1973), The Strength of Weak Ties, *American Journal of Sociology*, Vol. 78, No. 6, pp. 1360–80.

Greer, A.L. (1988), The State of the Art versus the State of the Science: The Diffusion of New Medical Technologies into Practice, *International Journal of Technology Assessment in Health Care*, Vol. 4, pp. 5–26.

Grönhaug, K. (1975), Search Behavior in Organizational Buying, *Industrial Marketing Management*, Vol. 4, pp. 15–23.

Grossman, J.B. (1970), The Supreme Court and Social Change, *American Behavioral Scientist*, Vol. 13, No. 4.

Gummesson, E. (1987), The New Marketing – Developing Long-term Interactive Relationships, Long Range Planning, Vol. 20, No. 4 (August), pp. 10–20.

Gupta, A.K. and D.L. Wilemon (1990), Accelerating the Development of Technology-Based New Products, *California Management Review*, Winter, pp. 24–44.

Haeffner, E.A. (1973), The Innovation Process, *Technology Review*, March/April, pp. 18–25.

Hagedoorn, J. (1990), Organizational Modes of Inter-Firm Cooperation and Technology Transfer, *Technovation*, Vol. 10, No. 1, pp. 17–29.

Håkansson, H. (ed.) (1982), *International Marketing and Purchasing of Industrial Goods: An Interaction Approach*, John Wiley and Sons, Chichester.

Håkansson, H. (ed.) (1987a), *Industrial Technological Development: A Network Approach*, Croom Helm, London.

Håkansson, H. (1987b), Product Development in Networks, in *Industrial Technological Development: A Network Approach*, H. Håkansson (ed.), Croom Helm, London, pp. 84–127.

Håkansson, H. (1989), *Corporate Technological Behaviour – Cooperation and Networks*, Routledge, London.

Håkansson, H. (1990), Technological Collaboration in Industrial Networks, *European Management Journal*, Vol. 8, No. 3 (September), pp. 371–9.

Håkansson, H. and J. Johanson (1989), Relationships in Industrial Networks, in *Research in Marketing: An International Perspective*, D.T. Wilson, S.-L. Han and G.W. Holler (eds), Proceedings of the 5th IMP Conference, Penn State University, Institute for the Study of Business Markets, 5–7 September, pp. 217–23.

Håkansson, H. and J. Laage-Hellman (1984), Developing a Network R&D Strategy, *Journal of Product Innovation Management*, Vol. 4, pp. 224–37.

Hamel, G., Y.L. Doz and C.K. Prahalad (1989), Collaborate with Your Competitors – And Win, *Harvard Business Review*, January–February, pp. 133–9.

Harding, M. (1966), Who Really Makes the Purchasing Decision?, *Industrial Marketing*, Vol. 51, September, pp. 76–81.

Harvey, E. and R. Mills (1970), Patterns of Organizational Adaptation: A Political Perspective, in *Power in Organizations*, M.N. Zald (ed.), Vanderbilt University Press, Nashville, Tennessee, pp. 181–213.

Hayward, G. (1978), Market Adoption of New Industrial Products, *Industrial Marketing Management*, Vol. 7, pp. 193–8.

Hayward, G., D.H. Allen, and J. Masterson (1977), Innovation Profiles: A New Tool for Capital Equipment Manufacturers, *European Journal of Marketing*, Vol. 11, No. 4, pp. 299–311.

Henderson, J.C. (1990), Plugging into Strategic Partnerships: The Critical IS Connection, *Sloan Management Review*, Spring, pp. 7–18.

Hill, R.M., R.S. Alexander, and J.S. Cross (1975), *Industrial Marketing*, 4th. ed, R.D. Irwin, Homewood, Ill.

Hise, R.T., C.M. Futrell, and D.R. Snyder (1980), University Research Centers as a New Product Development Resource, *Research Management*, May, pp. 25–28.

Hodock, C.L. (1990), Strategies Behind the Winners and Losers, *The Journal of Business Strategy*, September/October, pp. 4–7.

Holt, K. (1983), *Product Innovation Management*, Butterworths, London.

Hopkins, D.S. (1981), New-Product Winners and Losers, *Research Management*, May, pp. 12–17.

Hopkins, D.S. and E.L. Bailey (1971), *New Product Pressures*, The Conference Board Record, Vol. III, No. 6, June, pp. 16–24.

Hutt, M.D. and T.W. Speh (1989), *Business Marketing Management; A Strategic View of Industrial and Organizational Markets*, 3rd ed, The Dryden Press, Hinsdale, Ill.

Hutton, J. (1984), Hospital Purchasing Procedures Throughout the Community, in *The Health Service Market in Europe – Hospital Equipment*, R. Rapparini (ed.), Proceedings of an International Symposium, Luxembourg, 17–19 October, 1983, Elsevier Science Publishers B.V., Amsterdam, pp. 160–70.

Industrial Research Institute (1980), The Impact of Industrial Innovation on the Economic and Social Welfare of the United States, *Research Management*, November, pp. 10–13.

Het Instrument (1990), *Trendonderzoek t/m Derde Kwartaal 1990* (Trend Investigation up to Third Quarter 1990), Quarterly report published by Het Instrument, Soest, The Netherlands.

Jackson, B.B. (1985), *Winning and Keeping Industrial Customers: The Dynamics of Customer Relationships*, Lexington Books, Lexington, MA.

Jackson, D.W., Jr, J.E. Keith, and R.K. Burdick (1984), Purchasing Agents'

Perceptions of Industrial Buying Center Influence: A Situational Approach, *Journal of Marketing*, Vol. 48, Fall, pp. 75–83.

James, B.G. (1985), Alliance: The New Strategic Focus, *Long Range Planning*, Vol. 18, No. 3, pp. 76–81.

Jervis, P. (1975), Innovation and Technology Transfer – The Roles and Characteristics of Individuals, *IEEE Transactions on Engineering Management*, February, pp. 19–27.

Johanson, J. and L.-G. Mattsson (1985), Marketing Investments and Market Investments in Industrial Networks, *International Journal of Research in Marketing*, Vol. 2, pp. 185–95.

Johne, F.A. (1984), Segmenting Buyers on the Basis of Their Business Strategies, *International Journal of Research in Marketing*, Vol. 1, pp. 183–198.

Johne, F.A. and P.A. Snelson (1988), Success Factors in Product Innovation: A Selected Review of the Literature, *Journal of Product Innovation Management*, Vol. 5, No. 2, pp. 114–28.

Johne, F.A. and S. Rowntree (1990), High Technology Product Development in Small Firms: Does Marketing Matter?, in *Advanced Research in Marketing*, H. Mühlbacher and C. Jochum (eds), Proceedings of the 19th Annual Conference of the European Marketing Academy, Innsbruck, Austria, 22–25 May, pp. 307–23.

Johnson, S.C. and C. Jones (1957), How to Organize for New Products, Harvard Business Review, May–June.

Johnston, W.J. and T.V. Bonoma (1981), The Buying Center: Structure and Interaction Patterns, *Journal of Marketing*, Vol. 45, Summer, pp. 143–56.

Kamann, D.J.F. (1991), Network Behaviour of Actors in Economic and Geographical Space, *Environment and Planning*, forthcoming.

Kamann, D.J.F. and D. Strijker (1991), Mechanisms of Coordination in the Dutch Horticultural Complex, *European Review of Agricultural Economics*, forthcoming.

Kanter, R.M. (1989), *When Giants Learn to Dance*, Simon and Schuster, New York, NY.

Kantrow, A.M. (1980), The Strategy–Technology Connection, *Harvard Business Review*, July–August, pp. 6–21.

Kennedy, A.M. (1983), The Adoption and Diffusion of New Industrial Products: A Literature Review, *European Journal of Marketing*, Vol. 17, pp. 31–88.

Kennedy, E.J. (1987), Social Network Analysis: Potential for Marketing Application, in *'Marketing Theory'* – *Proceedings of the 1987 AMA Winter Educators' Conference*, R.W. Belk *et al.* (eds), Proceedings Series, AMA, Chicago, Ill, pp. 101–6.

King, C.W. (1966), Adoption and Diffusion Research in Marketing: An Overview, in *Proceedings of the American Marketing Association Conference*, R.M. Haas (ed.), American Marketing Association, Chicago, pp. 665–84.

King, R., O. Port, and Z. Schiller (1990), Een Slimmere Manier van Fabriceren (A Smarter Way to Manufacture), *Management Team*, 24 September, pp. 24–37.

Kline, S.J. (1985), Innovation is Not a Linear Process, *Research Management*, July–August, pp. 36–45.

Knight, K. (1967), A Descriptive Model of the Intra-Firm Innovation Process,

Journal of Business, Vol. 40, October, pp. 478–96.

Kok, J.A.A.M., G.J.D. Offerman, and P.H. Pellenbarg (1985), *Innovatieve Bedrijven in het Grootstedelijk Milieu* (Innovative Firms in the Urban Region), Geographical Institute of the University of Groningen, Groningen.

Kooy, B.J.G. van der (1983), *Management van Innovatie; De Mens als Vergeten Dimensie* (Management of Innovation; Man as Forgotten Dimension), Kluwer, Deventer, The Netherlands.

Kooy, B.J.G. van der (1988), *Innovatie Gedefinieerd; Een Analyse en een Voorstel* (Innovation Defined; An Analysis and a Proposal), Report of the Eindhoven University of Technology, EUT/BDK/33 Eindhoven.

Krieger, R.H. and J.R. Meredith (1985), Emergency and Routine MRO Part Buying, *Industrial Marketing Management,* Vol. 14, pp. 277–82.

Kuczmarski, T.D. (1988), *Managing New Products*, Prentice-Hall, Englewood Cliffs, NJ.

LaFief, W.C. and C.R. O'Neal (1987), The Process of Developing Commitment in the Industrial Buyer–Seller Relationship, in *'Marketing Theory' – Proceedings of the 1987 AMA Winter Educators' Conference,* R.W. Belk *et al.* (eds), Proceedings Series, AMA, Chicago, Ill., p. 121.

Lancaster, G.A. and M. White (1976), Industrial Diffusion, Adoption and Communication, *European Journal of Marketing,* Vol. 10, No. 5, pp. 280–98.

Lazarsfeld, P.F., B. Berelson, and H. Gaudet (1948), *The People's Choice,* 2nd ed, Columbia University Press, New York, NY.

Leiva, W.A. and J.W. Obermayer (1989), Commonsense Product Development, *Business Marketing,* Vol. 74, No. 8, August, pp. 44–8.

Link, P. (1987), Keys to New Product Success and Failure, *Industrial Marketing Management,* Vol. 16, pp. 109–18.

Lipnack, J. and J. Stamps (1987), A Network Model, *The Futurist,* July–August, pp. 23–25.

Lister, P. (1967), Identifying and Evaluating the Purchasing Influence, *IMRA Journal,* August, pp. 190–9.

Littler, D.A. and R.C. Sweeting (1985), Radical Innovation in the Mature Company, *European Journal of Marketing,* Vol. 19, No. 4, pp. 33–44.

Lyons, T.F., A.R. Krachenberg, and J.W. Henke, Jr (1990), Mixed Motive Marriages: What's Next for Buyer–Supplier Relations?, *Sloan Management Review,* Spring, pp. 29–36.

Mahajan, V. and E. Muller (1979), Innovation Diffusion and New Product Growth Models in Marketing, *Journal of Marketing,* Vol. 43, Fall, pp. 55–68.

Mahajan, V., E. Muller and F.M. Bass (1990), New Product Diffusion Models in Marketing: A Review and Directions for Research, *Journal of Marketing,* Vol. 54, January, pp. 1–26.

Maidique, M.A. and B.J. Zirger (1984), A Study of Success and Failure in Product Innovation: The Case of the U.S. Electronics Industry, *IEEE Transactions on Engineering Management,* Vol. EM-31, No. 4, November, pp. 192–203.

Maidique, M.A. and B.J. Zirger (1985), *The New Product Learning Cycle,* Research Report Series, Innovation and Entrepreneurship Institute, School of Business Administration, University of Miami, Coral Gables, FL., February, pp. 85–101.

Mansfield, E. (1968), *The Economics of Technological Change*, Norton & Co., New York, NY.

Mantel, S.J., Jr and J.R. Meredith (1986), The Role of Customer Cooperation in the Development, Marketing and Implementation of Innovations, in *The Art and Science of Innovation Management*, H. Hübner (ed.), Elsevier Science Publishers B.V., Amsterdam, pp. 27–36.

Mantel, S.J., Jr and G. Rosegger (1987), The Role of Third-Parties in the Diffusion of Innovations: A Survey, in *Innovation, Adaptation and Growth*, R. Rothwell and J. Bessant (eds), Elsevier Science Publishers B.V., Amsterdam, pp. 123–34.

Marquis, D.G. (1969), The Anatomy of Successful Innovations, *Innovation*, Vol. 1, November, pp. 28–37.

Marshall, A. (1920), *Principles of Economics*, Macmillan, London.

Martilla, J.A. (1971), Word-of-Mouth Communication in the Industrial Adoption Process, *Journal of Marketing Research*, Vol. VIII, May, pp. 173–8.

Martin, M.J.C. (1984), *Managing Technological Innovation and Entrepreneurship*, Reston Publishing Company, Inc., Reston, Virginia.

Materials Advisory Board (1966), *Report on the Ad-Hoc Committee on Principles of Research-Engineering Interactions*, National Academy of Engineering, Washington, DC, July.

Mattson, M.R. (1988), How to Determine the Composition and Influence of a Buying Center, *Industrial Marketing Management*, Vol. 17, pp. 205–14.

Mattsson, L.-G. (1985), An Application of a Network Approach to Marketing: Defending and Changing Market Positions, in *Changing the Course of Marketing: Alternative Paradigms for Widening Marketing Theory*, Research in Marketing, Supplement 2, N. Dholakia and J. Arndt (eds), JAI Press, Greenwich, CT, pp. 263–88.

Mattsson, L.-G. (1987), Indirect Relations in Industrial Networks – A Conceptual Analysis of Their Significance for the Firm's Strategic Activities, in *'Marketing Theory' – Proceedings of the 1987 AMA Winter Educators' Conference*, R.W. Belk *et al.* (eds), Proceedings Series, AMA, Chicago, Ill., pp. 127–32.

McDonald, D.W. and S.M. Gieser (1987), Making Cooperative Research Relationships Work, *Research Management*, July–August, pp. 38–42.

McKenna, R. (1985), *The Regis Touch*, Addison-Wesley, Reading, MA.

Meadows, D. (1969), Estimate Accuracy and Project Selection Models in Industrial Research, *Industrial Management Review*, Spring.

Meyer, M.H. and E.B. Roberts (1986), New Product Strategy in Small Technology Based Firms: A Pilot Study, *Management Science*, Vol. 32, No. 7, pp. 806–21.

Miaoulis, G. and P.J. LaPlaca (1982), A Systems Approach for Developing High Technology Products, *Industrial Marketing Management*, Vol. 11, pp. 253–62.

Midgley, D.F. (1977), *Innovation and New Product Marketing*, Croom Helm, London.

Ministry of Economic Affairs (1986), *Stimuleringsprogramma Medische Technology* (Stimulation Programme Medical Technology), June, The Hague, The Netherlands.

Mitsch, R.A. (1990), Three Roads to Innovation, *The Journal of Business*

252 *Managing innovation within networks*

Strategy, September/October, pp. 18–21.

Mogee, M.E. and A.S. Bean (1978), The Role of the Purchasing Agent in Industrial Innovation, in *Organizational Buying Behavior*, T.V. Bonoma and G. Zaltman (eds), American Marketing Association, Chicago, Ill., pp. 126–37.

Möller, K.E. and D.T. Wilson (1988), Interaction Perspective in Business Marketing: An Exploratory Contingency Framework, in *Research Developments in International Marketing*, P.W. Turnbull and S.J. Paliwoda (eds), Proceedings of the 4th IMP Conference, University of Manchester, Institute of Science and Technology, 7–9 September, pp. 394–443.

Moore, R.A. (1984), Control of New Product Development in UK Companies, *European Journal of Marketing*, Vol. 18, No. 6/7, pp. 5–13.

Moore, W.L. (1987), New Product Development Practices of Industrial Marketers, *Journal of Product Innovation Management*, Vol. 4, pp. 6–20.

More, R.A. (1984), Improving the Organizational Adoption Rate for High-Technology Industrial Products, *Journal of Product Innovation Management*, Vol. 1, pp. 182–98.

Moriarty, R.T. and J.E.G. Bateson (1982), Exploring Complex Decision Making Units: A New Approach, *Journal of Marketing Research*, Vol. XIX, pp. 182–91.

Moriarty, R.T. and R.E. Spekman (1984), An Empirical Investigation of the Information Sources Used During the Industrial Buying Process, *Journal of Marketing Research*, Vol. XXI, May, pp. 137–47.

Myers, S. and E.E. Sweezy (1978), Why Innovations Fail, *Technology Review*, March/April, pp. 41–6.

Nabseth, L. and G.F. Ray (eds) (1974), *The Diffusion of New Industrial Processes; An International Study*, Cambridge University Press, Cambridge.

NEHEM (1987), *Regelgeving voor Medische Technologie* (Regulations Concerning Medical Technology), 's-Hertogenbosch, January.

Nelson, R.E. (1988), Social Network Analysis as Intervention Tool, *Group & Organization Studies*, Vol. 13, No. 1, March, pp. 39–58.

Nevens, T.M., G.L. Summe, and B. Uttal (1990), Commercializing Technology: What the Best Companies Do, *Harvard Business Review*, May–June, pp. 154–163.

New, D.E. and J.L. Schlacter (1979), Abandon Bad R&D Projects with Earlier Marketing Appraisals, *Industrial Marketing Management*, Vol. 8, pp. 274–80.

Newall, J. (1977), Industrial Buying Behaviour; A Model of the Implications of Risk Handling Behaviour for Communication Policies in Industrial Marketing, *European Journal of Marketing*, Vol. 11, pp. 105–211.

Nicosia, F.M. and Y. Wind (1977), Emerging Models of Organizational Buying Processes, *Industrial Marketing Management*, Vol. 6, pp. 353–69.

Nijverheidsorganisatie TNO, De (1974), *Innovatieprocessen in de Nederlandse Industrie* (Innovation Processes in the Dutch Industry), TNO/COP study.

Nonaka, I. (1988), Creating Organizational Order out of Chaos: Self-Renewal in Japanese Firms, *California Management Review*, Spring, pp. 57–73.

Nonaka, I. (1990), Redundant, Overlapping Organization: A Japanese Approach to Managing the Innovation Process, *California Management Review*, Spring, pp. 27–38.

Nooteboom, B. (1989), Diffusion, Uncertainty and Firm Size, *International Journal of Research in Marketing*, Vol. 6, pp. 109–28.

Nooteboom, B. and M. Boorsma (1990), *Adoption Under Conditions of Rapid Technical Change and Risk of Implementation*, University of Groningen, School of Management and Organisation, Research Report 1990–1.

Normann, R. (1971), Organizational Innovativeness: Product Variation and Reorientation, *Administrative Science Quarterly*, Vol. 16, No. 2, pp. 203–15.

Norris, W.C. (1985), Innovation is Spelled Cooperation, *Business and Economic Review*, Vol. 31, No. 4, July, pp. 29–34.

Norton, J.A. and F.M. Bass (1987), A Diffusion Theory Model of Adoption and Substitution for Successive Generations of High-Technology Products, *Management Science*, Vol. 33, No. 9, September, pp. 1069–86.

NRC Handelsblad (1990a), Solo van Dwarse Onderzoeker (Solo from Contrary Scientist), 18 April, p. 1 and De 'Solotoer' van een Onderzoeker bij Philips (The 'Solo Performance' of a Scientist at Philips), 18 April, p. 11.

NRC Handelsblad (1990b), Philips Stapt uit Groot Chip-Project (Philips Quits Large Chip Project), 31 August, p.1 and Mega-Project Commerciële Flop voor Philips (Mega Project Commercial Failure for Philips), 31 August, p. 11.

NRC Handelsblad (1990c), Nieuwe Philips-Catechismus Moet Leiden tot Cultuurshock (New Philips Gospel Needs to Result in Culture Shock), 10 October, p. 14.

NRC Handelsblad (1990d), Eindhovense Rouw met Hemels Randje (Eindhoven's Cloud with a Silver Lining), 27 October, p. 15.

Nyström, H. (1985), Product Development Strategy: An Integration of Technology and Marketing, *Journal of Product Innovation Management*, Vol. 2, pp. 25–33.

Oakey, R., R. Rothwell, and S. Cooper (1988), *Management of Innovation in High Technology Small Firms*, Pinter, London.

OECD (1982), *Innovation in Small and Medium Firms*, Report of the Organisation for Economic Cooperation and Development, Paris.

Ohmae, K. (1989), The Global Logic of Strategic Alliances, *Harvard Business Review*, March–April, pp. 143–54.

Olson, P.D. (1990), Choices for Innovation-Minded Corporations, *The Journal of Business Strategy*, January/February, pp. 42–6.

Ozanne, U.B. and G.A. Churchill, Jr (1968), Adoption Research: Information Sources in the Industrial Purchasing Decision, in *Marketing and the New Science of Planning*, R.L. King (ed.), Proceedings Fall Conference, American Marketing Association, Chicago, pp. 352–9.

Ozanne, U.B. and G.A. Churchill, Jr (1971), Five Dimensions of the Industrial Adoption Process, *Journal of Marketing Research*, Vol. 8, August, pp. 322–8.

Pappas, C. (1984), Strategic Management of Technology, *Journal of Product Innovation Management*, Vol. 1, pp. 30–5.

Parkinson, S.T. (1982), The Role of the User in Successful New Product Development, *R&D Management*, Vol. 12, No. 3, pp. 123–31.

Peplow, M.E. (1960), Design Acceptance, in *The Design Method*, S.A. Gregory (ed.), Butterworth, London.

Peters, T.J. (1987), *Thriving on Chaos; Handbook for a Management Revolution*, Macmillan, London.

Peters, T.J. and R.H. Waterman (1982), *In Search of Excellence: Lessons from America's Best Run Companies*, Harper and Row, New York, NY.

Petroni, G. (1985), Who Should Plan Technological Innovation?, *Long Range Planning*, Vol. 18, No. 5, pp. 108–15.

Poutsma, E., P.M. van der Staal, F.W. van Uxem, A.H.C.M. Walravens, and A.B. Zwaard (1987), *Procesvernieuwing en Automatisering in het MKB* (Process Innovation and Automation in Small and Medium-Sized Firms), Research Institute for Small and Medium-Sized Enterprise/University of Technology Delft, Zoetermeer/Delft, June.

Quinn, J.B. (1985), Managing Innovation: Controlled Chaos, *Harvard Business Review*, May–June, pp. 73–84.

Rabino, S. (1983), Influencing the Adoption of an Innovation, *Industrial Marketing Management*, Vol. 12, pp. 233–41.

Rabino, S. and T.E. Moore (1989), Managing New-Product Announcements in the Computer Industry, *Industrial Marketing Management*, Vol. 18, pp. 35–43.

Rajagopal, S. and K.R. Deans (1990), Cooperative Relationship: The Next Chapter in the Buyer/Supplier Manual, in *Research Developments in International Industrial Marketing and Purchasing*, R. Fiocca and I. Snehota (eds), Proceedings of the 6th IMP Conference, SDA Bocconi, Area Marketing, 24–25 September, Milan, pp. 909–33.

Ramanujam, V. and G.O. Mensch (1985), Improving the Strategy–Innovation Link, *Journal of Product Innovation Management*, Vol. 4, pp. 213–23.

Riedle, K. (1989), Demand for R&D Activities and the Trade Off Between In-House and External Research: A Viewpoint from Industry with Reference to Large Companies and Small and Medium-Sized Enterprises, *Technovation*, Vol. 9, pp. 213–25.

Rijcke, J. de, and W. Faes (1982), Management in het Inkoopgebeuren: Noodzakelijk en Mogelijk (Management in Purchasing: Necessary and Possible), *Economisch en Sociaal Tijdschrift*, Nr. 4, pp. 419–42.

Rijcke, J. de, and A. van Weele (1980), Het Profiel van de Inkoper in de Jaren 80 (The Profile of the Purchasing Agent in the 80s), *Bedrijfsvoering*, December, pp. 674–8.

Roberts, E.B. (1988), Managing Invention and Innovation, *Research · Technology Management*, January–February, pp. 11–29.

Roberts, E.B. (1989), Managing Technological Innovation in the Medical Devices Industry, *Research · Technology Management*, July–August, pp. 34–41.

Roberts, E.B. and D.H. Peters (1982), Commercial Innovation from University Faculty, *Research Management*, May, pp. 24–30.

Robertson, A. (1974), Innovation Management, *Management Decision Monograph*, Vol. 12, No. 6.

Robertson, A., B. Achilladelis, and P. Jervis (1972), *Success and Failure in Industrial Innovation; Report on the Project SAPPHO*, Centre for the

Study of Industrial Innovation, London.

Robertson, T.S. (1971), *Innovative Behavior and Communication*, Holt, Rinehart and Winston, New York, NY.

Robertson, T.S. and H. Gatignon (1986), Competitive Effects on Technology Diffusion, *Journal of Marketing*, Vol. 50, July, pp. 1–12.

Robinson, P.J., C.W. Faris, and Y. Wind (eds) (1967), *Industrial Buying and Creative Marketing*, Allyn and Bacon, Inc., Boston, MA.

Rogers, E.M. (1962), *Diffusion of Innovations*, The Free Press of Glencoe, New York, NY.

Rogers, E.M. (1983), *Diffusion of Innovations*, 3rd ed, The Free Press, New York, NY.

Rogers, E.M. and F.F. Shoemaker (1971), *Communication of Innovations: A Cross-Cultural Approach*, The Free Press, New York, NY.

Ronkainen, I.A. (1985), Criteria Changes Across Product Development Stages, *Industrial Marketing Management*, Vol. 14, pp. 171–8.

Rothwell, R. (1979), Successful and Unsuccessful Innovators, *Planned Innovation*, Vol. 2, April, pp. 126–8.

Rothwell, R. (1984), Public Procurement and Technological Innovation, in *The Health Service Market in Europe – Hospital Equipment*, R. Rapparini (ed.), Proceedings of an International Symposium, Luxembourg, 17–19 October, Elsevier Science Publishers B.V., Amsterdam, pp. 178–92.

Rothwell, R. and W. Zegveld (1982), *Innovation and the Small and Medium-Sized Firm*, Frances Pinter Ltd, London.

Rubenstein, A.H., A.K. Chakrabarti, R.D. O'Keefe, W.E. Souder, and H.C. Young (1976), Factors Influencing Innovation Success at the Project Level, *Research Management*, May, pp. 15–20.

Ryan, B. and N. Gross (1943), The Diffusion of Hybrid Seed Corn in Two Iowa Communities, *Rural Sociology*, Vol. 8, pp. 15–24.

Ryan, J.F. and J.A. Murray (1977), The Diffusion of a Pharmaceutical Innovation in Ireland, *European Journal of Marketing*, Vol. 11, No. 1, pp. 3–12.

Samli, A.C., K. Palda, and A.T. Barker (1987), Toward a Mature Marketing Concept, *Sloan Management Review*, Winter, pp. 45–51.

Saren, M.A. (1984), A Classification and Review of Models of the Intra-Firm Innovation Process, *R&D Management*, Vol. 14, No. 1, pp. 11–24.

Sarin, S. and G.M. Kapur (1990), Lessons from New Product Failures: Five Case Studies, *Industrial Marketing Management*, Vol. 19, pp. 301–13.

Saxenian, A. (1988), The Cheshire Cat's Grin: Innovation and Regional Development in England, *Technology Review*, February/March, pp. 67–75.

Schiffman, L.G. and V. Gaccione (1974), Opinion Leaders in Institutional Markets, *Journal of Marketing*, Vol. 38, April, pp. 49–53.

Schmittlein, D.C. and V. Mahajan (1982), Maximum Likelihood Estimation for an Innovation Diffusion Model of New Product Acceptance, *Marketing Science*, Vol. 1, No. 1, Winter, pp. 57–78.

Schon, D.A. (1963), Champions for Radical New Inventions, *Harvard Business Review*, March/April, pp. 77–86.

Schon, D.A. (1967), *Technology and Change*, Delacorte Press, New York, NY.

Schumpeter, J. (1939), *Business Cycles*, McGraw-Hill, New York, NY.

Shaw, B. (1983), *The Role of Equipment Users in the Generation of Innovations in the UK Medical Equipment Industry*, Paper presented to the Workshop on Innovations in Health Care: Historical and Contemporary Perspectives, University of York, 23–5 March.

Shaw, B. (1985), The Role of the Interaction between the User and the Manufacturer in Medical Equipment Innovation, *R&D Management*, Vol. 15, No. 4, pp. 283–92.

Shaw, B. (1986), Appropriation and Transfer of Innovation Benefit in the UK Medical Equipment Industry, *Technovation*, Vol. 4, pp. 45–65.

Shaw, B. (1988), The Role of Networking in the Development of Successful Innovations by Small and Medium Sized Firms in the UK Medical Equipment Industries, in *Research Developments in International Marketing*, P.W. Turnbull and S.J. Paliwoda (eds), Proceedings of the 4th IMP Conference, University of Manchester, Institute of Science and Technology, 7–9 September, pp. 511–22.

Smith, D. and R. Taylor (1985), Organisational Decision Making and Industrial Marketing, *European Journal of Marketing*, Vol. 19, No. 7, pp. 56–71.

Snyder, D.R. and D.A. Blevins (1986), Business and University Technical Research Cooperation: Some Important Issues, *Journal of Product Innovation Management*, Vol. 3, pp. 136–44.

Souder, W.E. and S. Nassar (1990a), Choosing an R&D Consortium, *Research · Technology Management*, Vol. 33, No. 2, March–April, pp. 35–41.

Souder, W.E. and S. Nassar (1990b), Managing R&D Consortia for Success, *Research · Technology Management*, Vol. 33, No. 5, September–October, pp. 44–50.

Specht, G. (1989), *Effectivity and Efficiency of the Product Formation Phase of Technical Product Innovations for Industrial Markets with Regard to the Interface Between R&D, Manufacturing and Marketing*, Presentation at the 5th IMP Conference, Penn State University, Institute for the Study of Business Markets, 5–7 September.

Spekman, R.E. and G.T. Ford (1977), Perceptions of Uncertainty Within a Buying Group, *Industrial Marketing Management*, Vol. 6, pp. 395–403.

Spekman, R.E. and L.W. Stern (1979), Environmental Uncertainty and Buying Group Structure: An Empirical Investigation, *Journal of Marketing*, Vol. 43, Spring, pp. 54–64.

Spencer, W.J. and D.H. Triant (1989), Strengthening the Link Between R&D and Corporate Strategy, *The Journal of Business Strategy*, January–February, pp. 38–42.

Staehr Johansen, K. (1984), The Evaluation of New Medical Devices and the Dissemination of Information, in *The Health Service Market in Europe – Hospital Equipment*, R. Rapparini (ed.), Proceedings of an International Symposium, Luxembourg, 17–19 October, Elsevier Science Publishers B.V., Amsterdam, pp. 143–8.

Stalk, G., Jr and T.M. Hout (1990), Competing Against Time, *Research · Technology Management*, March–April, pp. 19–24.

Steele, L.W. (1989), *Managing Technology: The Strategic View*, McGraw-Hill, New York, NY.

Steinhöfler, K.H. (1986), Patterns of Innovation Processes in Small and

Medium-Sized Firms, in *The Art and Science of Innovation Management*, H. Hübner (ed.), Elsevier Science Publishers B.V., Amsterdam, pp. 261–72.

Stolte, J.B. (1984), Clinical Freedom and Purchasing Decisions, in *The Health Service Market in Europe – Hospital Equipment*, R. Rapparini (ed.), Proceedings of an International Symposium, Luxembourg, 17–19 October, Elsevier Science Publishers B.V., Amsterdam, pp. 171–7.

Strauss, G. (1964), Workflow Frictions, Interfunctional Rivalry, and Professionalism: A Case Study of Purchasing Agents, *Human Organization*, Vol. 23, No. 2, Summer, pp. 137–49.

Styles, P.R. (1984), Marketing Innovative Products, in *The Health Service Market in Europe – Hospital Equipment*, R. Rapparini (ed.), Proceedings of an International Symposium, Luxembourg, 17–19 October, 1983, Elsevier Science Publishers B.V., Amsterdam, pp. 113–19.

Sultan, F., J.U. Farley, and D.R. Lehmann (1990), A Meta-Analysis of Applications of Diffusion Models, *Journal of Marketing Research*, Vol. XXVII, February, pp. 70–7.

Summers, J.O. (1971), Generalized Change Agents and Innovativeness, *Journal of Marketing Research*, Vol. VIII, August, pp. 313–16.

Szakasits, G. (1974), The Adoption of the SAPPHO Method in the Hungarian Electronics Industry, *Research Policy*, Vol. 3, pp. 18–28.

Takeuchi, H. and I. Nonaka (1986), The New New Product Development Game, *Harvard Business Review*, January–February, pp. 137–46.

Talaysum, A.T. (1985), Understanding the Diffusion Process for Technology Intensive Products, *Research Management*, July–August, pp. 22–6.

Tauber, E.M. (1974), How Market Research Discourages Major Innovation, *Business Horizons*, June, pp. 22–6.

Taylor, W. (1990), The Business of Innovation: An Interview with Paul Cook, *Harvard Business Review*, March–April, pp. 96–106.

Teece, D.J. (1988), Capturing Value from Technological Innovation: Integration, Strategic Partnering, and Licensing Decisions, *Interfaces*, Vol. 18, No. 3, May–June, pp. 46–61.

Thomas, L.J. (1980), Available Light Movies – An Individual Inventor Made It Happen, *Research Management*, November, pp. 14–18.

Turnbull, P.W. and A. Meenaghan (1980), Diffusion of Innovation and Opinion Leadership, *European Journal of Marketing*, Vol. 14, No. 1, pp. 3–33.

Turnbull, P.W. and S.J. Paliwoda (eds) (1988), *Research Developments in International Marketing*, Proceedings of the 4th IMP Conference, University of Manchester, Institute of Science and Technology, 7–9 September.

Twiss, B.C. (1986), *Managing Technological Innovation*, 3rd ed, Pitman Publishing, London.

Upah, G.D. and M.M. Bird (1980), Changes in Industrial Buying: Implications for Industrial Marketers, *Industrial Marketing Management*, Vol. 9, pp. 117–21.

Urban, G.L., J.R. Hauser, and N. Dholakia (1987), *Essentials of New Product Management*, Prentice-Hall, Englewood Cliffs, NJ.

Utterback, J.M. (1971), The Process of Innovation: A Study of the Origination and Development of Ideas for New Scientific Instruments, *IEEE*

Transactions on Engineering Management, November.

Utterback, J.M. (1974), Innovation in Industry and the Diffusion of Technology, *Science*, Vol. 183, 15 February, pp. 658–62.

Utterback, J.M. and W.J. Abernathy (1975), A Dynamic Model of Process and Product Innovation, *Omega*, Vol. 3, No. 6, pp. 639–56.

vanden Abeele, P. and I. Christiaens (1987), De Klant als Generator van Innovatie in 'High-Tech' Markten – Een Conceptuele en Empirische Studie (The Customer as Generator of Innovation in 'High-Tech' Markets – A Conceptual and Empirical Study), *Economisch en Sociaal Tijdschrift*, Nr 1, pp. 27–56.

van den Muyzenberg, L. (1990), Fast Track Development, *European Management Journal*, Vol. 8, No. 2, June, pp. 227–33.

Vandermerwe, S. (1987), Diffusing New Ideas In-House, *Journal of Product Innovation Management*, Vol. 4, pp. 256–64.

van der Sluijs, A. and D.A. Hogenkamp (1987), Een Mobiele Niersteenvergruizer in Midden-Nederland (A Mobile Kidney Stone Pulveriser in the Central Netherlands), *Het Ziekenhuis*, Nr 23/24, 17 December, pp. 1049–51.

van Dierdonck, R., K. Debackere, and B. Engelen (1990), University–Industry Relationships: How Does the Belgian Academic Community Feel About It?, *Research Policy*, Vol. 19, pp. 551–66.

Vollering, J.B. (1986), Het Verkopen van Nog te Ontwikkelen Oplossingen (Selling Solutions that Still Need to be Developed), *Tijdschrift voor Marketing*, Vol. 20, January, pp. 2–8.

von Hippel, E. (1976), The Dominant Role of Users in the Scientific Instrument Innovation Process, *Research Policy*, Vol. 5, pp. 212–39.

von Hippel, E. (1977a), The Dominant Role of the User in Semiconductor and Electronic Subassembly Process Innovation, *IEEE Transactions on Engineering Management*, Vol. EM–24, No. 2, May, pp. 60–71.

von Hippel, E. (1977b), Transferring Process Equipment Innovations from User–Innovators to Equipment Manufacturing Firms, *R&D Management*, Vol. 8, No. 1, pp. 13–22.

von Hippel, E. (1978), Successful Industrial Products from Customer Ideas, *Journal of Marketing*, Vol. 42, No. 1, January, pp. 39–49.

von Hippel, E. (1982), Get New Products from Customers, *Harvard Business Review*, March–April, pp. 117–22.

von Hippel, E. (1985), Learning from Lead Users, in *Marketing in an Electronic Age*, R.D. Buzzell (ed.), Harvard Business School Press, Boston, MA, pp. 308–17.

von Hippel, E. (1986), Lead Users: A Source of Novel Product Concepts, *Management Science*, Vol. 32, No. 7, July, pp. 791–805.

von Hippel, E. (1988), *The Sources of Innovation*, Oxford University Press, New York, NY.

Voss, C.A. (1985a), The Role of Users in the Development of Applications Software, *Journal of Product Innovation Management*, Vol. 2, pp. 113–21.

Voss, C.A. (1985b), Determinants of Success in the Development of Applications Software, *Journal of Product Innovation Management*, Vol. 2, pp. 122–9.

Wagner, G.A. (1981), *Een Nieuw Industrieel Elan* (A New Industrial Elan),

The Hague, June.

Webster, F.E., Jr (1968), Word-of-Mouth Communication and Opinion Leadership in Industrial Markets, in *Marketing and the New Science of Planning*, R.L. King (ed.), Proceedings Fall Conference, American Marketing Association, Chicago, pp. 455–9.

Webster, F.E., Jr (1969), New Product Adoption in Industrial Markets: A Framework for Analysis, *Journal of Marketing*, Vol. 33, July, pp. 35–9.

Webster, F.E., Jr (1970), Informal Communication in Industrial Markets, *Journal of Marketing Research* Vol. VII, May, pp. 186–9.

Webster, F.E., Jr (1971), Communication and Diffusion Processes in Industrial Markets, *European Journal of Marketing*, Vol. 5, No. 4, pp. 178–88.

Webster, F.E., Jr and Y. Wind (1972), *Organizational Buying Behavior*, Prentice-Hall, Englewood Cliffs, NJ.

Weele, A.J. van and J. van Hespen (1987), *Professioneel Inkopend Nederland: Nu en Straks – Deelrapport 1: Inkoopfunctie in Industriële Ondernemingen* (The Professional Buying Netherlands: Present and Future – Volume 1: Purchasing Function in Industrial Firms), Report of a Joint Research Project by order of the Ministry of Economic Affairs, the Dutch Organization for Buying Efficiency and the Steering Committee Purchasing Large Firms, Kluwer, Deventer.

Weigand, R.E. (1968), Why Studying the Purchasing Agent is Not Enough, *Journal of Marketing*, Vol. 32, January, pp. 41–5.

Wigand, R.T. and G.L. Frankwick (1989), Inter-organizational Communication and Technology Transfer: Industry–Government–University Linkages, *International Journal of Technology Management*, Vol. 4, No. 1, pp. 63–76.

Willems, W. (1985), *Marktaspecten Medische Technologie* (Market Aspects Medical Technology), University of Technology Delft, Centre of Medical Technology, Delft, April.

Williams, A.J. and W.C. Smith (1990), Involving Purchasing in Product Development, *Industrial Marketing Management*, Vol. 19, pp. 315–19.

Willyard, C.H. and C.W. McClees (1987), Motorola's Technology Roadmap Process, *Research Management*, September–October, pp. 13–19.

Wilson, D.T. and M. Ghingold (1987), Linking R&D to Market Needs, *Industrial Marketing Management*, Vol. 16, pp. 207–14.

Wilson, D.T. and K.E. Möller (1988), Buyer–Seller Relationships: Alternative Conceptualizations, in *Research Developments in International Marketing*, P.W. Turnbull and S.J. Paliwoda (eds), Proceedings of the 4th IMP Conference, University of Manchester, Institute of Science and Technology, 7–9 September, pp. 573–97.

Wilson, D.T., S.-L. Han, and G.W. Holler (eds) (1989), *Research in Marketing: An International Perspective*, Proceedings of the 5th IMP Conference, Penn State University, Institute for the Study of Business Markets, 5–7 September.

Wind, Y. (1967), The Determinants of Industrial Buyers Behavior, in *Industrial Buying and Creative Marketing*, P. Robinson, C. Faris, and Y. Wind (eds), Allyn and Bacon, Inc., Boston, MA.

Wind, Y. (1978a), Organizational Buying Center: A Research Agenda, in *Organizational Buying Behavior*, T.V. Bonoma and G. Zaltman (eds), American Marketing Association, Chicago, Ill., pp. 67–76.

Wind, Y. (1978b), The Boundaries of Buying Decision Centres, *Journal of Purchasing and Materials Management*, Vol. 14, pp. 23–9.

Wind, Y., T.S. Robertson, and C. Fraser (1982), Industrial Product Diffusion by Market Segment, *Industrial Marketing Management*, Vol. 11, pp. 1–8.

Wissema, J.G. and L. Euser (1988), *Samenwerking bij Technologische Vernieuwing* (Cooperation at Technological Innovation), Kluwer Bedrijfswetenschappen, Deventer.

Wood, A.R. and R.J. Elgie (1976), *Early Adoption of Manufacturing Innovation*, University of Western Ontario, Canada.

Yin, R.K. (1989), *Case Study Research – Design and Methods*, Sage Publications, Beverly Hills, CA.

Zaltman, G. and T.V. Bonoma (1977), Organizational Buying Behavior: Hypotheses and Directions, *Industrial Marketing Management*, Vol. 6, pp. 53–60.

Zaltman, G., R. Duncan, and J. Holbeck (1973), *Innovation and Organization*, Wiley, New York, NY.

Zijlstra, J.J. (1985), Prijzige Prothesen (Expensive Prostheses), *Intermediair*, Vol. 21, No. 42, October 18, pp. 61–3.

Index

Notes: 1. Most references are to innovation and research, unless otherwise indicated. 2. Names of firms in inverted commas are disguised.

TJQO

B